Out of Sync and
Out of Work

Out of Sync and Out of Work

History and the Obsolescence of Labor in Contemporary Culture

JOEL BURGES

Rutgers University Press

New Brunswick, Camden, and Newark, New Jersey, and London

Library of Congress Cataloging-in-Publication Data

Names: Burges, Joel author.
Title: Out of sync & out of work : history and the obsolescence of labor in contemporary culture / Joel Burges.
Other titles: Out of sync and out of work
Description: New Brunswick : Rutgers University Press, 2018. | Includes bibliographical references and index.
Identifiers: LCCN 2017055193 | ISBN 9780813597119 (paperback) | ISBN 9780813597126 (paperback)
Subjects: LCSH: Working class in motion pictures. | Working class in literature. | Unemployed in literature. | Motion pictures—Social aspects—United States. | American fiction—20th century—History and criticism. | English fiction—20th century—History and criticism. | BISAC: PERFORMING ARTS / Film & Video / History & Criticism. | BUSINESS & ECONOMICS / Labor. | SOCIAL SCIENCE / Media Studies. | SOCIAL SCIENCE / Social Classes.
Classification: LCC PN1995.9.L28 B97 2018 | DDC 791.43/6520623—dc23
LC record available at https://lccn.loc.gov/2017055193

A British Cataloging-in-Publication record for this book is available from the British Library.

∞ The paper used in this publication meets the requirements of the American National Standard for Information Sciences—Permanence of Paper for Printed Library Materials, ANSI Z39.48-1992.

www.rutgersuniversitypress.org

Manufactured in the United States of America

Contents

**Out of Sync and
Out of Work**

Introduction

Falling into History

Across the history of capitalism, the obsolescence of labor has left ever-increasing numbers of people out of sync and out of work. Fueled by the unforgiving dialectics of technological change that automation, mechanization, and computerization have propelled, the obsolescence of labor is a process that leaves the unemployed behind the times. As machinery displaces and replaces workers, however, obsolete laborers discover themselves falling not out of history but into it. This fall is at the center of *Out of Sync and Out of Work*, which looks to contemporary culture to push back against the elitist idea that the technologically unemployed have no feeling for or currency with history. That currency is far more than, as some imagine it to be, a simple matter of just updating your skill set to find new work in a new economy. Instead, such historical currency is a collective experience of class, in which technological change brings obsolete workers up against the very limits of reproducing themselves, their families, and their communities in an era in which diminishing work and falling wages have made such reproduction harder and harder.

Out of Sync and Out of Work is about the temporal horizon that contemporary culture opens up in response to this indelibly historical experience. This book focuses on early twenty-first-century films and novels that call forth historical time, the feeling of being "out of sync," by exploring the obsolescence of labor, the fact of being "out of work." These novels and films come from both the United States and the United Kingdom and range across mediums and genres: Brian Selznick's children's novel *The Invention of Hugo Cabret* (2007) and Martin Scorsese's adaptation of it, *Hugo* (2011); Rich Moore's digitally animated film *Wreck-It Ralph* (2012); Wes Anderson's stop-motion film *Fantastic Mr. Fox* (2009); and China Miéville's political novel *Iron Council* (2004). Low, popular, and at times pulpy, noncanonical (not to mention unlikely ever to achieve canonicity), and shot through with childlike modes of irrealist perception, all of them spur—unexpectedly given the qualities just enumerated—an active experience of historical time in responding to the fact that the obsolescence of labor has acutely intensified since the end of the twentieth century.

What is so compelling about the historical experience these films and novels incite is their own relationship to history. Despite the extraordinarily recent vintage of all of them, despite how they all make legible that the obsolescence of labor has intensified in our contemporary moment of capitalism, all of them also activate both the distant and proximate past of capitalist history in response to that moment. In so doing, they reterritorialize the past, bringing it into relation with the present. They transform the deep time of our time—in particular, the techniques, technologies, and technicians that seem to have fallen out of the mode of production but in crucial ways remain within it—into the outmoded stuff of narration, perception, and figuration, thereby engineering for readers and spectators historical experience often said to be dead in the culture of the present. All of these works of culture, in short, fall into history, taking us along with them when they do. That fall is, moreover, why we have to look at the films and novels to which I attend in *Out of Sync and Out of Work*, for the way in which all of them aesthetically rework and politically reinvent the past crystallizes the intensification that the obsolescence of labor has undergone in the present, revealing a historical experience that, much as some retreat from this fact, more and more of us are confronting in the crisis that is capitalism now.

Falling into history is the central conceit of this book. Historical and temporal, it is the conceptual figure that cuts across the materials and methods that it advances for the study of culture in the range of fields—most visibly, literary criticism, media studies, cultural critique, and critical theory—on which it depends and to which it contributes from within a Marxist tradition of thought. Given its centrality as conceit and concept, then, falling into history requires our attention as a figure of thought from the outset. Indeed, it provides a generative point of departure to introduce readers to the book they hold in their hands. It does so in four ways. First, falling into history is how this book understands what it means for a worker to be rendered obsolete, along with the more stubbornly tendential process—the obsolescence of labor—of which any individual worker's "technological unemployment," as it is sometimes called, is an instance. This form of falling, in other words, will be described not only as an immediate experience for the worker who has his or her job taken by a machine but also as a structural tendency of capitalist history that has been intensified in recent decades. Second, falling into history is also how this book grasps the pressing and powerful work that culture does in response to that recent intensification. The cultural materials I assemble in this book all intensively embrace the outmoded: recombining and reemploying what is residual, obstinately playing with what seems to have been creatively destroyed, feeling out the out-of-date as a sensory medium timely and untimely alike, and making the obsolete into the simultaneously historical and contemporary wellspring of political imagination.

Falling into history is not only a feature of capitalist labor and cultural work in *Out of Sync and Out of Work*. It is also the foundation of the book's critical method and conceptual intervention. Third, then, is how my method aims to itself fall into history by close reading the novels and films in this book across the deep time of capitalism, especially as that mode of production intersects with the long history of technological change. However, the payoff of these close readings is not only what each of them reveals about how specific works of culture fall into history but also how each of them grounds a conceptual intervention of a more general nature in each chapter. This is thus the fourth way that the conceit of falling into history sets *Out of Sync and Out of Work* going. If the overriding figure of thought for the book is that of falling into history, then that figure leads each chapter to be similarly organized around a conceptual frame that more ambitiously offers a portable vocabulary for how culture falls into history. The hope is that these conceptual frames will be repurposed and reinvented by other critics and scholars, especially when such reuse involves engaged disagreement with (indeed, perhaps even the rejection of) the frames themselves—all in the name of the ongoing intellectual effort to collectively grapple with how culture and capitalism push and pull at one another in and over time.

Falling is an involuntary act for most of us. A gravitational compulsion, it typically happens *to* us, pulling us *toward* the ground in an attraction that cannot be dispelled. This is as true of the experience of slipping, when I lose my balance and find myself accelerating toward the base of a stairwell, as it is of the object thrown into the air that, from the moment it ascends, is already descending. In the absence of any countervailing force, that object cannot *not* descend. It is immediately drawn down toward the Earth by the forces of nature, suggesting that gravity itself is arguably the elemental source of the cliché that what goes up must come down. Even our moon is subject to this gravitational compulsion, falling toward the Earth in an astronomical version of the force that pulls us downward in daily life, keeping us steady on terra firma.[1] Or at least, keeping us steady for the great majority of daily life—a significant exception arising when the compulsory force of gravity intersects with the moment in which I stumble, leaving me battered and bruised at the bottom of the stairs. Falling is thus good evidence that gravity not only pulls me down all of the time but also pushes me over some of the time.

Out of Sync and Out of Work is about the times when we get pushed as much as pulled by forces beyond our control—not by the natural forces of the physical world but rather by the contradictory tendencies of the economic totality in which we find ourselves. This is the totality that Karl Marx once called, in a phrase this book will repeatedly use in capitalized form, "Capital itself."[2] Capital itself is not unlike the force of gravity when it comes to us, functioning as the cause of a form of falling just as involuntary as the one that acts upon us every day in the natural world.[3] Like gravity, Capital itself pulls us toward it, pulls us into it, because living within it means laboring in it if we want to sustain ourselves. Even if we want to work, even if we enjoy our work, then both our desire and pleasure in working are in the first instance necessary to our survival. This is not to level the differences between distinct classes of work and thus obfuscate both the politics of class by which some of us get to do what we want for decent pay and some of us do not and the economics of inequality by which some of us have reserves that enable the work we want to do and some of us don't. An academic professoriate, professional managerial class, industrial proletariat, and gendered and racialized precariat are not identical to one another; indeed, each of these classes of the variously employed, unemployed, and underemployed is itself internally differentiated in crucial ways that are hard to properly describe—whatever one's empirical commitments. The great majority of the people within all of these classes, however, cannot separate themselves from the fact that laboring is a "structural coercion" that dominates us in capitalist life if we want to keep on living.[4] In the absence of any countervailing economic structure, we cannot *not* sell our labor.

There are times, however, when we end up unable to sell our labor due to the contradictions of Capital itself. For even as it pulls me into work, it just as often tries to push me out of it. From the moment I gain employment, then, unemployment looms as a possibility. For reasons that will be explained at greater length in chapter 1, the push and pull of Capital itself spring from the fact that, while the living labor of human beings is the primary source of value in capitalism writ large, that labor is also one of the central costs that an individual company must seek to reduce in order to remain competitive with other firms. Over the seven-century *durée* of capitalism, technological change is one of the singular forms through which this reduction of living labor has taken place, through which we are pushed as much as pulled by Capital itself. That push has gained striking momentum again and again since the end of the eighteenth century in particular, intensifying the tendential process that I call the "obsolescence of labor" since the first Industrial Revolution seized hold of the Western world.

When this push gains momentum, laborers find themselves falling into history. Or to put the matter differently, this is a push that pulls workers out of the present and thrusts them into the past by taking away the work by which we reproduce ourselves from day to day. This is not to say that falling into history means we simply vanish from the present or that we never put up a fight once pushed. Instead, to cite two other oft-evoked metaphors for this experience, it means that we find ourselves left behind—and more balefully, forgotten—when the work we used to do is now done by a more efficient machine; when the anachronistic skills we still have are no longer synchronized with what is necessary in this economic moment; when the industries that used to employ us are transformed into what Dora Apel calls "beautiful terrible ruins," from which most traces of living labor are gone because technological change has moved jobs to more up-to-date and less labor-intensive factories elsewhere in the world.[5] In these situations, we have fallen into history because the present feels like the past, confronting us with the question of how to sustain ourselves. Falling into history thus names an immediate experience and a structural tendency: the involuntary way in which we are rendered obsolete through technological change, pulled down by the gravitational force of Capital itself such that we often find ourselves embedded in the past, unable to fulfill the pull that wanting to work exerts over us if we are to get by in the present.

Both this experience and this tendency are also historically specific. In fact, the period of capitalist history through which we are living, typically dated to circa 1973, is often described using the language of falling. Take Robert Brenner's highly influential *The Economics of Global Turbulence: The Advanced Capitalist Economies from Long Boom to Long Downturn, 1945–2005*. Brenner traces the worldwide shift from decades of upturn after World War II to decades of downturn after 1973, speaking of a "descent into crisis" in the late 1960s and early 1970s that has led to declines in aggregate profitability in the advanced capitalist world (itself a version of Marx's infamous law of the tendency of the rate of profit to fall in volume 3 of *Capital*). Or consider the title of Robert J. Gordon's *The Rise and Fall of American Growth: The U.S. Standard of Living since the Civil War*, a book "the central thesis" of which "is that *some inventions are more important than others*" to economic growth. More specifically, Gordon argues that "there was virtually no economic growth for millennia until 1770, only slow growth in the transition century before 1870, remarkably rapid growth in the century ending in 1970, and slower growth since then." This is a fall that Gordon attributes, interestingly, "to the pace of innovation since 1970 [not being] as broad or as deep as that spurred by the inventions of the special century [since 1870]," a situation of economic slowdown compounded by rising inequality after 1970 in which automation plays an important role. As Jason E. Smith has observed of the period since 1973, "As it turns out, the capitalist mode of production has experienced a slowly unfolding crisis of accumulation over the past forty years, punctuated by sudden, and near lethal, *collapses*: since the early 1970s, we have witnessed *diminishing* productivity, *falling* profit rates, and *stagnant and even declining* real wages."[6] While the scholarship of Brenner, Gordon, and Smith is all data driven, these titles and this sentence capture the nearly postlapsarian sense of a world-historical collapse having taken place. Based on them, advanced capitalist economies since the 1970s, especially the United States, have found themselves pushed from a Golden Age characterized by factory production into an Age of Falling beleaguered by financial speculation. While cultural critics have often pursued the idea that history evaporates and historical thought collapses in the late twentieth century, with space overtaking time, the economic scholarship suggests the exact opposite: that we have fallen into history since 1973.[7]

The obsolescence of labor is a critical source of grave levels of both unemployment and underemployment in the present, levels that the most commonly cited statistics notoriously conceal, indeed, that they deliberately *forget* in their calculations. This obsolescence has nonetheless played an immiserating role in our contemporary moment, which is increasingly accepted in both economic and cultural circles as belonging to a post-1973 era of capitalism.[8] Along with global outsourcing, the combined forces of automation, mechanization, and computerization have functioned as a crucible for the agonizing economic developments of that era. However, the history of automation in our time also disrupts this more conventional periodization, especially when it comes to the cultural domain that is the primary concern of *Out of Sync and Out of Work*. "It may be that the history of capitalism is the history of automation," writes Smith in his essay "Nowhere to Go: Automation, Then and Now." In the twentieth century, Smith suggests, that history is one that points to cyclical moments of material and discursive intensification, largely related to the obsolescence of labor in manufacturing. Coming every three decades or so in Smith's accounting, the most recent of those moments of intensification, the decades circa 2000, has registered how thoroughly manufacturing labor has fallen into history in the United States and the United Kingdom in particular; that moment has, at the same time, led many since the 1990s to predict the automation of the service sector that has comprehensively replaced factory work in the American and British labor markets.[9]

In significant part due to this intensified moment, what happens is that the obsolescence of labor—the technological and economic crisis of human beings falling into history—achieves what is arguably a fuller cultural legibility than it ever has before. Central to what makes this legibility fuller than before is how it involves culture itself falling into history, tapping into the stuff of both the recent and distant pasts of Capital itself because of the obsolescence of labor intensifying as a problem in the very late twentieth and very early twenty-first centuries. Thus in the chapters to come, even the most ephemeral of cultural works produced in response to seemingly fleeting manias of the moment—a poster for a steampunk bazaar (chapter 2) and an animated film about video games, *Wreck-It Ralph* (chapter 3)—spiral into the past, tapping and transforming a deeper history in which machines replace humans and humans wreck machines over and over again.[10]

This falling into history by cultural means, however, does not mean that *Out of Sync and Out of Work* disputes the actuality of the post-1973 period. But it does mean that this book works both *with* and *against* this increasingly routine periodization. It works *with* it in that it takes this period to be a demonstrable epoch in capitalist history that has produced acute effects in the declining cores of the world system, especially the United States and the United Kingdom. It works *against* it in that it sees in contemporary culture, especially the mass culture of the early twenty-first century, a powerful tendency to move in less than linear forms in, through, and across capitalist history, revealing its propensity to turn back upon itself, repeating and recalling earlier moments, especially to the degree that it has been motored by technological change that expels laborers from work as a result of the contradictory force of Capital itself. The fall into history that workers have experienced ever more profoundly as the post-1973 era of capitalism has progressed has, I am arguing, brought about an even deeper fall into the history of Capital itself within the culture of the post-2000 era. In so doing, this book further contends that culture puts paid to both *post-1973* and *post-2000* as historical markers that do sufficient or supple justice on their own to the aesthetic and political work of historical time in our moment. That work is the work of culture, which activates in even the lowest of cultural forms the deepest of capitalist histories, generating a relationship between past and present that we were supposed to have forgotten how to have when, according to the cultural logic of late capitalism, history came to an end and space displaced time.

The cultural works that *Out of Sync and Out of Work* close reads at the greatest length date to an eight-year period between 2004 and 2012. Not even referring to a full decade, however, *period* seems like too grand a term for this duration. Historically speaking, *interval* or *instant* is more like it. Nonetheless, this interval or instant just after 2004 does follow from a significant moment for us, a decade of intensification in the history of automation roughly during the 1990s, which itself belongs to an almost fifty-year period in the history of capitalism that began to take shape during the 1970s. Thus *The Invention of Hugo Cabret, Hugo, Wreck-It Ralph, Fantastic Mr. Fox,* and *Iron Council* belong to the brief interval between 2004 and 2012, emerge out of a technologically momentous decade, and can be situated in the post-1973 era. However, from Selznick and Scorsese to Moore and Miéville, the ultimate period to which these novels and films truly belong is the longer and wider *durée* of Capital itself. Although they fascinatingly do not restrict themselves to even the following period(s), these novels and films primarily fall backward into what Joshua Clover has elegantly called the "long metacycle of productive capital" that extends from approximately 1830 to 1973, signs of which were on the rise in the late eighteenth century—or in Giovanni Arrighi's relatedly elegant periodization, the long nineteenth and twentieth centuries of political and economic hegemony enjoyed by the United Kingdom and the United States, respectively, as subsequent cores of the capitalist world system.[11] From *Invention* to *Iron,* the cultural works explored here are simply illegible until they are read and viewed not only in terms of our contemporary moment of capitalist history but also in terms of this much longer *durée*, given how riotously they fall into it.

This fall is apparent if we preview the omnibus of moments that rise up in the chapters to come as a result of the metacyclical reach of the films and novels that *Out of Sync and Out of Work* examines. In chapter 1, "Culture by Outmoded Means," I analyze—as exemplary of all the films and novels in subsequent chapters—a poster from a 2010 fair for steampunk enthusiasts. The poster depicts a mechanical robot as Leonardo da Vinci's Vitruvian Man, leaping from the start of the twenty-first century to the end of the fifteenth century, centuries prior to the metacycle through whose end we are living. Brian Selznick's 2007 *The Invention of Hugo Cabret* and Martin Scorsese's 2011 *Hugo* are my subjects in chapter 2, "Reading by Residual Means." The novel in particular invites us to turn its pages in the present according to the rhythms of the past by immersing us in the technological forces and representational forms of late nineteenth- and early twentieth-century film history that it reuses and recombines. And simultaneously, it tells a story of reemployment about what, ironically, it means to be unemployed and underemployed today through a major figure, the French filmmaker Georges Méliès, from that history. Chapter 3, "Narrative by Obstinate Means," revels in the violently playful energies of the 2012 film about video games, *Wreck-It Ralph*. This animated film unites the ludic history of gaming since around 1973 with the Luddite history of technological destruction since around 1811, not to mention mining the more immediate tempos of planned obsolescence by which technological goods and cultural commodities rapidly come and go in the marketplace.

In chapter 4, "Cinema by Dated Means," I trace how the 2009 masterpiece, *Fantastic Mr. Fox*, embraces the technics and aesthetics of what I call a *'70s feeling* at the same time that it tunes into rioting as a late twentieth- and early twenty-first-century political form that materializes in the film through the millennia-old story of a classic trickster: the wily fox that we moderns have inherited from ancient and medieval sources, especially beast fables. Finally, chapter 5, "Politics by Obsolete Means," ends *Out of Sync and Out of Work* with a novel, China Miéville's 2004 *Iron Council*, which builds a world filled with obsolete technologies drawn from at least the last three centuries at the same time that it tells a story about a railroad strike. As a result, it narratively foregrounds a mode of political antagonism that has been in statistical free fall since the late twentieth century by evoking a late nineteenth- and early twentieth-century form of it, though in the United Kingdom at least, struggles between labor and capital remain a recurrent conflict of the contemporary railway system. These are all novels and films in which falling into history is aesthetically and politically fundamental to the cultural work they perform in relationship to our moment. In them, the motion of history is backward as much as forward, and the work of culture is the labor of tuning into the presence of the past in the present.

The fact that these novels and films fall into history means that my mode of interpretation does as well in *Out of Sync and Out of Work*. The phrase "the presence of the past" above hints at the interpretive debt that mode has to Walter Benjamin. As writings such as "Surrealism: The Last Snapshot of the European Intelligentsia" and the *Arcades Project* reveal, what often fascinated Benjamin were the ruins of the past surfacing in the present to remind us of the alternative modernities that we have rendered obsolete—of the revolutionary experience built up in that rubble, which might rescue us from catastrophe with what it can teach.[12] While this materialist pedagogy remains an essential part of Benjamin's thinking on the past, my mode of interpretation is closer to Benjamin's belief that, as Kristin Ross has characterized it, "there are moments when a particular event or struggle [from the past] enters vividly into the figurability of the present," though the figurability of the past by the present is just as significant in the chapters to come.[13] In them, I bring my critical eye to bear on how the culture of the present falls into the past, showing it entering that past to reactivate and remix earlier moments for their figurability and narratability alike such that, in turn, it reterritorializes the present. I do so, moreover, less with alternative modernities in mind than with a focus on the historical experience that contemporary culture has the potential to stir by falling into history, especially by refracting the intensification of obsolescence in the here and now when it turns back to the there and then. In this respect, my mode of interpretation is also Benjaminian to the extent that, as with the children of capital he describes in his writing on "the mimetic faculty," it traces how contemporary culture is at play in the fields of the outmoded that obsolescence has cultivated across capitalist history by superannuating products and people alike for centuries.

As such, *Out of Sync and Out of Work* lays claim to a mode of interpretation that reads culture across the deep time of capitalism, also syncing up with the intervention of Wai Chee Dimock in *Through Other Continents: American Literature across Deep Time*. There Dimock argues that "literature is the home of nonstandard space and time" to which scholars need to attend. Rightly pointing out that "the uneven pace of modernity suggests that standardization is not everywhere the rule," Dimock nominates "deep time," a geological and astronomical concept, to describe culture, especially American literature, as embracing "a set of longitudinal frames, at once projective and recessional, with input going both ways, and binding continents and millennia into many loops of relations, a densely interactive fabric."[14] However, as a mode of interpretation, falling into history in this book remains more resolutely materialist than Dimock does in hers because it insists that the backward motion of the films and novels it close reads cannot be set free from the intensification of the obsolescence of labor in our moment. As a critical method, then, falling into history is tethered to the present *and* tuned into the past. The double historicity of this materialist method thus also affiliates my approach with the "ultimate horizon" of Marxist interpretation that Fredric Jameson proposed as "the mode of production" thirty-five years ago in *The Political Unconscious: Narrative as a Socially Symbolic Act*. If for Jameson, reading texts within this horizon made them intelligible as sites forged from a "vaster historical rhythm," legible as loci of "*cultural revolution*, that moment in which the coexistence of various modes of production becomes visibly antagonistic, their contradictions moving to the very center of political, social, and historical life,"[15] then falling into history, for me, commits interpretation to making visible how culture moves with little linearity in actively interrelating past and present, even as our (or any) contemporary moment necessarily conditions the range of cultural activities in which we engage (reading, storytelling, moviegoing, and political action will be the ones engaged in the chapters to come). What becomes aesthetically and politically tangible in the process is how often the work of culture involves historical movements and temporal passages, sliding around in time, repeating earlier moments with a difference, anachronizing, self-dating, and obsolescing in relation to the struggles of the present such that an active experience of historical time takes hold of us.[16] To echo Carolyn Lesjak's brilliant essay "Reading Dialectically," as a mode of interpretation, falling into history is a means of keeping faith with history.[17]

The faithful fall on which I wager in *Out of Sync and Out of Work* gambles, moreover, on a conceptual intervention that aligns with the book's critical method. That intervention is not unlike the one that Amy Elias and I have sought to achieve through the twenty essays we brought together in *Time: A Vocabulary of the Present* in acknowledgment of a field of scholarship that we define in our introduction to that volume as "time studies." That field also includes such recent studies as Amir Eshel's *Futurity: Contemporary Literature and the Quest for the Past*, Loetz Koepnick's *On Slowness: Toward an Aesthetic of the Contemporary*, Bliss Cua Lim's *Translating Time: Cinema, the Fantastic, and Temporal Critique*, Theodore Martin's *Contemporary Drift: Genre, Historicism, and the Problem of the Present*, and Sarah Sharma's *In the Meantime: Temporality and Cultural Politics*. This burgeoning field challenges the ubiquitously calcified claim that space has superseded time in contemporary life, with the essays in *Time* collectively articulating the historical idioms and temporal languages of the late twentieth and early twenty-first centuries in the name of that intervention. *Out of Sync and Out of Work* challenges this claim as well. It also refutes the idea that we currently inhabit, as Jonathan Crary has unimaginatively put it, a "non-time," a "time without time, a time extracted from any material or identifiable demarcations, a time without sequence or recurrence." Insisting that this "non-time" is not our time by falling into history, *Out of Sync and Out of Work* ultimately articulates a vocabulary not purely of the present but of how the past gets reworked in and by the present.

Although each chapter involves often intricate close readings of films and novels, those readings are themselves the medium for providing various fields today with a conceptual vocabulary for thinking through the experience of historical time those readings bring to the surface as the work of culture. This introduction has proffered falling into history as what I hope will be one of this book's useful legacies. All of the other concepts extend from that, with each chapter delving into what we might understand as a sequence of historicisms produced in and by the present as it activates the past: an intensive historicism, a hermeneutic historicism, a ludic and Luddite historicism, a phenomenological historicism, and an imaginative historicism. Out of these historicisms arise a set of terms. Those terms are the adjectives—*outmoded, residual, obstinate, dated,* and *obsolete*—that modify *means* in the titles of all of the chapters as a way of characterizing the cultural activity at the center of a given chapter: culture, especially mass culture, then reading, narrating, moviegoing, and political action. Culture leads my argument to the *irrealist* reception of the past in a present in which obsolescence has been *intensified* to a new point of legibility, reading to *reuse* and *reemployment* of that past, narrating to the past as an arena of *play and destruction*, moviegoing to *feeling* the past in ways both historical and haptic, and politics to *imagining* the role of the past in present-day struggles. By the end of *Out of Sync and Out of Work*, then, I hope that my readers will have a vocabulary of portable concepts through which they can fall into history themselves: a temporal and historical language that articulates how out of sync the present inevitably and intensively is with itself due to the urgency of what has melted into air *and* what has stubbornly persisted; due to the energies of what we can sense but not see *and* what is visibly being mobilized against the grain of its original use; and due to the exigency of what is present as aesthetic remnant only *and* what is active as political possibility still.

1

Culture by Outmoded Means

———————————————————•

Capitalism [is] a society marked by a temporal duality—an ongoing, accelerating flow of history, on the one hand, and an ongoing conversion of this movement of time into a constant present, on the other. Although socially constituted, both temporal dimensions lie beyond the control of, and exert domination over, the constituting actors.

—Moishe Postone, *Time, Labor, and Social Domination*

Dreams, the world of children, and artistic creation are privileged sites of playful disobediences, misbehaviors, and even malfunctions (tellingly, they are frequently grouped together). Here the movement of bodies and animation of images generate what Gilles Deleuze once referred to as the *movement of the world*: a shift away from the paralysis of reality, toward an oneiric realm of motion and possibility.

—Scott Bukatman, *The Poetics of Slumberland*

Statistical Hieroglyphs

In 2013 and 2014, Carl Benedikt Frey and Michael A. Osborne authored two studies that predicted that in the United States and the United Kingdom labor markets, respectively, 47 percent and 35 percent of current jobs are at "high risk" of automation, especially as a result of computerization.[1] These two statistics, especially the 47 percent figure, have received widespread attention as evidence that the robots are coming to replace us in multiple publications and on social media. They have circulated in the United States and United Kingdom as potential evidence of a few possible futures—a future of mass unemployment and underemployment, a future of polarizing income inequality, and sometimes a more utopian future in which work has come to an end, basic incomes are the norm, and capitalism never ends as a result. We will return to these statistics with more precision later. However, the currency with which they have circulated indicates how anxiously legible the obsolescence of labor has become in these two advanced capitalist economies in the early twenty-first century.

What is also legible is that this anxiety is both discursive and material. As two 2015 magazines show—a July/August special issue of *Foreign Affairs* entitled "Hi, Robot: Work and Life in the Age of Automation" and a July/August issue of the *Atlantic* with a cover story entitled "A World without Work"—the obsolescence of labor is discursive in that the media are talking intensively about the problem of automation. A conversation occurring on air in addition to in print (see, for example, *Planet Money*'s series on automation, also from 2015), that discourse provides analytical and narrative frameworks to mass audiences wrestling with the question of whether more and more of us are falling into history—in fact, falling into history yet again. For these articles and studies tend to rehearse the deeper and longer genealogy of technological change that capitalism has undergone as a mode of production for hundreds of years. Sometimes pointing to seventeenth- and eighteenth-century beginnings, the past origin that these articles and studies consistently establish as leading to the present moment is the much-mythologized Luddite riots of the 1810s. This is thus a discourse about the obsolescence of labor in past and present alike, with researchers and journalists struggling to understand both in order to make sense of the future.

However, the obsolescence of labor is not purely discursive in our contemporary moment. Among the definitively sobering things we can say about the post-1973 era of capitalist history, especially since the 1990s, is that the obsolescence of labor has become evident as a more terminally material tendency than ever before. In no small part due to automation, it has thoroughly rusted out industrial employment in manufacturing in the United States and the United Kingdom. It has, significantly, also turned toward other sectors of the economy once imagined to be immune to it, from logistics and transportation to retail, finance, and parts of the "creative economy," such as journalism. Whatever their possible imprecision may be, then, the statistics regarding 47 percent and 35 percent of future U.S. and U.K. employment being at high risk have gained such currency because of the intensified material and discursive legibility of the obsolescence of labor in our time (providing a figure, moreover, that runs counter to the U.S. unemployment rate in which so much misguided faith is put, given how much that statistic conceals from view). In this respect, 47 percent and 35 percent constitute statistical hieroglyphs of the fall into history that not only threatens present classes of labor in the future but also has already shoved people out of work in the past. These are people who have sometimes been propelled into lower-paying, shorter-term, and less-protected employment—and sometimes not.

The discursive and material legibility of the obsolescence of labor, especially as a result of the intensification of automation in the decades around 2000, is integrally related to that obsolescence assuming a newfound and pervasive cultural legibility as well since the turn of the millennium. It is no surprise that *mass* culture is a powerful locus at which *mass* unemployment becomes a readable dimension of the contemporary moment. This site of mass legibility makes even more sense when we consider how various culture industries—for example, publishing and bookselling, filmmaking and moviegoing, and gaming, which are the industries relevant to the films and novels explored in *Out of Sync and Out of Work*—have themselves undergone extensive forms of computerization that overlap with the technological changes rendering laborers and their skills obsolete throughout the late twentieth and early twenty-first centuries. This book is focused on five such mass-cultural works, novels and films authored and directed by people who have themselves lived and labored through these changes, including the corresponding political vicissitudes of these technological and economic transformations.

Despite a sometimes direct relationship to these changes, however, *The Invention of Hugo Cabret, Hugo, Wreck-It Ralph, Fantastic Mr. Fox*, and *Iron Council* are nonetheless surprising sites for this cultural legibility in that they take us so far afield of the traditions of documentary realism that have more canonically represented the obsolescence of labor and, more broadly, the economic immiseration of which it is itself an instance. What differentiates the mass-cultural works here from those traditions is how profoundly they fall into history in both their form and content, as if in tandem with the workers who are themselves doing so. When they fall, moreover, they are less focused on conventionally representing the ruins of the industrial past or creating traditional portraits of the redundant worker than they are on reworking and reinventing the past through irrealist receptions of it in which the outmoded is central (*irrealist* being a term I adapt from Gaston Bachelard, Scott Bukatman, and China Miéville). These films and novels thus embody a fascinating tendency in contemporary culture that I call "culture by outmoded means."

This chapter describes and historicizes culture by outmoded means through an exemplary instance of it: a poster for an event organized around steampunk, a contemporary mode that fetishizes the technologies and trends of nineteenth-century capitalism. This poster embodies the fundamental traits of culture by outmoded means. Mass cultural in origin, these means partake of an irrealist aesthetic in which affinity predominates over referentiality. That irrealism is central to how headily culture by outmoded means reworks the past in relationship to the obsolescence of labor—and obsolescence more generally—in the present. Because of that relationship to obsolescence, the past here is defined as outmoded. The concept of the outmoded has a close relationship to products by way of centuries-old French usage, in which *mode* refers to fashions that are variously *à la mode* or *démodé*. However, taking a cue from Hal Foster, this chapter conceptualizes the outmoded "in the sense not only of fashion but also of mode of production." But where Foster is interested in how doing so draws out "the tension between cultural objects and socioeconomic forces, between mode as fashion and mode as means of production," this chapter pursues the outmoded in this double sense with an alternative set of stakes in mind.[2]

In the pages to come, *the outmoded* does at times refer to cultural trends once *á la mode* but now *démodé*. Beyond trends, however, *the outmoded* more significantly refers to techniques, technologies, and technicians across the deep time of capitalist history that seem to have fallen *out* of the mode of production but remain in some powerful sense *within* it, especially in the mass-cultural works to which this book turns and that the poster in this chapter exemplifies. Beckoning us into an intensive historicism for culture and economy alike, the intensely anachronic figuration of the outmoded in these works—their profound relationships to so many moments in the capitalist and sometimes even precapitalist past—arises in response to the intensification of obsolescence in the capitalist present. Thus these works not only confirm the cultural legibility of the obsolescence of labor circa 2000 but also do so by leaping into moments as far-ranging as the 1400s and the 1800s such that a chronologically complex experience of historical time develops in nonsynchronous and nonlinear forms. What this chapter's delineation of the traits shared by the films and novels in *Out of Sync and Out of Work* gives us, then, is a conception of culture in which the irrealist fall into the past makes of the outmoded the very means of cultural production, especially the cultural production of historical experience. This is an experience of historical time that challenges much of what scholars have said about temporality and historicity in our current moment. In so doing, it also challenges some of the more conventional ways of periodizing the relationship of culture to that moment.

The Irreality of the Outmoded, or, Culture and the Movement of Historical Time

Steaming ahead in the marketplace and the factory alike for centuries now, obsolescence is the capitalist process by which both products and people become outmoded. A function of stylistic trends that come and go and revolutions in the means of production, it is the polyrhythmic motion by which goods fall out of fashion and laborers find themselves out of work. It is the multicadenced current by which products and workers fall into history such that they seem no longer to belong to it, seem to have been pushed out of the mode of production in its current state, but nonetheless remain within it, persisting and subsisting—dead tech gathering dust in closets and obsolete laborers with defunct skill sets struggling to find new employment. Producing generations of dated technologies and defunct technicians, obsolescence is thus a historical and temporal process that overtakes objects and subjects alike, outmoding both of them. From *The Invention of Hugo Cabret* to *Iron*

Council, these outmoded products and people are the stuff of culture itself, especially the cultural production of a historical experience in which the obsolescence of labor in our time becomes legible through an irrealist movement across the deep time of capitalist history as it unfolds by way of technological change, principally automation, mechanization, and computerization. This irrealist reception of the past takes exemplary form in a poster advertising a 2010 Steampunk "Bizarre" in Hartford, Connecticut, by Joey Marsocci, who also more playfully goes by "Dr. Grymm" (figure 1.1).

Marsocci is the proprietor of Grymm Laboratories, which has embraced the trend of steampunk popularly found in a number of culture industries. As a mass-cultural phenomenon that cuts across the late twentieth and early twenty-first centuries, reveling in the fads and tech of nineteenth-century capitalism, steampunk extends from novels by William Gibson and Bruce Sterling (*The Difference Engine*), Thomas Pynchon (*Against the Day*), and Cherie Priest (The Clockwork Century series) to films by Hayao Miyazaki (*Howl's Moving Castle*) and Guy Ritchie (*Sherlock Holmes*). The steampunk phenomenon is also fueled by less prominent, but no less interesting, cultural producers such as Marsocci. Marsocci has published books on how to draw steampunk imagery and the neo-Victorian gear and gadgets that people make on their own, made a documentary entitled *I Am Steampunk*, and been part of the lead design team for a theme park attraction constructed around Jules Verne's *20,000 Leagues under the Sea*. He has also curated an exhibition of steampunk design and art at the Mark Twain House and Museum and other locations in Hartford, Connecticut, multiple times, from which the marvelous poster for the 2010 Steampunk Bizarre comes.[3] That poster is paradigmatic of culture by outmoded means, especially of how it falls into history, making legible how that which seems to have been pushed out of the mode of production has been pulled into a fourth dimension of it due to the dual movement of time in capitalism.

The poster features a playful pastiche of Leonardo Da Vinci's late fifteenth-century drawing *The Vitruvian Man*, which it calls the Vitruvian Steam-bot. Replacing the perfected man that Da Vinci envisioned with an old-fashioned image of a steam-powered robot, the poster falls into the 1400s and the 1800s alike. In so doing, it draws on the outmoded most visibly through its ludic riff on the latter century's technological innovations. These were the innovations central to the capitalist world-system over which the United Kingdom presided in the long nineteenth century, itself part of the longer U.S.-U.K. metacycle from the late eighteenth to the late twentieth centuries. That riff also invites us to consider man and machine in parallel. In a highly figural form, it beckons us into considering how often inhuman machinery has displaced, deskilled, and replaced human beings in the name of productivity and profit in that metacycle. The image of the Vitruvian Steam-bot, in other

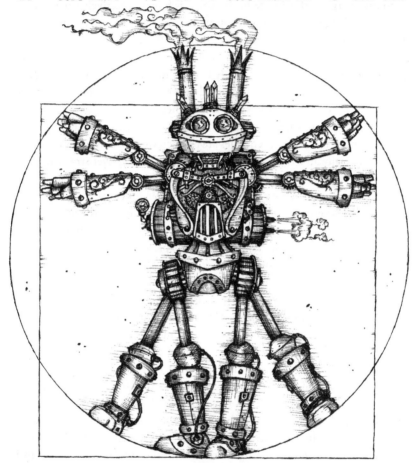

FIGURE 1.1 By Joey Marsocci, owner and lead designer of Grymm Studios, the Vitruvian Steam-bot in *I Am Steampunk*, poster for the 2010 Steampunk Bizarre, Hartford, Connecticut. Courtesy of the artist.

words, emphasizes that the robotic machine has overtaken not only the idealized human being that Da Vinci once drew but also the living labor of the past two centuries that is an absent presence in this image. Having rendered both Vitruvian man and workingman obsolete, if you will, the Steam-bot is also a figure for its own obsolescence. It is a hieroglyph, not unlike "47 percent" and "35 percent," ironically pointing to what has already outmoded it. Elemental to the charge of this image in the 2010s is how it effectively carries within it the knowledge that computerization has overtaken mechanization—that electrons, not steam, power the machinery of the early twenty-first century. Culled from the past and present of capitalist history, the technological correspondences thus multiply profligately here. With intensely figural and fantastic energies, the poster pulls us backward into the fifteenth-century prehistory of capitalism even as it pushes full steam ahead across the more than two-century metacycle of capitalism since the end of the eighteenth century.

Such figural and fantastic energies are characteristic of culture by outmoded means, especially an irrealism that both runs roughshod over straightforward chronology and disrespects referential representation. This irrealist aesthetic—its intense fall into history and its intensively figural quality—comes into sharper relief when we contrast the Vitruvian Steam-bot to the more canonically realist modes that have been ubiquitously used to document the obsolescence of labor. Those modes famously include pictures of workers, machinery, and factories alike, images of the kind to be found in photographer Bill Bamberger and scholar Cathy Davidson's elegiac book *Closing: The Life and Death of an American Factory*. Evoking the social realism of James Agee and Walker Evans's *Let Us Now Praise Famous Men* and the conceptual realism of Bernd and Hella Becher's industrial typologies, Bamberger's style of portraiture in *Closing* points to the rich varieties of realism to which not only photographers but also filmmakers (e.g., the video work of Tacita Dean, Kevin Jerome Everson, and Sharon Lockhart), the creators of television series (e.g., David Simon's *The Wire*), and novelists (e.g., Phillip Meyer's *American Rust*) have recently turned to represent the obsolescence of labor.[4] The variety on which Bamberger draws in documenting the human and mechanical ruins of deindustrialization in *Closing* is a romantic tradition of social realism, as can be seen in a moving two-page spread (figure 1.2).

The left page of that spread reproduces a simple portrait, entitled "Avery Apple," of a laborer who has lost his job when a factory closed, and the right page reprints a similarly simple "portrait" of a defunct factory entitled "Conveyors in the finishing department, one month after the auction." Side by side, the two photographs create an analogy between man and machine that the juxtaposition simultaneously works to undo in its more troubling aspects. On the one hand, the spread communicates that Avery Apple is about as valuable as much-used equipment that did not sell at auction. On the other hand, as

FIGURE 1.2 Photographs by Bill Bamberger, "Avery Apple" and "Conveyors in the finishing department, one month after auction," double-page spread from *Closing: The Life and Death of an American Factory* (W. W. Norton, 1998). Copyright © Bill Bamberger and Cathy N. Davidson, 1998. Courtesy of the artist.

Avery Apple gazes out at us from the portrait, it humanizes him as an individual caught up in the dehumanizing process of losing his job because the factory where he worked for years fell prey to the economic developments of the late twentieth century, which *Closing* rightly characterizes as "an era of disposable work and disposable workers."[5] Whichever perspective one assumes, the correspondence between man and machine created by the juxtaposition here functions in both cases to index the harsh reality of Avery Apple's fate. In this, these two photographs expose a realist impulse in *Closing*, with this two-page spread embracing a documentary aesthetic to sympathetically depict the disposable worker left behind by the closing of the furniture factory where he used to be gainfully employed.

Although they both address the obsolescence of labor, Bamberger's realism and Marsocci's irrealism are strikingly different, with one of the most important differences being the historicity of photograph and poster, respectively. Although Avery Apple is himself falling into history, Bamberger's portrait of him hardly is falling by comparison to Marsocci's image, even if traditional portraiture is now something of an outmoded genre.[6] It needs to be noted here that *Closing* writ large tells the story of the rise and fall of the furniture factory where Avery Apple worked, with Davidson charting its history from 1881 to 1993 in prose. Although it contains chapters organized around the memories of individual workers, Davidson structures the history in a largely linear style. In effect, her prose situates the portrait of Avery Apple, along with the many other portraits of workers and the factory where they worked in *Closing*, as the end of the line for that history, as the deeply human moment when that history comes to an inhumane close. The diachronic and the synchronic thus join temporal forces in *Closing* for a far more traditionally realist relationship to historical time as a series of moments that can be portrayed in a linear fashion.

In contrast, Marsocci's relationship to historical time is more dizzyingly anachronic, invested in temporal and technological correspondences. The Vitruvian Steam-bot is both *less* historically specific and *less* historiographically situated—as well as *more* forcefully caught within the crosscurrents of capitalist history—than "Avery Apple." Possessed of an intensive historicism that the hand-drawn aesthetic only deepens, the poster operates according to what Gaston Bachelard calls the *irreality function*. Scott Bukatman has beautifully summarized this function as generating "what Gilles Deleuze once referred to as the *movement of the world*: a shift away from the paralysis of reality, toward an oneiric realm of motion and possibility."[7] If Bamberger's photograph sympathetically captures the paralyzing moment in which a laborer becomes obsolete, then Marsocci's image irrealistically refuses to be paralyzed through the *movement of time*, especially an intensively oneiric movement into historical time through outmoded means. Of the present but plunging into multiple pasts, Marsocci's poster falls into the deep time of capitalist history in response to the obsolescence of labor (perhaps even the obsolescence of the human, given the Da Vinci allusion).

In these respects, the image of the Vitruvian Steam-bot is indicative of the irrealism of culture by outmoded means, putting this popular and pulpy mode in the gravitational orbit of what Walter Benjamin calls "the mimetic faculty." As with the irreality function in Marsocci's poster, that faculty is at a distance from the impulse to document reality, immersing itself in a stranger mode of mimesis in which affinity, not representation, is of the irreal essence when it comes to both form and content. As Miriam Bratu Hansen has masterfully accounted for it, this faculty springs from a conception of the mimetic not as "a category of representation, pertaining to a particular relationship with a referent, but a *relational* practice—a process, comportment, or activity of 'producing similarities' (such as astrology, dance, and play); a mode of access to the world involving the sensuous, somatic, and tactile, that is, embodied, forms of perception and cognition." Dependent on an active interpreter—perhaps even a "mimetically gifted reader," like an astrologer deciphering the stars in the sky—this irreal mode of access often turns on what Benjamin calls "nonsensuous similarities," akin to those between a constellation and a mythological character.[8] This predisposition for nonsensuous similarities in the poster is evident in a further replacement within its verbal rhetoric. It cleverly substitutes *bizarre* for *bazaar*, employing a homophonic pun that shows that this poster is far more enamored of the strange correspondences in which the mimetic faculty playfully revels than *Closing*. Following Hansen, then, what this model of mimesis indicates for culture by outmoded means is that it is not committed to "resemblance that appears overt and self-evident," as in the two photographs from *Closing* that picture a disposable worker and an old machine in realist form. Instead, culture by outmoded means operates "on the order of affinity," seeking out the irreal that beckons us to enter more fully into nonsensuous similarities as readers and interpreters, as in the androgynous Steam-bot that replaces the perfected man in the Steampunk Bizarre poster's pastiche of Da Vinci, generating multiple correspondences across past and present that exist in anachronic relationship to one another.[9]

By generating these anachronic intensities, Marsocci's Vitruvian Steam-bot—and culture by outmoded means—takes us into a childlike mode of perception. Here, too, Benjamin's understanding of the mimetic faculty proves generative because of his interest in how the children of capital play with the outmoded stuff that obsolescence generates. In Hansen's cogent summary, according to Benjamin, "the *physis* mimetically engaged by children is not that of an immutable organic nature, but the historically formed, constantly changing nature of urban-industrial capitalism, with its growing heap of ever-new—and increasingly obsolescent—commodities, gadgets and masks, and images. Children practice an inventive reception of the world of things in their modes of collecting and organizing objects, in particular discarded ones, thus producing a host of bewildering and hidden correspondences, tropes of creative miscognition."[10]

In its valorization of an old-fashioned vision of a steam-powered robot, the hand-drawn poster for the Steampunk Bizarre offers one such image of the inventively childlike reception of the "increasingly obsolescent." Festivals like the Bizarre advertised by the poster are themselves childishly inventive in this way and express the relational love of affinities Benjamin sees as central to the mimetic faculty. Recalling what the children of capital do with the outmoded in the passage above, the attendees of some of these festivals, most often adults, dress up in the *démodé* fashions from the eras of the first and second Industrial Revolutions in fantastic acts of historical mimicry. As I discovered as an observer at one such festival at the Charles Rivers Museum in Waltham, Massachusetts, around 2010, some of those attendees participate in fashion shows at the festivals to display their mimetic riffs on the costumes of those two Industrial Revolutions to other attendees, while others buy carefully made goods and gadgets that stylize those obsolete periods of technological change as part of their mechanical substance and aesthetic appearance alike. The modes of perception and cognition that Benjamin identifies with the children of capital can thus persist into adult forms of childlike and childish being, making for creative encounters in which otherwise devalued stuff is revalued through the inventively irrealist reception of the outmoded.

Such childlike encounters are key to the works of culture by outmoded means on which this book focuses, all of which, it is striking, are directed at children or have some association with the childlike. *The Invention of Hugo*

Cabret, Wreck-It Ralph, and *Fantastic Mr. Fox* address children as their primary readers and spectators—though parents are likely to read Brian Selznick's
book as well as Roald Dahl's 1970 novel, the source of Wes Anderson's film, to
their children in some cases, and adults are almost always part of the imagined
audience of commercial animation in the late twentieth and early twenty-first
centuries. Anderson's *Fantastic* and Martin Scorsese's *Hugo* more clearly imagine an intergenerational audience that is simultaneously juvenile and mature.
Meanwhile, China Miéville's *Iron Council* is the only work directed at an adult
audience. But its relationship to the genre of fantasy, especially the dark mode
of that genre known as "weird fiction," pulls the novel into the often mimetically irreal radius of the childlike and even the childish in the most compelling of ways.[11] While culture by outmoded means is not restricted to children,
then, the orientation of these novels and films toward a childlike and childish
sensorium is crucial to how they fall into history with so much irrealist creativity and to how they bring that creativity to bear on the encounters with the
outmoded that they stage for readers and spectators in the early twenty-first
century. Just as the Vitruvian Steam-bot moves to-and-fro among the 1400s,
the 1800s, and the 2000s, these films and novels resourcefully involve readers and spectators in irreal encounters with the black-and-white stills from
early film history that *The Invention of Hugo Cabret* reuses and recombines;
with retro video games turned into characters equal parts zanily obstinate and
destructively cute in *Wreck-It Ralph*; with analog tech that imbues the world
of *Fantastic Mr. Fox* with a beautifully dated feeling; and with an industrial
proletariat that successfully revolts in *Iron Council*, laying claim to a steam
train when they do—much as culture by outmoded means pushes into a past
that pulls upon us in the present due to the scores of products and people rendered obsolete for centuries now.

This is one of the crucial senses in which techniques, technologies, and
technicians that appear to have fallen out of the mode of production remain
within it. While a good does not simply vanish because it is no longer *à la
mode*, while a worker does not stop having a residual set of skills simply because
his craft has been mechanized, the material persistence of the outmoded that
these two examples represent from different spheres of the economy finds a
correlative in culture by outmoded means. There the outmoded discovers an
afterlife, becoming the stuff out of which culture springs as a result of a worker
falling into history in the way that Marsocci's Vitruvian Steam-bot prototypically exemplifies. The outmoded becomes not only the very means of cultural
production in such an image (and in the novels and films to which subsequent
chapters turn) but also, more specifically, the means for the cultural production of historical experience in forms inseparable from the obsolescence that
products and people undergo as capitalist history unfolds. In this sense, the
use of the term *means* here and elsewhere in the book is intended as an allusion

to the idea of means of production in Marxist thought, where it covers raw materials and living labor, tools and machines, and the structures where these are brought together to produce goods. Unlike these means of production, however, the ones employed by culture by outmoded means are involved not in the industrial manufacture of goods but in the cultural production of historical time out of the goods—and the workers who make the goods with certain tools and machines—that are rendered obsolete day in and day out across centuries of technological change in capitalism.

In our everyday lives, the outmoded often telegraphs the past as a function of how it intersects with the present. A fashion from a decade ago brings to mind what was once all the rage but is now at best retro. The sight of a telephone booth does not yet evoke industrial ruin along the lines of an abandoned factory, but it can't help but make us aware of the smartphones superannuating an older telecommunications infrastructure. The sound of a typewriter clacking recalls a mechanical past in a digital present—not to mention pools of clerical workers displaced by computers that demand new technical skills and new technicians. Technologies, techniques, and technicians superseding one another are thus so many signals that time is moving and history is passing at a variety of paces that punctuate the rhythms by which we consume and create goods made by workers less and less necessary to their manufacture. And those unnecessary workers show that as time moves, as the gadgets of yesterday yield so many moments of historicity for us, it also passes people by, expanding the ranks of those who have fallen into history. The past thus builds up in the passé daily.

Culture by outmoded means depends on that quotidian buildup across centuries, manufacturing a chronologically complex experience of historical time as a result. In his influential study, *Time, Labor, and Social Domination: A Reinterpretation of Marx's Critical Theory*, Moishe Postone writes that "historical time in capitalism can be considered a form of concrete time that is socially constituted and expresses an ongoing qualitative transformation of work and production, of social life more generally, and of forms of consciousness, values, and needs." In considering capitalism as deeply intertwined with the level of productivity in an economy, Postone further states that capitalism is distinctive in that it is "a society marked by a temporal duality—an ongoing flow of history, on the one hand, and ongoing conversion of this movement of time into a constant present, on the other."[12] Culture by outmoded means resists this movement, irrealistically making time appear before our eyes, in our hands, and within our minds. It propels us backward as much as forward. It moves against the ongoing flow, keeping us within historical time, repeatedly drawing us into the past in the present such that these two moments, no matter how near or far, must be concretely experienced in anachronic relation to one another.

As such, culture by outmoded means challenges the accounts of historical experience we have with regards to the contemporary moment. For decades, the most influential accounts stressed how space had superseded time, amnesia had overtaken us, and historicity was in crisis in the culture of late capitalism. Fredric Jameson, for example, has consistently argued that subjects of late capitalism have lost access to "the temporal manifold" of past, present, and future, a loss that fractures the capacity of their "cultural productions" to have cogent relationships to time and history; he has further argued that a "spatial dialectic" is now of the essence in light of this loss if we are to make sense of whatever "new kind of time" is the legacy of late capitalism. In the related argument of Andreas Huyssen, that loss leads to the collapse of "the constitutive tension between past and present, especially when the imagined past is sucked into the timeless present of the all-pervasive space of consumer culture."[13] The thinking of both Jameson and Huyssen on historicity and temporality is far richer than these quotations alone can communicate, and a new generation of critics has moved the study of time and history in new directions. However, both scholars nonetheless epitomize one of the lessons that their many scholars and students most profoundly took away from them over the last few decades: that culture is no longer capable of adequately figuring, much less granting access to, the temporal manifold of past, present, and future in relationship to capitalism. The intensive historicism of culture by outmoded means shows that not all cultural productions absorbed this lesson and that some cultural producers just won't learn. But what is the reason they can fail to learn? What in the material conditions of our time enables the irreality of the outmoded to take on the force of historical experience? How do we historicize the intensively historical in relation to the period through which we are living and laboring? Answers to these questions about historicizing and periodizing turn on a process that has itself intensified in our contemporary moment: the obsolescence of labor.

Intensive Historicism and the Obsolescence of Labor

As the Vitruvian Steam-bot exemplifies, culture by outmoded means revels in an irrealist reception of the past, upending the linearity of past, present, and future by moving backward as much as forward across capitalist history—intensively repeating a technical omnibus of moments that have come before. In challenging much of what we used to say about the experience of historical time in the contemporary period, moreover, the intensive historicism of culture by outmoded means raises real questions about its relationship to that period. How do we periodize culture by outmoded means, situating it historically in light of its own refusal to stay within any given period by embracing techniques, technologies, and technicians that have fallen into obsolescence?

The answer is to take a periodizing cue from the intensive historicism of culture by outmoded means by falling into history with it, especially the deep-rooted history of the obsolescence of labor. What falling into that history for the purpose of periodizing here involves is twofold. On the one hand, it entails retaining a date that has become ever more central to periodizing our present culturally and economically. That date is 1973. Following the era that began around 1945, this is the year to which many critics and historians now date the period of capitalist history through which we are living, with 1973 playing a defining role in the economic and political scholarship of Robert Brenner, Giovanni Arrighi, Judith Stein, Jackson Cowie, Joshua Clover, and others. In cultural scholarship—especially the materialist mode pursued in these pages—one of the most vivid uses of this date to periodize the present occurs, again, in Jameson's writing, specifically in the 1991 preface to the book *Postmodernism, or, The Cultural Logic of Late Capitalism*, where he also most conclusively diagnosed the crisis of historical experience being rethought in these pages. "Meanwhile," says Jameson, in one of his long sentences, "it is my sense that . . . the economic system and the cultural 'structure of feeling' . . . somehow crystallized in the great shock of the crises of 1973 (the oil crisis, the end of the international gold standard, for all intents and purposes the end of the great wave of 'wars of national liberation' and the beginning of the end of traditional communism)." Positing 1973 as a critical year, Jameson immediately takes a figurative turn that is notably spatial in its imagery of the post-1973 era that gave rise to postmodernism in his account, writing in the same sentence that "now that the dust clouds have rolled away, [they] disclose the existence, already in place, of a strange new landscape."[14] That landscape is the culture and economy of our time, which in *Postmodernism* is a landscape disfigured by pastiche, lacking in historical affect for the past and overflowing in nostalgia for the present, and dominated by Capital itself to the detriment of our ability to imagine a better mode of production (a disfigurement, lack and overflow, and domination that another date from this period—1989—would only reinforce).

On the other hand, falling into history to periodize culture by outmoded means entails resisting 1973 because the development to which it responds—the obsolescence of labor—discursively and materially intensifies in the decades around 2000 such that it takes on newfound legibility at that moment. By around that year, the obsolescence of labor had not only decimated the sphere of production over the course of the post-1973 period, with technological change colonizing factories and curtailing factory jobs, but it had also begun to turn to sectors of the economy traditionally believed to be immune to it. That turn will also strikingly include culture industries to which Marsocci, Selznick, Scorsese, Moore, Anderson, and Miéville belong. This intensification thus explains why all the works of culture in this book are post-2000 works (just think of the 2010 date on Marsocci's poster). While the significance of 2000 thus becomes clear, however, that date is also not adequate on its own to periodize culture by outmoded means in resisting the 1973 date. We need to think of the moment of intensification at that point in the post-1973 era as being consistent with cycles of automation that repeat with animated fervor in a much longer history of automation, the genealogy of which extends back at least to the late eighteenth- and early nineteenth-century ascent of the 1830–1973 metacycle of productive capital. Dealing with this chronological complexity is thus what intensively historicizing culture by outmoded means requires: seeing that the period of this form of cultural production is both very close and extremely far and that its intensive historicism only achieves interpretive legibility when viewed from within the *longue durée* of Capital itself.

Pursuing this intensive historicism requires that we define obsolescence, especially the obsolescence of labor, more precisely than we have so far. Generally, obsolescence is associated with innovation as a central aspect of technological change. The dynamic of innovation and obsolescence, moreover, is usually presented as a smooth, linear sequence of technical advances that so improve functionality and efficiency (innovation) as to depreciate and displace a prior technology (obsolescence). Yet as Michael B. Schiffer has shown, this dynamic is rarely a "rout [in which] 'old-fashioned, inferior' technologies [are] swiftly replaced by 'new and better' ones in a linear process." The history of technological change is instead one of "protracted competitions, often lasting decades, centuries, or longer," in which a variety of apparatuses may—or may not—"die out." This is as true in capitalism as it is in any other economic system. As David Harvey writes, "Innovations at one point in a supply chain—for example, power loom fabric production—required innovations elsewhere—for example, the cotton gin—if overall productivity was to be improved. But it sometimes took and still takes awhile for a whole domain of economic activity to be reorganized on a new technological basis." What this protracted problem of interrelatedness can mean is that such a domain of economic activity ends up migrating elsewhere—in the phenomenon we now call "globalization"—because a more recently developing region is in a position to adopt innovations with less cost to it than an older one dependent on technologies that are falling into obsolescence.[15]

Obsolescence, moreover, works differently depending on the economic sphere in which it is to be found. In political economy as it descends from the critique of that discipline in Karl Marx, there are two major spheres: the sphere of production and the sphere of circulation, with the transport of goods from the former to the latter occupying a much debated place in between. The classic site of the sphere of production is the factory where goods are made and surplus value is created through the exploitation of living labor in capitalist economies. The classic site of the sphere of circulation is the marketplace where goods are exchanged, with the value created in production hopefully realized as profit through the sale of those goods in commercial transactions. This sphere also includes the stock exchange, that marketplace of high finance. Transportation and distribution reside between these two sites, with the infrastructure of trains, planes, ships, and the like facilitating the movement necessary from one sphere to another. Neither of these spheres ever exists in the absence of the other, even if the unity they form is a contradictory one.[16] Obsolescence, as I mean it, occurs in both of these spheres, enveloping products and people alike across the *longue durée* of capitalist history, creating the stuff of culture by outmoded means.

We are all unduly familiar with how obsolescence operates in the sphere of circulation, with the sale of commodities from cars to computers in the marketplace shaped by planned obsolescence, especially in the twentieth and twenty-first centuries. Over the course of the twentieth century, "planned obsolescence" became "the catch-all phrase used to describe the assortment of techniques used to artificially limit the durability of a manufactured good in order to stimulate repetitive consumption."[17] These techniques began to spread into various industries in the early twentieth century, with the automobile industry in particular starting to think about cars like clothes in the 1920s in response to the success of the textile and fashion sectors of the economy in this period. This strategy was important because the industry was producing more cars than it could sell. By foregrounding technological and stylistic obsolescence, the automobile industry found a solution in the sphere of circulation to the problem of overproduction caused by factories that were consistently technologically advancing due to the innovations of the first and second Industrial Revolutions.

Planned obsolescence truly began to flourish after World War II, extending to more and more industries.[18] The automobile industry is nonetheless one of the best examples from the post-1945 era as well, for during this era, that industry codified a rhythm that remains deeply familiar to us today: the three-year styling change that "would eventually define the lifespan of all so-called durable goods in America. Between these major styling changes, annual face lifts rearranged minor features, such as chrome work. But even these minor moves created the illusion of progress and hastened the appearance of datedness that obsolescence required."[19] By the 1950s, the annual style change had become the standardized rhythm for the production and circulation of cars, converting whatever had been current, say, five years before to the datedness that stylistic obsolescence often materializes for the consumer.[20] Such a regulated rhythm plays an enormous role in the production and circulation of a vast manifold of commodities now, showing how integral planned obsolescence has become since the middle of the twentieth century. It is, for instance, a key component of what in marketing circles is known as the "product life cycle." This is the cycle by which "the growth of a product follows a systematic path from initial innovation through a series of stages: early development, growth, maturity, and obsolescence," the last being the "inevitable" point at which demand for the good "slackens."[21] The inevitability of the point at which this cycle terminates reinforces how much planned obsolescence is an inescapable fact of the capitalist marketplace in the late twentieth and early twenty-first centuries.

Another inescapable fact in the late twentieth and early twenty-first centuries is the obsolescence of labor. This phrase is not offered as a synonym for the end of work altogether. Instead, "the obsolescence of labor" describes, first, the capitalist tendency to deskill and displace workers through technological change so as to diminish the cost of living labor, especially by automating the production of goods. Second, the phrase further highlights the broader and more insidious process by which, as political economists Aaron Benanav and John Clegg argue, "the proletariat tendentially becomes an externality to the process of its own reproduction, a class of workers who are 'free' not only of the means of production, but also of work itself." This "freedom" from work—this obsolescence of labor—is a result of the displacing effects of technological change growing asymptotically worse over time, such that those effects come to include workers being replaced for good. Following Marx, Benanav and Clegg argue that this violently terminal motion is a tendency of capitalist history for two reasons. First, once a new technology is introduced to increased profitability at a given firm, "*labor-saving technologies tend to generalize, both within and across the lines*, leading to a relative decline in the demand for labor." Second, they continue, "these innovations are irreversible: they do not disappear if and when profitability is restored. . . . Thus left unchecked this relative decline in labor threatens to outstrip capital accumulation, becoming absolute."[22] This obsolescence of labor emerges out of a dialectics of technological change. The change is dialectical because it mediates the motion of "Capital itself." "Capital itself is the moving contradiction," writes Marx in notebook 7 of the *Grundrisse*, "[in] that it presses to reduce labor time to a minimum, while it posits labor time, on the other side, as sole measure and source of wealth. Hence it diminishes labor time in the necessary form so as to increase it in the superfluous form; hence posits the superfluous in growing measure as a condition—question of life or death—for the necessary."[23] Marx here lays out the law of value, by which the hours contributed by living labor to the manufacture of goods in the sphere of production are the sole source of surplus value in capitalism, with the creation of surplus value being the pre-condition for systemic accumulation. But those hours and that labor are what individual firms, unconcerned with systemic accumulation because they are forced to be concerned with their economic survival, aim to reduce as they compete for profits in the sphere of circulation. Thus one form the moving contradiction of Capital itself takes, admirably described by Joshua Clover, is that of "intercapitalist struggles to economize all processes," which "iteratively replace labor power with more efficient machines and organizational forms, and so over time increase the ratio of constant to variable capital, dead to liv-ing labor, expelling the source of absolute surplus value [that leads to systemic accumulation] in the struggle for its relative form [at the level of individual firms]."[24] It is this iterative replacement of labor power with more efficient machines that marks technological change as dialectical, making that change into a volatile process that Capital itself propels.

The obsolescence of labor is thus a fourfold process. It is (1) a process of technological change by which workers are deskilled and displaced. Although workers often move into other classes of labor, this process is (2) "tenden-tially jobless," especially when it comes to industrial employment, because the process (3) dialectically mediates the moving contradiction of Capital itself, compelling the expulsion of living labor primarily in the sphere of production despite its necessity as a source of surplus value to systemic accumulation.[25] As more and more workers are ejected from industrial employment due to the dialectics of technological change, the obsolescence of labor becomes (4) both cause and effect of a qualitative transformation of work and production over time. In fact, such a transformation is precisely the source of an experience of historical time in material reality, with what Postone earlier called "an ongoing flow of history" being what these workers encounter as an ongoing fall into history in the obsolescence of labor.

This fourfold process has vividly determined the late twentieth and early twenty-first centuries, with there being good reasons to use 1973 as the date around which the ongoing fall of countless people into history that the obso-lescence of labor propels in our time began. For so many, 1973 is epochal because it was, to start, the year in which the OPEC oil crises shook the global order, the United States officially withdrew from Southeast Asia, and the Bretton Woods Agreement fully dissolved—all of which set the stage for the neoliberal turn of economic policy by the late 1970s and early 1980s. Most importantly, however, 1973 was a watershed moment in which declines in aggregate profitability and economic growth since the middle of the 1960s in the advanced capitalist world started to critically affect the health of that world, initially most intensely in the manufacturing sector of the United States due to international competition. This "descent into crisis," as Brenner characterizes it, eventually set off the agonizing transformations of the nearly half a century since 1973, including a seismic shift from manufacturing to services and from factories to finance as the main sources of profits in major capitalist economies such as the United States and United Kingdom.[26] The obsolescence of labor is a key feature of that seismic shift. But it is one that demands we periodize culture by outmoded means both with and against the idea of a "post-1973 era" that has come to inform economic and cultural scholarship on the late twentieth and early twenty-first centuries.

We must periodize with it because the obsolescence of labor in the United States and the United Kingdom is impossible to separate from deindustrialization in the crisis-ridden epoch through which we have been living since 1973. Deindustrialization is the process by which, as Jasper Bernes has usefully summarized it, "people, by and large, turn from work based on making things or objects to work oriented around the performance of administrative and technical processes or the provision of services to customers."[27] The statistics confirm that this turn has occurred. Since the 1970s ended, advanced capitalist economies have seen industrial employment cut by 50 percent in relationship to total employment alongside the massive expansion of precariously low-wage work, formal and informal, in the service sector. While the collapse of industrial employment cannot be disentangled easily from automation, especially computerization, the dialectics of technological change have not singularly propelled deindustrialization on their own since 1973.[28]

In one of the earliest studies of deindustrialization in the United States, *The Deindustrialization of America: Plant Closings, Community Abandonment, and the Dismantling of Basic Industry*, published in 1982, Berry Bluestone and Bennett Harrison carefully document how transformations in the nature of work through the 1970s and early 1980s were driven by "a widespread and systematic divestment in the nation's productive capacity," in part due to the fact that a great deal of that capacity was at best aging and at worst already obsolete. Much of this divestment involved the simultaneous movement of capital "into unproductive speculation, mergers and acquisitions, and foreign investment." Thus throughout the 1970s and then into the 1980s and 1990s, a given conglomerate would purchase "a profitable company, [milk] it of its cash, [run] it into the ground, and then [close] it altogether," while an industrial company would move production to a newer and more technologically efficient factory with cheaper labor elsewhere, ranging from domestic locations such as the American South to offshore locales such as Singapore. By the early 1980s, Bluestone and Harrison estimate, such financial and spatial fixes resulted in the loss of thirty-eight million jobs in the United States. Whatever solutions the service sector would increasingly offer as the post-1973 period progressed, then, mass unemployment was hardly some fantasy in that period's first decade due to the ruinous process of deindustrialization by which factories were shut down and factory workers lost their jobs.[29] Indeed, the human dimension of deindustrialization is a central aspect of what Bamberger and Davidson's *Closing* makes visible.

Closing, of course, is also a portrait of the obsolescence of labor, representing how deindustrialization outmoded men and women as much as the aging machines and dated factories in which they once worked. The reference to *Closing* thus compels us to ask more precisely how the obsolescence of labor belongs to the post-1973 era. There is no question that the dialectics of technological change, as propelled by automation, were progressing apace in this period. However, they did not gain momentum until the late 1970s and early 1980s. Indeed, part of what drove the capital flight Bluestone and Harrison describe was how, in a word choice apposite to the concept central to this chapter, *outmoded* factories, machinery, and tools had inefficiently become in the United States in the 1970s.[30] As Stanley Aronowitz and William DiFazio describe it in their classic study, *The Jobless Future*, "The major employers in the U.S. steel, auto parts, and machine tool industries, among others, did not introduce [the basic technologies of automation] until the late 1970s," when they were forced "to undertake serious modernization, especially computer mediation into almost every aspect of life." This "meant that millions of workers were permanently displaced from industrial production," with the steel industry, for instance, shedding four hundred thousand jobs primarily in the 1980s even as it intensified productivity.[31]

The obsolescence of labor that the U.S. steel industry underwent in the 1980s would turn out to be part of a larger trend in the sphere of production that intensified the disparity in the ratio of human workers to inhuman machines and technical processes by what Aronowitz and DiFazio fittingly characterize as "quantum measures" throughout the late twentieth and early twenty-first centuries.[32] Since 1987, for instance, the productivity of the manufacturing sector of the U.S. economy has increased by nearly 155 percent while the employment rate in the same sector has decreased by just less than 30 percent. Put differently, the manufacturing sector now makes 85 percent more than what it made in 1987, and it does so with only 70 percent of the labor. The trend in the United Kingdom has been similar. The rate of employment growth in U.K. manufacturing has tended to decline unevenly since the 1840s, even though the absolute number of workers employed in that sector increased from the same period until the early 1960s. At that point, however, the absolute number of workers began a precipitous fall from around fifty million people working in the sphere of production in 1961 to less than twenty million in 1991.[33] By the 1990s in the United States and the United Kingdom, the obsolescence of labor was no longer a Luddite fantasy from the world of 1811. It was both fact and force in the post-1973 landscape.

We can see, then, how the obsolescence of labor is integral to the post-1973 epoch through which economic historians and cultural critics say we have been getting by for nearly half a century. However, the gesture to the Luddites, who obstinately and belatedly fought the machines introduced to replace them in the early nineteenth century, underscores the fact that the obsolescence of labor is not a force historically specific to the landscape that has disclosed its existence since 1973. It is a force that points to how capitalism is defined from its very origins, though most saliently for our purposes from the eighteenth century onward, by the drive to make as many classes of work as unnecessary as possible by harnessing the ancient impulse to create mechanical life—in short, to automate. As one of the twentieth century's leading historians of this drive, David Noble, writes in *Forces of Production: A Social History of Automation*, "Ancient enchantment with automation ultimately became interwoven with the emergent logic of capitalism," especially once that logic conceived of labor as a commodity. Thus "the reduction of labor through so-called labor-saving devices came to mean not only the lessening of drudgery for working people (a traditional and noble human impulse to liberate, uplift, and dignify human beings), but also the elimination of working people themselves by employers." From very early in capitalist history, Noble shows that "the primitive enchantment with automation [was turned] to practical and pecuniary ends, where it now fuelled fantasies not of automatic birds and musicians but of automatic factories." Noble is not alone in this perspective. The absorption of automation into capitalism is a technological history that is central to none other than Marx's account of our mode of production in the first volume of *Capital*, especially the magisterial chapter entitled "Machinery and Large-Scale Industry." Although deeply tuned into the nineteenth century in that chapter, Marx could be describing our own historical moment in that now, too, the "poor devils" rendered obsolete by machinery "are worth so little outside their old trade that they cannot find admission into any industries except a few inferior and therefore over-supplied and under-paid branches."[34]

The obsolescence of labor in our moment is therefore nothing new. It is instead a repetition and an intensification of a much longer capitalist history, if a history that has arguably begun to approach a powerful limit, granting it a material and discursive legibility fuller than ever before. This legibility is a legacy written into culture by outmoded means, giving genuine force to the historical experience those means set into temporal motion. The obsolescence of labor is thus not unlike that culture. It unsettles the dates by which we periodize the present because it repeats the past with intensifying difference. It demands that we historicize it by tuning into that intensity in our time and across the deep time of capitalism.[35] When it comes to intensively historicizing the obsolescence of labor and its relationship to culture by outmoded means, then, the post-1973 era is both too short and too long. It is too short because it does not acknowledge the cycling history of intensification through which the obsolescence of labor has gone for centuries. It is too long because the most recent moment of that cycling history crystallized circa 2000, with the 1990s being a profoundly important decade of historical truth, the effects of which remain with us today. Without these more contracted and more expanded scales of time, the dates—the 1490s, the 1800s, 2010—that proliferate in Marsocci's image, not to mention the omnibus of technological moments that rise up in so many works of culture by outmoded means, are illegible, merely appearing as yet more instances of the amnesiac crisis of historicity and asymptotic end of temporality putatively at work in postmodernism.

As we saw at the outset of the chapter, the obsolescence of labor has been anxiously legible in the United States and the United Kingdom in the 2010s due to factors material and discursive alike. Central to this legibility is how that process now seems to be enveloping classes of work once thought to be robustly immune to it. The key classes here come from the "almost universally poorly paid and precarious" sector of the economy known as services. As Jason E. Smith writes in his urgent two-part essay "Nowhere to Go: Automation, Then and Now," this sector includes "a hotchpotch of occupations that lumps together retail and restaurants with other, vast sectors like education and healthcare," all of which produce "no discrete or detachable object that can be kept" but rather a commodity that "is produced and consumed in the same instant or interval." As Smith shows, this is a sector of the economy that has come to define huge quantities of the labor markets in the United States and the United Kingdom (the obsolescence of labor in the sphere of production being one major cause of this redefinition). And it is this sector of the economy that increasingly fuels visions of mass unemployment in the 2010s, with the much-cited studies of Frey and Osborne being a go-to resource in this regard today. While some persistent forms of industrial labor do appear in Frey and Osborne's list of 702 jobs that risk computerization in the next couple decades, consider that among the top twenty jobs most likely to be automated in the United States is a preponderance of service occupations: first and foremost, telemarketers, followed by a manifold of clerks (order, brokerage, new accounts, insurance claims and processing), alongside library technicians, cargo and freight agents, and tax preparers.[36] Meanwhile, in the near future of the United Kingdom, computerization threatens "office and administrative work [and] sales and services." According to the Frey-Osborne study commissioned by Deloitte, in London, "jobs where the annual rate of pay is less than £30,000 are more than eight times more likely to be replaced by automation than jobs paying more than £100,000. In fact, 63% of these jobs are in the high-risk category compared with 30% for all London jobs. In the U.K., the ratio is less than five times. This is surely a matter of some concern."[37]

Woefully understated as that last sentence is—this level of automated inequality is surely an exigent matter of economic and political crisis—the Frey and Osborne studies are indicative of how the obsolescence of labor is now turning more and more toward classes of labor outside of the sphere of production. Such classes are, in the end, more difficult to automate than manufacturing jobs, with Smith noting that the 47 percent statistic goes down dramatically with regards to those classes when a distinction is drawn between "tasks and jobs—that is, between discrete activities and occupations."[38] The dialectics of technological change nonetheless *have* enveloped tasks and jobs in service work. The example of Amazon, which is heavily computerized, provides strong evidence in the retail sector. Not only does Amazon indicate the major online shift away from brick-and-mortar retail (a shift that does not make up for job losses in the latter yet), but robots have also begun to work side by side with employees there in forms that may predict the different shapes that the obsolescence of labor will take in banking, health, education, law, journalism, management consulting, taxes, auditing, data analysis, and even architecture.[39] We thus find ourselves back where we began, if with a great deal more precision: 47 percent and 35 percent are statistical hieroglyphs for our time because the obsolescence of labor is ever more readable within our material and discursive reality. This readability, however, began to gain serious traction in the 1990s. That decade is, actually, the moment of historical truth for the obsolescence of labor as we have traditionally known it, allowing us to understand culture by outmoded means as a more intense development circa 2000 as much as it is a part of the post-1973 era.

Marked by an intensification of discourse about the automated end of service work, with Jeremy Rifkin's 1995 *The End of Work* being exemplary of that discourse, the 1990s were equally marked by a measurable intensification in the effects of technological innovation on the economy, especially in the United States. In *The Rise and Fall of American Growth*, Robert Gordon documents this phenomenon, showing that the ten years between 1994 and 2004 witnessed a "spurt of productivity and innovation." This spurt resulted from a surge in manufacturing productivity due to computerization, most intensely in the information and communication technology sectors, and from the declining prices and growing power of computers through the 1990s and early 2000s. It also had much to do with a "productivity revolution" in retail, a big-box and now online phenomenon that technologically "transformed supply chains, wholesale distribution, inventory management, pricing, and product selection," computerizing work and deskilling labor in ways that have laid the groundwork for robots in the sphere of circulation today. As Gordon points out, however, the gains of this third Industrial Revolution were short-lived, being largely unique to the 1990s and never yielding the kind of economic growth that the technological innovations of the first and second Industrial Revolutions did.[40]

Culture by outmoded means is a response to the 1990s in this regard, with all the films and novels of which Marsocci's image is exemplary emerging after the 2004 end to that period. Indeed, they arise in the interval between 2004 and 2012, their own intensive historicism a refracted response to the intensification of the obsolescence of labor that the spurt of productivity and innovation that Gordon describes in part involves. They also predict the increased legibility that studies such as those by Frey and Osborne help discursively fuel with empirical predictions, with the first of those studies having been released in 2013, which is just one year after the date of the most historically recent cultural work considered here. In addition to being a post-1973 development, then, culture by outmoded means is by more intense measure a circa-2000 phenomenon.

But if the intensification of the obsolescence of labor materially and discursively from the 1990s to the 2010s shores up the point that the post-1973 era is in significant part too long to periodize culture by outmoded means, then the very intensification circa 2000 to which it is a response—indeed, in which it actively participates—also tells us that post-1973 is too short. In "Nowhere to Go: Automation, Then and Now," Jason E. Smith has persuasively argued that for about the last century, the discourse about the obsolescence of labor has heated up every three decades or so, typically in lockstep with the dialectics of technological change leaping forward in the sphere of production: in the 1930s, the 1960s, the 1990s, and the 2010s. Although it seems as if the 1990s and the 2010s may be part of one longer moment of intensification, the point here is that the cyclical history of intensification means that the obsolescence of labor is not strictly a contemporary experience. It is one that has been unevenly developing for centuries, enveloping people and inducing discourse across the first, second, and third Industrial Revolutions. What may be special about our moment is that it constitutes a limit to that history. On the evidence of how temporary the 1994–2004 spurt of productivity and innovation was and how little enduring impact it has had on economic growth, Gordon's contention is that this much longer history has come to an end. The technological momentum of what he calls the "Special Century," which he dates from 1870 to 1970—with origins extending back to 1770—has run out of steam. The Special Century has thus reached a limit consistent with more materialist accounts such as the one this book prefers: the 1830–1973 metacycle of productive capital that Clover has posited, which also has origins in the late 1700s and early 1800s and has also reached a limit since the 1970s, if one marked by political crisis as much as economic stagnation.

Whichever dating of this *longue durée* one adopts, the limit that two centuries of technological and economic growth appears to have reached actually provides one rich way to explain the material and discursive legibility of the obsolescence of labor circa 2000, especially the obsession with the automation of services—for that obsession is one symptom that this much longer history has run its course. The obsolescence of labor has so thoroughly and so successfully unfolded in the sphere of production since the end of the eighteenth century that by the 1990s, it sought more systematically to free people from work in the service sector that has since the 1970s served as a laborious refuge for those in search of employment. Culture by outmoded means is as much a response to this much longer two-century history as it is to the moment at the end of the twentieth century and the beginning of the twenty-first, the evidence for which is exactly all the outmoded technologies and obsolete times that materialize from the metacycle of productive capital within contemporary culture. At the limit of that metacycle, the culture of our moment falls into its history.

Culture by outmoded means is thus a chronologically complex affair to periodize, its intensive historicism datable not only to the post-1973 era but also to circa 2000 and to circa the last two hundred years. The most compelling evidence for this chronological complexity is to be found in the historical experiences of the times and technologies that culture by outmoded means puts to temporal work as a matter of form and content in stories from *The Invention of Hugo Cabret* to *Iron Council*. But we can also be more literal in accounting for why Selznick, Scorsese, Moore, Anderson, and Miéville make novels and films that end up doing that work—and often marvelously so. In the first instance, they all belong to culture industries that have seen the dialectics of technological change, especially computerization, alter the very nature of their mediums: writing and publishing, filmmaking and animation, not to mention gaming. An homage to early cinema, Scorsese's *Hugo*, for instance, was released in theaters as Kodak was collapsing, the 140,000 people it used to employ outmoded along with the obsolescence of the photochemical film stock on which films were made for nearly a century. After college, Selznick began his years as an illustrator and writer by supporting himself as a bookseller at the Manhattan store Eeyore's Books for Children, which fell prey to Barnes and Noble, which itself has (along with Borders) fallen prey to Amazon—economically and technologically displacing knowledgeable booksellers in favor of merchandise pickers over the course of the 1990s and 2000s. And Anderson worked part-time as a film projectionist while going to college in the late 1980s, a period during which that profession was turning into an increasingly part-time gig as it became more and more automated until its nearly total disappearance in the 2010s.[41] While cultural labor remains difficult to automate in comparison to factory work, the experiences of these filmmakers and novelists in their own employment histories indicate that the obsolescence of labor has turned not only toward the service sector but also toward the work of culture in ways that are more and more directly experienced by those who write novels, draw pictures, and make movies. This, in fact, may well be one of the legacies of the intensification of the obsolescence of labor circa 2000—a newfound cultural legibility for that historical experience that speaks to the limits that the past two hundred years of rendering people obsolete in the sphere of production have reached in our time.

Of course, this is not the first time the obsolescence of labor has been materially, discursively, culturally, and, indeed, politically legible for the past two centuries at various intervals. In the early 1960s, before the service sector grew to absorb so many, James Boggs wrote in *American Revolution: Pages from a Negro Worker's Notebook*, "America today is headed towards an automated society, and it cannot be stopped by featherbedding, by refusal to work overtime, by sabotage, or by shortening the work week a few hours. America today is rapidly reaching a point where . . . there will be automation on top of automation." In the 1930s, a pair of strange bedfellows with very different—if equally utopian—visions saw, on the one hand, technological unemployment leading to a future freed of work in the name of liberatory leisure (John Keynes, "Economic Possibilities for Our Grandchildren") and, on the other, so much revolutionary energy to fuel anticapitalist politics in the increasingly visible presence of the "outmoded" in everyday life and avant-garde art (Walter Benjamin, "Surrealism: The Last Snapshot of the European Intelligentsia"). And even farther back, at what is a major point of origin for the history into which culture by outmoded means falls, songs from the 1810s such as "General Ludd's Triumph" contain obstinately angry lines like these: "These Engines of mischief were sentenced to die / By unanimous vote of the Trade / And Ludd who can all opposition defy / Was grand Executioner made."[42] Nonetheless, there is something different about the engines of mischief confronting us this time, with the obsolescence of labor coming for new kinds of work a sign that the two centuries of toil and struggle embodied in the writings of Boggs, Keynes, Benjamin, and the author of "General Ludd's Triumph" are approaching a limit intense enough to end in culture by outmoded means.

2

Reading by
Residual Means

In that moment, the machinery of the world lined up. Somewhere a clock struck midnight, and Hugo's future seemed to fall perfectly into place.
—Brian Selznick, *The Invention of Hugo Cabret*

Steve Tohill, a business agent for IATSE Local 348, used to be a boxer in his youth before becoming a film projectionist. "I'm now getting $15.50 an hour," says Tohill. "Not big pay for the amount of skills I have." Today, his gloves are off in a fight with an employer who wants to turn his profession into a minimum-wage job with little training.
—Carole Pearson, "Infamous Players: Film Projectionists Battle the Big Boys"

A Hermeneutics of Historical Time

Brian Selznick's 2007 novel, *The Invention of Hugo Cabret*, is a distinctively bookish book, simulating an old-fashioned, leather-bound volume in order to remind us of books of the past. And that volume is most definitely voluminous. *Invention* is a heavy book, the weight of which you cannot avoid as you read, especially if you're the juvenile reader for whom the novel is primarily intended. The paper on which the novel is printed, moreover, is high quality, and the book is thread sewn rather than glued. As a result of all these features of its material form, *Invention* insists that a bookish past—a literary past of printed matter—remains durably active even as the experience of reading moves from printed page to digital screen in the present at quantum measures not unlike those that have been insistently displacing workers both in our time and across the deep time of capitalism. While print media are not yet fatally obsolete due to the proliferation of such screens, especially in the advanced capitalist world, they are no longer singularly prevailing in how consumers read anymore, especially if reading is understood to include a continuum of genres and modes from novels and newspapers to social networks and text messages. The practice of reading that print media evoke, the habits of mind and body they entail (as Maura Nolan would elegantly put it), is more and more residual as computers become more and more dominant in cultural activities of all sorts.[1] The residual is a concept borrowed, as many will recognize, from Raymond Williams's influential scheme of residual, dominant, and emergent in *Marxism and Literature*. Distinguishing it from the archaic, there he states that the "residual, by definition, has been effectively formed in the past, but it is still active in the cultural process, not only and often not at all as an element of the past, but as an effective element of the present."[2] While its bookish qualities conform to this definition, the efficacy of the past in Selznick's *Invention* points to a conception of the residual that more specifically turns on how the experience of reading *Invention* involves us in the reuse, recombination, and remediation of outmoded products and obsolete people—in what is ultimately the reemployment of the past in the present of reading.

Reemploying the past is fundamental to both the formal and narrative dimensions of the novel. Formally, what we discover inside of the book are residual media of multiple sorts reused and recombined in the readerly present of the book as printed matter: not only prose printed on high-quality paper in a book stitched rather than glued but also the illustrations hand drawn by Selznick and black-and-white stills reproduced from films of the late nineteenth and early twentieth centuries. Narratively, what we discover is a double story about, first, the impoverished orphan Hugo Cabret as he tries to survive in 1930s Paris by secretly maintaining the clocks of a train station. There he encounters—this is the second narrative in the double story—a man he eventually learns is Georges Méliès, an important early filmmaker who in the 1930s of the novel has fallen from the heights of his cinematic career into repairing gadgets and selling toys at the margins of the train station where Hugo lives. But both Hugo and Méliès get comic endings. The once-famous filmmaker and his family adopt Hugo, the young boy eventually becoming both a magician and a writer, and Méliès is rediscovered, his films restored to their former glory and Méliès himself given a job teaching film history. Like the film stills reused and recombined in the form of the material book, Hugo and Méliès end up reemployed in the double story that the novel tells. Material form and narrative content alike are thus committed to reemploying the past, especially the cinematic past, as part of a historical experience that this chapter calls "reading by residual means."

With reading by residual means defined by its commitment to reuse, recombination, remediation, and, most importantly, reemployment of the obsolete and the outmoded, it more specifically engenders an experience shaped by a hermeneutics of historical time. This hermeneutics develops in two ways within reading by residual means. The first, which I call "reading the residual," focuses on the products that have fallen into film history in the form of those stills the novel reuses and remixes; the second, which I call "reading residually," focuses on the people that fall into film history through the physical activity of page turning, which here turns us into film projectionists. These two dimensions of reading by residual means are hermeneutic because they involve us both in decrypting the cinematic past reproduced across the pages of the book in the stills (reading the residual) and in reviving the now redundant labor of that past by turning the pages (reading residually).

Reading by residual means is a hermeneutics because it takes the interpretive and sensory activity of reading so deeply—and so playfully—as a matter of form, drawing us intensively into the cognitive activity of deciphering and the physical activity of handling that together define the mental and material process of making sense of a book. It is a hermeneutics of historical time because in making sense of *Invention*, reading by residual means is caught up in the present efficacy of the outmoded products (the stills) and obsolete people (the projectionists) of the cinematic past. As a result, the process of obsolescence, especially as it displaces techniques, technologies, and technicians, is legible in the experience of reading the book, aligning *Invention* with the legibility of obsolescence circa 2000. Decoding that legibility is central to the project of this chapter, which, taking a cue from *Invention*, pursues a hermeneutic historicism that sometimes entails getting too interpretively and historically close—indeed, perhaps even for too long—to the stuff of the cinematic past reemployed in Selznick's book. Indeed, this critical proximity and critical duration may be among the debts that falling into history has to Walter Benjamin as a methodological means. Theodor Adorno famously characterized Benjamin as "permitting thought to get, as it were, too close to its object," such that "the object becomes foreign as an everyday, familiar thing under a microscope."[3] That microscope is, here, a hermeneutic historicism in which close reading residual forces and forms defamiliarizes things by falling into history with them.

As readers will have in all likelihood already gleaned, the centrality of the term *reemployment* and its cognates in this chapter is integrally bound to the obsolescence of labor that *Out of Sync and Out of Work* argues intensified circa 2000 as part of a post-1973 epoch, not to mention the *longue durée* of Capital itself. As we shall see, reemploying the past in *Invention* commits Selznick's book to resisting the obsolescence of labor, which is not surprising given that Williams famously attributes oppositional potential to the residual. That opposition is not out-and-out politics by obsolete means in *Invention*, falling far short in this respect of what erupts in all of the other films and novel in *Out of Sync and Out of Work*. However, resisting residually through reemployment is nonetheless vividly apparent in the double story that the novel tells, for which it will be useful to consider Martin Scorsese's 2011 adaptation of *Invention*, simply entitled *Hugo*. That story draws out how the historical experience materialized in reading by residual means is, in the first instance, determined by the obsolescence of labor both historically and currently. In keeping with culture by outmoded means as delineated in chapter 1, *Invention* and *Hugo* tell a post-1973 story circa 2000 by tapping into a narrative mix of fact and fiction from earlier in the metacycle of productive capital through employing Méliès and Hugo as figures for the obsolescence of labor. In so doing, what crystallizes is how the centrality of reemployment to reading by residual means is about reversing that obsolescence, not to mention repressing the contradictions of Capital itself. For what the double story of Méliès and Hugo ultimately emplots is a "comedy of reemployment" in which those who have lost their jobs—indeed, those who no longer have access to the faltering formal wage relation but remain within history—happily regain work and wages alike.

Reading the Residual, Reading Residually

As any reader can attest, the time that we pass when we read a book has a set of material and stylistic rhythms that can't be disaggregated from what we mean when we think of ourselves as reading that book. Page turning creates a tactile tempo. Prose style mediates the pace at which we take in sentences, which affects the rate at which we turn pages. The typographic layout of the page punctuates the rhythms of reading, quickening it now, slowing it then, all depending on how typographically and thus temporally dense the space of a given page is. The rhythm of reading is in this sense an artifact of what Leah Price describes as "the manual dimension of reading itself: books handled, pages turned." This dimension is what Price calls, in an elegant phrase, a "hermeneutics of handling," which is one of the ideas by which she posits a distinction between the literary work as a textual and verbal construct in which characters are imagined and stories written and the literary work as a material form and physical object that readers handle and touch.[4] In *Invention*, those hermeneutics are shaped by the fact that this book is "a novel in words and pictures."[5] Inventively modulating between different levels of readerly ability among children, as embodied by the illustrated book and the chapter book, respectively, and pleasurably breaking boundaries between text and image for adult readers, what the word-picture relationship produces in *Invention* is a word-picture rhythm: illustration and then prose, prose and then illustration, illustration and then prose, prose and then film still, film still and then prose—and so on until the end of reading. The material form of our reading time (to riff on Marx) is thus punctuated by a visual-verbal rhythm inseparable from the printed pages on which the plot advances at its own semiautonomous pace.

That rhythm, moreover, is evocatively cinematic but in a distinctly residual form of that medium. For example, following a "Brief Introduction" in which one Professor H. Alcofrisbas asks us to imagine ourselves in a movie theater

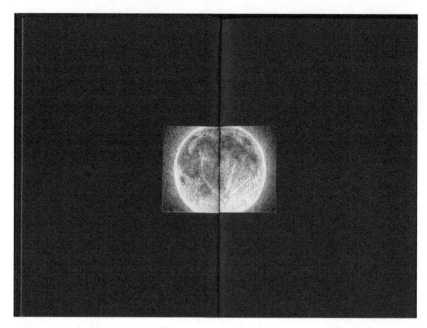

FIGURE 2.1 From Brian Selznick, *The Invention of Hugo Cabret* (Scholastic Inc., 2007). Copyright © Brian Selznick. Used with permission.

FIGURE 2.2 From Brian Selznick, *The Invention of Hugo Cabret* (Scholastic Inc., 2007). Copyright © Brian Selznick. Used with permission.

FIGURE 2.3 From Brian Selznick, *The Invention of Hugo Cabret* (Scholastic Inc., 2007). Copyright © Brian Selznick. Used with permission.

FIGURE 2.4 From Brian Selznick, *The Invention of Hugo Cabret* (Scholastic Inc., 2007). Copyright © Brian Selznick. Used with permission.

FIGURE 2.5 From Brian Selznick, *The Invention of Hugo Cabret* (Scholastic Inc., 2007). Copyright © Brian Selznick. Used with permission.

FIGURE 2.6 From Brian Selznick, *The Invention of Hugo Cabret* (Scholastic Inc., 2007). Copyright © Brian Selznick. Used with permission.

FIGURE 2.7 From Brian Selznick, *The Invention of Hugo Cabret* (Scholastic Inc., 2007). Copyright © Brian Selznick. Used with permission.

FIGURE 2.8 From Brian Selznick, *The Invention of Hugo Cabret* (Scholastic Inc., 2007). Copyright © Brian Selznick. Used with permission.

"zooming towards a train station" (Selznick, ix), the first sequence of illustrations establishes the setting of the novel as a Parisian train station in the 1930s and the protagonist as an orphaned boy who inhabits its walls (figures 2.1–2.8; Selznick, 4–19). That boy, Hugo, secretly and wagelessly maintains all of its clocks so that he won't become a ward of the state. The first illustration is a two-page spread depicting a portion of a moon drawn in pencil. The picture is much smaller than the rectangle of bound pages on which it appears. The pages are black rather than white in a gesture to that technical material, photochemical film stock, which the computerization of culture has rendered obsolete, leaving it to currently live a mostly residual life.[6] Turning the page, the picture enlarges. The moon shifts fully onto the right page. The sky expands into the left. Then once we flip the page again, an aerial view of Paris—just as well described as an establishing shot—comes into our line of sight, followed by a "cut" to the exterior of a train station. While it does not do so at the rate of twenty-four times per second, the picture is enlarging every time the reader turns the page, remediating a black-and-white film that locates us in the diegetic space and time of the historical past, until we finally reach a double-spread close-up of Hugo casting his eye over his shoulder at the reader.

This rhythmic sequence of pages embodies the two major dimensions of reading by residual means, which create a double subjectivity for the reader. The reader is a moviegoer—a reader-spectator residually sutured, almost, into the world of the novel.[7] And the reader is also a film projectionist—a reader-laborer whose page turning sets in residual motion the movie written on the pages of this novel. Partaking of a hermeneutics of historical time, this dual conception of the reader as both a moviegoer and a projectionist engages us in a *retrograde remediation*, to borrow Pavle Levi's apt term, in which we read the residual and we read residually such that a historical experience unfolds as we turn the pages of the book.[8] In that turning, reading the residual depends on reusing and recombining the products of film history such that the technological forces and representational forms inscribed within them, not unlike the statistical hieroglyphs of chapter 1, make obsolescence itself legible. In that turning, moreover, reading residually depends on reemploying the people of the cinematic past such that the legibility of obsolescence becomes a historical experience of the obsolescence of labor written into contemporary culture.

One of the most striking features of *Invention* is that it incorporates black-and-white stills from the first few decades of film history. These stills are central to how *Invention* remakes its readers into moviegoers deciphering the cinematic past in the present of their reading—that is, they are central to reading the residual. During one of his visits to the bookstore where some of the action of the novel unfolds, for example, Hugo recounts to Etienne and Isabelle, a young man and girl he befriends, the time that he went to the movies to see the 1923 slapstick film *Safety Last!* with his now deceased father. This recounting occurs in prose. But immediately after his recounting, a photographic still flashes up, appearing when the reader turns the page (figure 2.9; Selznick, 174–175). The first to appear in the book, this still is one among a number of black-and-white stills in *Invention*, including two that occur later in the novel, from 1902's *A Trip to the Moon* and 1895's *Arrival of a Train at La Ciotat* (figures 2.10 and 2.11; Selznick, 352–353, 348–349). The latter two appear in a book of film history that Hugo and Isabelle read at the Film Academy Library. Although not figured as the flashing up of a personal memory in the way the still from *Safety* is, the placement of these other stills within historiographical discourse nonetheless means that they embody the same thing: a memory of moviegoing taking shape as a readerly constellation that commemorates film history as a reusable past across the pages of *Invention*.

The appearance of these stills in the novel is often textually motivated in that, as in the above stills, they represent the mental operations of characters either remembering moviegoing or learning about film history. However, the stills are also potent elements of the material form of the book, photographic sites at which we read the residual through reuse and recombination. These sites have a series of material properties that emerge both independently and relationally in *Invention*. The most visible property of the stills is, of course, their tonality. All of them are in black and white, affiliating them

FIGURE 2.9   Still from *Safety Last!* (1923), film by Harold Lloyd, as it appears in Brian Selznick, *The Invention of Hugo Cabret* (Scholastic Inc., 2007). Copyright © Harold Lloyd Entertainment, Inc. Used with permission.

FIGURE 2.10 Still from *A Trip to the Moon* (1902), film by Georges Méliès, as it appears in Brian Selznick, *The Invention of Hugo Cabret* (Scholastic Inc., 2007).

FIGURE 2.11 Film Lumière Number 653: *Arrivée d'un train à La Ciotat* (France, 1895) Copyright © Institut Lumière, as it appears in Brian Selznick, *The Invention of Hugo Cabret* (Scholastic, Inc., 2007). Used with permission.

with what Miriam Hansen calls "outdated representational styles."[9] The datedness of this tonal style is the result of technological shifts that correlate to
aesthetic transformations. The shift in question began most significantly in the
1950s and concluded in the 1970s. By the end of the later decade, 96 percent
of U.S. feature films were being shot using color film stock.[10] Generally speaking, these types of shifts materially date spectators' experiences of films because
the technological forces of development in the film industry are so deeply
keyed to the representational forms of cinema at any given historical moment.
This technological and aesthetic correlation is more pronounced over shorter
periods of time in film history than, say, literary history, though the material
form that *Invention* gives to the book—with its thread-sewn binding, high-
quality paper, and simulation of a heavy, leather-bound book—does self-
consciously key it to a prior moment of publishing.

In this instance, the important point is that for any contemporary reader
of *Invention*, the cinematic intersection of forces and forms is most obvious
in the black-and-white stills that project them materially—and readers of
the book with them—into an experience of the past shaped by a hermeneutics of historical time. That past is not gone for good here, not an archaism
of the most inert and inactive sort, but rather residual in that these movies
retain a material purchase on the present, reactivated for a new use by *Invention*. Generally, the obsolete and the outmoded tend to persist into the present
because dated technologies and passé clothes, for instance, do not simply melt
into air but rather build up in our drawers and closets. This is even true of old
films at times, including those of Méliès, which can be found decaying after
the original mania for them has passed, awaiting discovery by preservationists
and cinephiles who turn them into classics. Here, however, that persistence is a
bookish rediscovery, part and parcel of the way in which culture by outmoded
means inventively adapts the past in the present, with *Invention* in particular
drawing the past into an experience of reading in which the reader is also a
spectator, indeed, a reader-cum-spectator who is invited to look with obsolete
eyes when she reads the residual in the tonality of these black-and-white stills.

To the extent that reading the residual entails looking with obsolete eyes in
Invention, however, that readerly act of outmoded spectatorship is not fueled
by a fantasy that we have direct access to cinematic sights that early moviegoers experienced with their own senses. This is not what it means to experience the past, which can only appear as past because subsequent presents
have left it behind. Thus reading the residual is an act in which one deciphers
the cinematic past in the readerly present, pointing to how the reuse of these
stills as a central feature of the material form of *Invention* makes reading the
residual into a hermeneutics of historical time. Such a hermeneutics develops
most immediately due to the tonality of the stills dating them as not belonging
to, if still persisting in, the present—as being the products of, if you will, an

outmode of cinematic production. However, this hermeneutics also develops because reading the residual pulls us into a more mediated dimension of the stills than their tonal surfaces: a material nexus of technological forces of production and aesthetic forms of representation that, although artifacts of the cinematic past, remain residually active in the ones reprinted in *Invention*. As we shall see, the hermeneutics of historical time that *Invention* realizes perceptually and cognitively in its reader-spectators is especially powerful to the degree that these stills are recombined in constellation with one another.

The stills from *Arrival* and *Trip*, for instance, share the basic compositional principle of the tableau, even as they point in different directions in their uses of it: one deep and perspectival and thus away from it, one flat and frontal and thus toward it.[11] There are cultural reasons for this principle, especially in *Trip*. The tendency toward tableau, radicalized in its flatness and frontality in the great majority of his films, was an effect of Méliès emerging out of a tradition of theatrical showmanship in France, with the typically lateral arrangement of actors and actions in his films pointing as well to the *tableau vivant*.[12] But this is not the reason for the quality of tableau in *Arrival*, which possesses depth that most of Méliès's films do not, including *Trip*. The rationale for tableau in *Arrival*—though tableau in depth, I should say—is more closely bound to factors that would have enforced greater fixity of and less movement from the camera in shooting films at the end of the nineteenth century and beginning of the twentieth century. A static shot predominated in early film aesthetics, with the still from *Arrival* heralding what would become professional norms about the value of a stable image as indicative of technical skill in filmmaking.[13] A second factor behind the tableau was the technological state of early cinema. While the sixteen-pound camera the Lumière brothers used was by all means portable, it was not yet fully mobile, not yet an agile-enough apparatus technologically and aesthetically to turn camera movement into a representational form in its own right.[14] In their time, then, *Arrival* and *Trip* tended toward versions of the tableau due to a variety of factors that led to static shots, with dynamism emerging instead out of diegetic action (a train seemingly moving toward the screen in *Arrival*) and special effects (the editorial tricks that land the rocket in the eye of the moon in *Trip*) rather than camera movement.[15] The state of camera technology along with cultural ideals of technical skill related to that state (so many forces of production) thus converged in the past to produce differing versions of the tableau as one of the privileged shots of early film (a form of representation), with these forces and that form residually enduring in the shots, if at a standstill of sorts, which *Invention* quotes from *Arrival* and *Trip* as part of the present of our reading.

Reproduced and remixed in one book, these stills allow the residual to be read in the sense that the forms and forces inscribed within them refer us backward in cinematic time to the origins of film history from the vantage point of our present. Their residual qualities are, moreover, strengthened by the fact that, across the reading of the book, they exist in constellation with the still from *Safety Last!* that reader-spectators would have already encountered earlier in the novel. Recalled during this later moment in the reading of *Invention*, the still from *Safety* deepens the historicity of those from *Arrival* and *Trip* when we encounter them, making what is residual about them readable because it constitutes an advance over them in the technological and aesthetic motion of film history in the early decades of the twentieth century. To begin with the 1895 film, a basic compositional parallel between the shots quoted from *Safety* and *Arrival* stresses this point. A diagonal line runs from the bottom-left area toward the upper-right portion of both of the stills. But the depth of field that the line traces in the still from *Safety* makes for a composition that appears to have superseded *Arrival* technically and aesthetically. For one, the still from *Safety* is in much greater focus. This is a formal feature that was to some degree enabled by developments in the forces of cinematic production by the 1920s, especially in film stock and camera technology, which expanded the material wealth of visual information that moviegoers could decipher once the film was being projected in theaters. But this point should not be unduly stressed. A crisp depth of field was technologically possible as early as 1895 even if later cameras did steadily improve upon that possibility. Moreover, the visual intelligibility of the image in *Safety*, the depth of its focus, would have been consistent with the generic concern to depict action with extreme clarity in slapstick cinema.[16] It is true that the still that *Invention* uses from *Arrival* looks, comparatively speaking, as if it is technologically less advanced when it comes to optics. The enlargement is blurrier and, therefore, apparently backward in relation to the still from *Safety*. But this could easily be an artifact of the provenances of the prints used and restoration processes applied (or not) to them at the archives where they originated (Selznick, 531–533). It is nonetheless significant that the relative blurriness of the still selected for reuse in Selznick's book inscribes the residual sense of a more backward time in the forces of production than film had available to it in terms of clarity and focus.

This residual sense of backward time is more robustly in play due to the additional fact that the still from *Safety* embodies the forward momentum of forces of production and forms of representation across the early decades of film history, in particular advances in technical skill that were involved in the shooting of a film, especially in how workers used the camera. In fact, the shot quoted in *Invention* does not even require the reader-spectator of the novel ever to have seen *Safety* to decipher this more advanced relationship to using the camera in more dexterously mobile ways to represent the virtuoso physicality of the slapstick star. An exterior shot of Harold Lloyd hanging from a clock is no longer committed to the fixed camera of early cinema, requiring in addition a complicated on-location setup involving multiple cameras and a camera tower that would have been a major step forward for the Lumière brothers and Georges Méliès alike.[17] That shot, moreover, also mobilizes the depth of field technologically possible in the forces of cinematic production in order to play formally with the diagonal line that the composition of *Safety* shares with *Arrival* but that, in the end, is far more technically and aesthetically complex in Lloyd's film. In filming, the cameramen used the camera beautifully, capturing Lloyd looking out into the profilmic space implied in the upper-right space beyond and exterior to the still that the reader encounters almost a century later in Selznick's book. Along with the hand of the clock from which he hangs, which is almost pointing to 3:00 p.m., Lloyd's line of sight, his direct address out at us from the page on which the still is reprinted, constitutes so much brilliant slapstick play on the line of perspective that moves backward from the left center at the bottom of the still toward the upper-right quadrant of it. In comparison to the one from *Arrival*, the still from *Safety* playfully pictures what was a techno-aesthetic leap forward in how filmmakers employed the forces of cinematic production, the formal power of which materializes in the ludic delineation of a highly focused depth of field in which the reader-spectator's eye can roam along the lines that animate the shot quoted by *Invention*.

So far, then, reading the residual is a twofold activity. First, through the simple reuse of any one of these stills, it involves the reader-spectator of *Invention* in deciphering the past in the present by stirring him or her to look with obsolete eyes, as with the tonality of the stills. Second, through the recombination of those stills, reading the residual also involves the reader-spectator in decrypting how the cinematic past was itself made up of a series of technologically and aesthetically advancing presents, the furious motion of which leaves behind so many residual marks, like hieroglyphs, which we continue to decode from those now-bygone presents, as in the constellation of stills. Not insignificantly, reading the residual takes a third form related to these, for the hermeneutics of historical time that it promotes draws the reader-spectator into an experience of reading not only the successive technological forces and representational forms of film history in the stills but also what, in fittingly heated language, Jonathan Crary calls "the transient elements in an accelerating sequence of displacements and obsolescences" produced by "the delirious operations of modernization" in capitalist history writ large.[18] These are the broader operations by which the cinematic image is transformed in and over time in concert with technological change steaming ahead in other industries, with new technologies displacing older ones due to the capitalist commitment to render as much obsolete as possible in the search for profit. In film history, these operations also outmode certain representational forms as new ones arise in a cycle that inexorably leads, for instance, from the more "primitive" technics and aesthetics of *Arrival* and *Trip* to the more "modern" ones of *Safety*—not to mention, nearly a century later, *Hugo*, the virtuoso 3-D adaptation of *Invention* from Scorsese, in which the deliriousness of cinematic modernization has hurtled digitally ahead in technological time. *Hugo* explicitly represents that delirium in a spectacular montage in which the title character dreamily imagines film history across its early decades while reading a book about the birth of cinema. In fact, the source of this montage is exactly the constellation of reemployed stills from *Invention*. As in the montage from *Hugo*, if with less techno-aesthetic spectacle, the delirious operations of modernization are delineated in that constellation such that they, too, become a residually readable feature of their form and content. What is delineated, in short, is obsolescence itself, that process by which products and people fall into history becoming legible.

I employ the verb *delineate* in asserting how this process becomes legible in *Invention* because, reinforcing how they exist in constellation with one another, line is a major element of the geometry of all of the stills, recurring across them in two ways. First, line produces one-point perspective in two of the stills and is related to the idea of perspective in the third, in which line is more suggestive than productive of depth. This representational form—the delineation of perspective—is at delightfully skillful work in the *Safety* still, with part of the skill of that shot being its slapstick play not only on the line of perspective inside of it but also on the paintings of bourgeois modernity, such as 1880's *Un balcon* by Gustave Caillebotte, which it recalls. But of course, in between *Un balcon* and *Safety Last!* is *Arrival of a Train at La Ciotat* in 1895, with one-point perspective being a feature of the diagonal line that organizes the geometry of that still as well, which the camera generated automatically and indexically as a material aspect of the film. However, while line delineates perspective in *Safety* and *Arrival*, the line of interest in the still from *A Trip to the Moon* is different. The rocket ship poking out of the eye of the moon in it creates a line that moves from the upper right leftward, toward the center of the two-page spread, organizing the geometry of the still. But although it hints at it, it does not produce the perspectival depth indexed in *Safety* and *Arrival*. The shot that *Invention* quotes from *A Trip* is, in keeping with its powerful tableau aesthetic, characterized by flattened frontality due to the minimal relations between foreground (the clouds that frame the still) and background (the face of the moon at the center of the still). Between these two dimensions is the rocket, where, in the middle, it suggests one-point perspective without ever fully marking it out such that it opens up. Nonetheless, as Tom Gunning (with whom Selznick spoke in his research for *Invention* [Selznick, 530]) writes in an essay on Méliès and modern vision, "The sequence [of edits leading up to this shot] functions like a point-of-view shot, the view of the explorers [in the rocket] as they speed toward the moon." This, contends

Gunning, is actually "a nonhuman point of view, the view precisely of the projectile as it arcs toward the moon. More than simply indicating a view, the shot makes palpable a trajectory. In effect, this is a peculiarly technological and modern viewpoint, the viewpoint of the speeding rocket."[19] The diagonal line in this still is thus the culminating trace of a sequence of edits that plays with the idea of perspective, mediating and meditating on the practices of looking that modernity develops by technological means when it suggests the point of view of a spaceship in employing techniques for generating such points of view in early film aesthetics.

But we can also say that the lines of perspective in both *Arrival* and *Safety* are such technologically generated points of view themselves. Perspectival depth in *Arrival* precisely *is* the nonhuman point of view of the speeding rocket. The ontological thrust of this sentence makes sense especially if we understand the rocket as a figure for modern technology not unlike the invention of the film camera in this period, which, as with all photographic media, automatically creates lines of perspective as a material dimension of the image rather than committing what André Bazin calls the "sin" of creating it by hand.[20] Meanwhile, *Safety* represents a more aesthetically agile delineation of depth of field, resulting from the advancing trajectory of technical skill in the use of cameras between the 1890s and the 1920s alongside the development of a more state-of-the-art system of editing. Relative to both *Trip* and *Arrival*, in other words, the more deeply focused delineation of perspective in the still from *Safety* was in its time the realization of a once-future practice of technological looking that could see much farther and much better, not unlike what was obviously in the early twentieth century still the wholly science-fiction fantasy of seeing the moon up close in the way that *Trip* imagines. To us, of course, none of these perspectives, points of view, and practices of looking—none of these forms—is anything new, including seeing the moon up close, since we now have actual photographs of lunar landscapes, none of them populated by the "natives" *Trip* imagines. But in their time, these forms were embodiments of a technological modernity in cinema—of so many forces of production—embodiments that even the most up-to-date models of cars fail to be to the most eager of car enthusiasts today, except perhaps for those autonomous eighteen-wheelers that spell the end of long-haul trucking as a profession much as containerization has overhauled the work of stevedores by eliminating the need for much of their labor.[21]

This reference to shipping containers and eighteen-wheelers is admittedly abrupt. But so is the disruption such innovations can create. As such, this reference calls attention to the third form of reading the residual here. We are reading not only the cinematic past in our readerly present. We are reading not only the forces and forms by which film history moves from past to present technologically and aesthetically. We are also reading the residual in the sense that these stills delineate the vast quantities of stuff that technological change, with little in the way of relief, leaves behind as obsolete and outmoded in the motion of capitalist history. This point crystallizes when we focus on the fact that line is not only a major force in the form of the stills but also a matter of their content—what we might think of as their residual mise-en-scène—for the diagonal is delineated, more specifically, by what are now so many outmoded generations of transportation technology that we still use, though our use occurs in forms more closely synced to the current state of the forces of production: a nineteenth-century steam train, automobiles of 1910s and 1920s vintage, and a rocket ship that is very much an old-fashioned future for space travel. For the original spectators of *Arrival* and *Safety*, the train and the cars indexed historical moments in which technologies such as these were creating new markets and reorganizing space and time, in which they were restructuring everyday life with scheduled departures and arrivals that were increasingly synchronizing various locales as well as reshaping street life with newfangled vehicles and new forms of traffic.[22] The rocket in *Trip*, of course, did not concretely index anything technologically quotidian but rather projected a fantasy of future transportation that might render trains and cars obsolete—or at least make them forms of travel entirely quaint by comparison. In this respect, trains, rockets, and automobiles figured a more potent modernity and a more present contemporaneity, not to mention an imagined futurity, when these films were released than they ever could for the reader-spectator of *Invention*.

For that reader-spectator, what they converge to create is a line of perspective not only manufactured by that diagonal but also written anachronically out of that delirious sequence of obsolescences that the modernization of forces and forms in all kinds of industries intensively enforces across the deep time of capitalist history. In fact, that sequence and those operations are themselves delineated along the diagonal across these stills, since the lines of perspectives they variously trace are made out of the obsolete stuff of the technological past. To push this point further, locomotives, spaceships, and automobiles are the diegetic signals of a signifying system in residual operation across these stills, a system that the diagonal line repeatedly delineates. That system is less immediately perceptible than the train, rocket, and cars, though those technologies of transportation very well may be hieroglyphs of it. And if so, then there is so much historicity in the hieroglyphic.[23] This is yet another way of saying the stills invite us to read the residual as part of a hermeneutics of historical time: to decipher the past in the present, to decrypt that the past was itself made up of so many bygone presents still active today, and to decode the motion by which the new is so rapidly turned into the old and the once gloriously dominant is only somewhat less swiftly transformed into the at best residual—a technical and aesthetic trace left behind in the pictures of the past that, in *Invention*, we read as we turn the pages of the novel. Reading the residual is thus a retrograde motion into film history in *Invention* by which obsolescence itself becomes legible. Tapping into that process, the book culls from it so many outmoded products—the three film stills—so as to inventively give that past a residual life in reading by propelling us backward in historical time to look with obsolete eyes and, in the process, to decrypt the forces and forms that made those eyes obsolete in the first place.

If reading the residual reuses and recombines the past such that a hermeneutics of historical time arises in which obsolescence itself becomes perceptually legible, then reading residually reemploys the people of that past through page turning such that those same hermeneutics give rise to a nonsynchronous experience in which the obsolescence of labor materializes. Delving into page turning (or what Price earlier called "the hermeneutics of handling") means shifting focus from how *Invention* conceives of its reader as a moviegoer to how it historicizes that reader as a film projectionist (or in the ranking of Carl Benedikt Frey and Michael A. Osborne's 2013 study of technological unemployment, number 45 out of 702 of the jobs most likely to be computerized).[24] As with the "Brief Introduction," page turning more generally plays a major role in producing a cinematic rhythm in the reading of *Invention* that is residual due to its mimesis (or remimesis) of a black-and-white film. This mimesis recurs throughout the novel. Late in the novel, for instance, the original experience of *Arrival of a Train at La Ciotat* is remediated in a chapter entitled "A Train Arrives in the Station." The myth of the original experience is that the first film spectators believed a real locomotive was about to hurtle out at them from the screen, causing them in some versions to flee the screening. This myth is probably a hyperbolic version of what Gunning has more carefully described as those not-quite-yet-moviegoers' startled pleasure at witnessing a still image becoming mobile—an aesthetics of astonishment that Scorsese's *Hugo* reenacts in a flashback, a dream sequence, and in the climax to this adaptation.[25] *Invention* also reenacts these aesthetics by offering the reader a great deal of pleasure as she turns the pages and the train appears to get ever closer to bursting from the book (figures 2.12–2.16; Selznick, 460–469). But here, of course, it is the technics of page turning that brings those aesthetics about, yielding a hermeneutics of historical time because of the way in which the physical rhythm of reading mobilizes an originary moment of film history. That rhythm is reinforced by the high narrativity of this moment of page turning, in which Hugo is almost hit by the onrushing locomotive before being rescued in the nick of time as part of a longer sequence that is itself the climax of the novel.

On the one hand, the dramatically plotted character of this moment of reading time narrativizes the original experience of *Arrival*, a notably nonnarrative film, in its more hyperbolically mythic form at the textual level of the novel as a real threat to the human body. On the other hand, the page

FIGURE 2.12 From Brian Selznick, *The Invention of Hugo Cabret* (Scholastic Inc., 2007). Copyright © Brian Selznick. Used with permission.

FIGURE 2.13 From Brian Selznick, *The Invention of Hugo Cabret* (Scholastic Inc., 2007). Copyright © Brian Selznick. Used with permission.

FIGURE 2.14 From Brian Selznick, *The Invention of Hugo Cabret* (Scholastic Inc., 2007). Copyright © Brian Selznick. Used with permission.

FIGURE 2.15 From Brian Selznick, *The Invention of Hugo Cabret* (Scholastic Inc., 2007). Copyright © Brian Selznick. Used with permission.

FIGURE 2.16   From Brian Selznick, *The Invention of Hugo Cabret* (Scholastic Inc., 2007).
Copyright © Brian Selznick. Used with permission.

turning at the same time evokes the corporeal wonder of creating movement
out of stillness at the material level of handling the book. Interestingly, this
dialectic of bodily threat and physical wonder leads *Invention* to repeat the
dialectic of modern trauma and technological reparation that Walter Benjamin located in the medium of film as a "room-for-play" or *Spielraum*.[26] But
here that room opens up at the juncture of the textual and material forms of
the book as a medium. As a reader, when I turn the pages of *Invention*, it is
as if I am seeing pictures of the filmic past move by. But because I am moving
the pictures as I read, because I am the one turning the pages of the past with
my hands, it is also as if I were a film projectionist operating an old-fashioned
film projector that required manual cranking. Thus where reading the residual
revolves around a conception of reader as spectator in which the book's inventive adaptation of the products of the past yields a hermeneutics of historical
time wherein I decipher the past in the present, reading residually turns on a
conception of the reader as projectionist in which I find myself irrealistically
figured as a person of the past in the present of my reading.

What we are seeing in reading residually, then, is the propensity of culture
by outmoded means to engage the mimetic faculty (not to mention the irreality function that interests Gaston Bachelard and Scott Bukatman). In his suggestive fragment, "On the Mimetic Faculty," Benjamin delineates the human
capacity both to produce and to perceive similarities, including the drive to

become similar to something other than oneself. According to Benjamin, "Play is to a great extent [the mimetic faculty's] school," making children key figures in this fragment. "Children's play," he writes, "is everywhere permeated by mimetic modes of behavior, and its realm is by no means limited to what one person can imitate in another. The child plays at being not only a shopkeeper or teacher, but also a windmill and a train."[27] And in *Invention*, the reader, most likely a child, plays at being a film projectionist as a result of the "nonsensuous similarity" between turning the pages of this book and the act of physically moving pictures in the way that film projectionists once had to hand crank projectors.[28] Reading residually thus allows us also to inhabit historical time hermeneutically in the sense of playfully reemploying, to borrow some language from Moishe Postone's discussion of the double time of capitalism, the "accumulated knowledge and experience of humanity," especially the "knowledge, skills, and labor" of the film projectionist conjured here.[29] In reading *Invention*, in delving into its hermeneutics of historical time, we are possessed by the *ghost*, a word that recurs in both the novel and film, of the now largely obsolete worker who once operated an apparatus that mechanically clacked and luminously flickered—with both the defunct technician and the technology he used to operate described and depicted in myriad ways throughout *Invention* as well as *Hugo*.

Precisely that apparatus clacks and flickers in a major scene of both novel and film. Just prior to this point, Hugo and Isabelle have discovered that the identity of her godfather, Papa Georges, is in fact Georges Méliès, a largely forgotten father of cinema in the 1930s of the novel, during a visit to the Film Academy Library. In the scene in question, the children reveal their discovery to both him and his wife with the help of a film historian and preservationist, René Tabard, who comes to their home. The revelation to Méliès in particular hinges upon him hearing a film being projected in his home. "'I would recognize the sound of a movie projector anywhere,'" he says in both novel and adaptation (Selznick, 392). In the latter, that sound plays a prominent aural role that can only be described in the book, both in this scene and in a truly remarkable earlier one. During that earlier visit, Hugo and Isabelle learn the cinematic identity of Méliès by reading Tabard's book, *The Invention of Dreams: The Story of the First Movies Ever Made*. As they read, Tabard's fictitious history is translated into a spectacular montage of shots from early film, with pages turning and pictures moving interlaced, with a bookish hermeneutics of handling intercalated with shots swiftly succeeding one another as Hugo and Isabelle turn the pages, and with the relation between film and book sutured together by a soundtrack in which the clattering of early film projectors is the basic rhythmic unit. The cone of light that classically emanates from the film projector also appears in both film and novel as incandescent illustration and image, luminously projecting out at us from an illustrated two-page spread in one instance in the book (figure 2.17; Selznick, 198–199, 345). In *Hugo* and *Invention*, then, reading a book is nonsensuously similar to projecting a film.

To put a finer point on it, reading a book is non*synchronously* similar to projecting a film, a hermeneutics of historical time that *Invention* is able to more fully enact because it is a book with pages we turn with our hands. In this nonsynchronous similarity, moreover, *Invention* reemploys its reader in a job that has fallen into history. The nascent elements of the film projectionist's technological unemployment, not to mention the decline of their political power vis-à-vis unions, were already taking hold in the early 1960s. But the automation of booth technology throughout the 1970s with the introduction of platter systems made the writing on the increasingly multiplex wall of the 1980s quite clear, even if projectionist unions would, as Steve Tohill indicates in the second epigraph to this chapter, keep duking it out well into the turn of the twenty-first century in a description of class struggle more resonant of films by Scorsese other than *Hugo* such as *Taxi Driver* (1976) and *Raging Bull* (1980).[30] Platter projection eventually gave way to digital projection, which saved on labor costs not only by turning the projector into "'just a big computer with a light bulb inside'" but also by turning the projectionist into an unskilled operator who assisted in the computer's "ingestion" of "content," much of which was remotely monitored and controlled.[31] In the 2010s, even

FIGURE 2.17 From Brian Selznick, *The Invention of Hugo Cabret* (Scholastic Inc., 2007). Copyright © Brian Selznick. Used with permission.

though the profession lingers here and there in archival contexts, film projectionists have become an obsolete class of workers. Because "everything that 35mm presentation had left to the projectionist's care and judgment is now automated," as David Bordwell has observed, their art has waned.[32] Their labor has been expelled from their traditionally skilled role at the theatrical point of circulation for films, and the training of new generations of projectionists and the transmission of knowledge to them are no longer necessary since films are files you essentially drag and drop in order to screen them. And projectionist unions have been disempowered by corporate conglomerates invested by the 2000s in the "digital revolution" that would allow less-skilled and worse-paid workers to assume their tasks. The computerization of culture in the film industry has meant not the flattening of the workplace that too-hasty hagiographers of the digital once imagined but rather the nearly total elimination of a class of workers by automated means that heightens conflicts between labor and capital.

This narrative of technological unemployment reveals how reading residually is a rhythmic experience of historical time that draws an obsolete class of laborers into itself. In reading *Invention*, we are irrealistically reemployed in the work of the recent past—in the dual sense of both the labor that projectionists used to do and the hermeneutic production of historical time—by means of the material tempo of page turning. However, *Invention* can only draw these "ghosts" into the reading of this book in this way because they have been expelled from the marketplace of the movie theater in the first place. Reading residually thus incorporates two antithetical tendencies into itself in *Invention* because turning its pages pulls the reader into a strange process of human possession and technical exorcism. Reading this book *repeats* the steady death of film projectionists since the 1970s by *reviving* them. As a function of this irrealist play of nonsynchronous similarity between reader and projectionist, reading residually is marked by a contradiction, indicating that the historical experience to which it gives rise goes beyond mediating the dialectic of trauma and repair that technological modernity unleashes and that cinema engages for Benjamin. Far more crucially, reading residually also mediates the dialectics of technological change, propelled by the moving contradiction of Capital itself, which have made the obsolescence of labor a destabilizing feature of capitalist history. That obsolescence takes tactile form in the hermeneutics of historical time that physically turning the pages of the book embodies as we read. And in that form, this obsolescence both has *and* has not taken place because the film projectionist is both revived *and* made redundant all over again in the process of reading. In this respect, reading residually is a weird and wonderful object, to paraphrase Matthew Garrett, one in which we are reemployed in the work of the past *and* are rescued from suffering the consequences of that work having passed into history in the present.[33]

Taken together, then, when we read the residual and read residually—when we read by residual means—the time we pass is historical time. That time, however, also sits at a safe remove from the intensification of the obsolescence of labor in contemporary reality, with the cruelly contradictory quality of that reality, if not exactly repressed, then at least given hermeneutic room to play as so much historical irreality when the film projectionist is revived from obsolescence and rendered obsolete all at once in reading by residual means. Moreover, the idea that reading by residual means is a historical experience determined by the obsolescence of labor finds yet more evidence in the double story both *Invention* and *Hugo* tell. Falling into film history for that story, Georges Méliès and Hugo Cabret provide *Invention* and *Hugo* with narrative figures for our time from the deep time of capitalism, which has unremittingly left living labor out of sync and out of work for centuries. That narrative is as driven by a strategy of reemployment as the material form of the book is, aligning the plot most closely with reading residually. By the end of that narrative, however, it becomes clear that all this reuse and recombination of the cinematic past—this technological, aesthetic, and even economic impulse to reemploy—is about resisting and reversing the obsolescence of labor, making *Invention* and *Hugo* fascinating examples of comedy in its most classic senses.

The Obsolescence of Labor and the Comedy of Reemployment

In 2002, Famous Players, a large Canadian chain of movie theaters owned by the even larger U.S. conglomerate Viacom, locked out Local 348 of the International Alliance of Theatrical Stage Employees, Moving Picture Technicians, Artists and Allied Crafts, a small union of film projectionists in British Columbia whose numbers have declined exponentially throughout the late twentieth and early twenty-first centuries. The lockout was instituted because Famous Players insisted that the film projectionists accept a $10-an-hour wage. This hourly rate was down from the $15.50 that Tohill cites as his wage in the second epigraph to this chapter, which was itself a decrease from the range of $18–$33 after a prior dispute between Local 348 and Famous Players in 1998. Repeating another effort of the 1998 dispute, the 2002 one also involved Famous Players demanding that fewer and fewer projectionist jobs fall under union jurisdiction as part of the corporation's ongoing attempt to curtail the protections of organized labor. Famous Players saw such demands as warranted because the technically skilled labor that film projectionists used to practice had been falling into history due to automation and computerization in various forms over the final decades of the twentieth century. With their profession having become a statistically negligible quantity of the labor market by the early twenty-first century, film projectionists are one among many of the workers across vast numbers of industries over the past half century who have found themselves rendered obsolete and thus pulled into the destabilizing vortex of contradictions that growing technological unemployment has wearingly normalized.[34]

Film projectionists, however, are hardly the workers to which we normally turn in telling the story of work in the late twentieth and early twenty-first centuries, especially when it comes to the obsolescence of labor. Certainly, the automation of their profession is one way in which the obsolescence of labor has taken on increased legibility in our time because of how it has enveloped the kind of cultural work that filmmakers and novelists might have once done. However, since around 1973—actually, since around 1811—the typical protagonist of the obsolescence of labor has been the industrial proletariat. That proletariat is not overly represented in the double story that *Invention* and *Hugo* tell. However, the telling in both novel and film nonetheless narratively figures the post-1973 decline of manufacturing and the concomitant rise of not only a service sector but also what is often called *wageless life*. Both of these are bound up with the obsolescence of labor that has become so palpable since circa 2000, with this 2007 novel and 2011 film pushing into the past to emplot the present.

As already noted, the plot of *Invention* and *Hugo* is double, with two intertwining narratives focused, respectively, on a fictional version of the early French filmmaker, Georges Méliès, and the titular protagonist, Hugo Cabret, an urchin and orphan reminiscent of the child characters of sentimental literature and culture in prior centuries.[35] Set in a Parisian train station in 1931, both novel and film begin with an image of Méliès looking dejected and bored in a toy booth, an unknown commodity and forgotten filmmaker isolated from the bustle of commerce and travel in the rest of the station. We get this image of Méliès from Hugo's perspective as he gazes at the toy booth from behind a clock in the wall. Hugo's clockwork point of view is a device that stresses his lonely separation from the train station—depicted here as a sphere of economy, especially of circulation, with trains carrying people and products into and out of its space—in which he struggles to survive by secretly maintaining the clocks of the station after the death of his entire family. From the start of the novel and the film, then, the doubled quality of the plot is stressed. With Méliès and Hugo both depicted as marginal to the sphere in which they eke out their existences, both novel and film emplot not only the obsolescence of labor through Méliès but also, through Hugo, the related phenomenon of what—in an incongruously lovely phrase—Aaron Benanav calls the "twilight of irregular employment." This is a twilight in which significant numbers of people now subsist as members of what has come to be known as "wageless life" in the wake of deindustrialization since the 1970s.[36]

More directly than Hugo's story, Méliès's addresses the obsolescence of labor that has intensified as the post-1973 era has progressed by turning back to the turn of the twentieth century and the invention of cinema in the second Industrial Revolution. At a climactic point in the novel and film, for example, we learn how he ended up in the toy booth, in the scene in which the unmistakable sound of the movie projector has a prominent role. While Scorsese expands Selznick's original treatment of the scene, including its acoustics, it is important in both novel and film because the various threads of the plot start to resolve in it: the children, Hugo and Isabelle, have realized that Papa Georges is Georges Méliès; Tabard, the film historian, comes to the home of Méliès and screens the only remaining copy of *A Trip to the Moon* for Hugo, Isabelle, and Mama Jeanne, the wife of Méliès; and overhearing the projector clack, Méliès emerges from his room, eventually telling the story of his rise and fall after spending the duration of the film unsettled by the ghosts of that story. The novel tells the story in Méliès's own voice, in a dialogue depicted as being primarily between him and the children, and using a metadiegetic form of narration that relies very little on illustrations (Selznick, 404).[37]

Recounting his past, Méliès explains to Hugo and Isabelle that he came from a family that owned a shoe factory in the nineteenth century. Hating shoes but loving machinery, Méliès sold his share of the factory and entered the world of theater as a magician, playing with devices of wonder like the automaton that figures throughout the book. With the invention of the movies, he fell in love with cinema: "Many of us recognized a new kind of magic had been invented, and we wanted to be a part of it. My beautiful wife became my muse, my star. I made hundreds of movies, and we thought it would never end. How could it? But the war came, and afterward there was too much competition, and everything was lost," forcing him to fire his employees and, in an ironic twist, "sell my movies to a company that melted them down and turned them into shoe heels" (Selznick, 405, 406). Scorsese's adaptation will allow this detail to literally resonate in the movie theater by drawing aural attention to the echo of high heels. *Hugo* thus amplifies the pathos of the following passage from *Invention* in which Méliès explains how his magical career of making movies concluded with a sound that, for him, is clearly the opposite of the unmistakable timbre of the movie projector that inspires him to tell the tale of his decline: "With the money I made from the sale of my films, I bought the toy booth, where I've been trapped ever since, listening to the sounds of shoe heels clicking against the floor . . . the sound of my films disappearing forever into the dust. I was haunted by those ghosts for so many years" (Selznick, 406).

The details of Méliès's recounting above are somewhat fictionalized. Competition ruined the filmmaker before, not after, World War I, and many consider the height of his career in terms of quality and popularity to be circa 1903–1904. While World War I did play a role in the movement of the productive center of filmmaking to the United States as that nation-state began its steady march to political and economic hegemony in the twentieth century, what actually led to the outmoding of Méliès was threefold. First, the historical Méliès exhibited a persistent attachment to the genre of *féerie films* that he only reluctantly ceded as other narrative genres became fashionable. Second, he depended on an artisanal and filial mode of industrial production that was losing traction by the beginning of the twentieth century as other modes more fully subsumed into capitalism emerged. In contrast to the production processes being developed at Pathé, for instance, Méliès's mode was highly labor-intensive and increasingly costly. As this second factor suggests, the third source of his fall into history was the growing power of a corporate model of standardized industrial production that was technologically and economically outmoding the model of capitalist organization structured around the family, which looked back to the nineteenth century and, in the case of Méliès, entailed an obstinate attachment to film as art, not business.[38] As these three factors indicate, the outmoding of Méliès took shape at the nexus of "mode as fashion and mode as means of production" at the turn of the century in the midst of the second Industrial Revolution.[39] Méliès, then, fell into obsolescence as a result of interrelated causes originating in both the sphere of circulation and the sphere of production, with trends in the marketplace and changes in the factory joining forces to leave him behind.

This is only loosely the story that the fictional Méliès recounts about his rise and fall in *The Invention of Hugo Cabret* and *Hugo*. But there are nonetheless interesting traces of it in the novel's version of events, which the film narratively and visually elaborates such that Méliès emerges as a figure for those who have fallen into history due to obsolescence. Consider the detail of the shoes. It is true that the Méliès family manufactured shoes in the nineteenth century, especially boots, but the filmmaker did not sell his films in the ironic twist that the novel invents. The reality of the irony was far harsher. The military seized some of his leftover films during World War I, and "the celluloid was used to make boot heels for the army."[40] But in having to sell his films to a shoe manufacturer, as the novel has it, *Invention* stresses the outmoding of Méliès by making him actively peddle his wares to the very industry he sought to escape; this was an industry that successfully adapted to methods of mass production and circulation in ways that Méliès did not, embracing both the dialectics of technological change that displaced and deskilled labor in the factory and the rhythms of fashion that helped ensure a given shoe company's competitiveness in the sphere of circulation.[41]

Employing both voiceover and visuals, *Hugo* shores up our sense of the obsolescence of the early filmmaker when it significantly expands this invented detail in the cinematic version of Méliès's recounting. Carefully and caringly made with too much labor, a process that *Hugo* depicts at far greater length and with much more elegiac texture than *Invention*, Méliès's films become the raw material for what Scorsese's adaptation explicitly represents as a partially automated industrial process in which no remarkable skill is required of the workers. After we watch workers throw the now-fungible film into canisters where it is set on fire with none of the techno-aesthetic care that went into the moving pictures inscribed on the material, we then see liquefied celluloid smoothly and swiftly pouring into molds for the casts of shoe heels. This latter aspect of the process seems to have done away with human beings altogether. Like the machinery in Marx's chapter on that subject in the first volume of *Capital*, the mechanical operations depicted are stripped of the artisanal pleasure and artistic skill that the film delights in portraying when it shows Méliès crafting his movies in the longer sequence of which this moment of melting down is a part. The film, moreover, reassigns the gender of the shoes made, left vague in the novel, from boots designed for military men to high heels for women.

The combined effect of these details—the liquidation of Méliès's laboriously made films after his decline in popularity and profitability; their feminized transformation into a mass commodity, women's shoes, which could not embody the stylistic cycles of planned obsolescence any more perfectly; how that transformation depends on the dialectics of technological change that displace living labor—is to draw out how the Georges Méliès of *Invention* and *Hugo* is a figuration of the outmoded. Like the Vitruvian Steam-bot offered up as paradigmatic of culture by outmoded means, the fictional Méliès has a mimetically figural affinity with the industrial worker rendered obsolete in the post-1973 era. To apply the spectral idiom that the Méliès of novel and film uses over and over again, the ghost of that worker effectively haunts the frames of *Hugo* when the movie depicts those essentially deskilled workers dumping his films into canisters before a machine takes over for them, pouring the casts of the shoes without their labor. As it substitutes the artisanal Méliès for the factory worker, as the industrial laborer is replaced by an automated machine, it is almost as if this succession of shots is reenacting the dialectics of technological change by which living labor dies off when production processes become steadily more mechanized in the inexorable motion of Capital itself in its search for profits—a motion that has clearly enveloped the fictional Méliès such that he becomes a figuration of the outmoded resonant with workers rendered obsolete in the name of that search.

His figuration as such is intensified further in the film by the fact that Méliès's metadiegetic narration of his story in the novel is dramatically analeptic in *Hugo*. It takes temporal shape as a vividly extended flashback that, compared to the novel, seizes upon the narrative with a memory of making movies that doubles as a memory of manufacturing. The flashback in the film emplots the French magician and filmmaker performing in popular magic shows we get to see, discovering cinema in the 1890s in a moment to which we are privy, and opening his famous glass studio and reveling in making his films there until World War I, when, he says, "Tastes had changed. But I had not changed with them"—a failure to adapt that leads his studio to fall into ruin, a process that we witness unfold in a time-lapse sequence elegiac in the tempo of its visual narration of decline. Watching this extended flashback, especially in the form of a time-lapse sequence, is not unlike surveying all the unused factories that have piled up one after another in landscapes real and representational alike since 1973. But this sequence figures rather than represents the ruins of manufacturing that mechanization, automation, and computerization have made a facet of our time, all in the name of emphasizing the obsolescence into which one laborer, Méliès, has fallen. That the stories of both *Invention* and *Hugo* address these aspects of the post-1973 epoch, that the fictional Méliès is a character with affinities to the obsolete workers of our time, is also evident in that his own narrative trajectory from movie studio to toy booth is extraordinarily difficult to read as anything but an allegory of the motion of capitalist history from the labor of material making in the sphere of production to the work of retail services that has characterized the shift from the post-1945 boom to the post-1973 bust in advanced capitalist economies in the twentieth and twenty-first centuries.

The story of Georges Méliès as *Invention* and *Hugo* tell it, then, indicates the determinate role that the obsolescence of labor in both our and prior eras of capitalist history plays in Selznick's book and Scorsese's film, with this fictional character emerging as nothing less than a figuration of that obsolescence. But how does Hugo's story address the obsolescence of labor? How does this character, the main character, emerge as a figuration of the outmoded? Unlike Méliès, Hugo cannot be understood as a character that has affinities with the industrial laborer who discovers himself out of work and out of sync. Neither is he a figure who was once employed but now is not. Nor is he only a twenty-first-century pastiche of those orphans and urchins to be found in works of the eighteenth, nineteenth, and twentieth centuries. Such sentimental characters figured the economic immiseration and intimate deprivations of their own moments in various historically specific forms. But while he is related to that genealogy, he is ultimately a figuration of the outmoded because he embodies, in the words of Michael Denning, "the end of work as we have known it," especially the expulsion of increasing numbers of workers from the formal wage relation that flourished more readily in the heyday of manufacturing. Indeed, if we recall Tohill and the battle over film projectionist wages at the outset of this section, we even see how the wage relation has been radically attenuated for those still being paid by the hour as a function of the dialectics of technological change by which certain kinds of work are brought to automated ends.

In his useful essay "Wageless Life," Denning shows that one of the central characters of "the end of work" in the post-1973 era is "not the child in the sweatshop that is our most characteristic figure [for capitalist exploitation], but the child in the streets, alternately predator and prey."[42] A more fitting description of Hugo could not be found, as the analeptic narration of how he came to be living a wageless life in a Parisian train station, keeping its clocks synchronized for no pay at all, reveals. In what almost feels like a gesture to the threats faced by early film projectionists due to combustible film, we learn through the analepsis that his father died in a fire, trapped in a room engulfed in flames as he repaired an automaton he had discovered at the museum where he worked part time. With his mother already dead, Hugo's uncle adopts him, forcing him to steal food in the train station to eat and to attend to the clocks in the train station in his stead until the uncle disappears. When his uncle doesn't return, Hugo initially decides to escape. But then he comes across an automaton in the burned wreckage of the museum where his father died. Seeing it as his inheritance, he takes "the ruined machine" and returns to the train station, believing if he fixes the automaton, it might produce a message from his father—its mechanical trick is that it can write—and "he wouldn't be so completely alone" (Selznick, 130, 131). But he also knows that if he is going to stay out of an orphanage, not to mention feed himself, he must maintain the clocks perfectly, keep out of the station inspector's way, and steal to live, doing "his best to remain invisible." Conspicuously, he also has enough foresight to know that he must "take his uncle's paychecks from the office when no one was looking (although he didn't know how to cash them)" (Selznick, 132). This child character thus steals to survive but is under a constant threat that he will be imprisoned by the state as an orphan. However, the single most meaningful aspect of Hugo's backstory is the paycheck that he invisibly collects but that he is cruelly unable to cash, forcing him to be both predator and prey, if not in the streets, then in the train station. The uncashed paycheck is a remarkable detail in the context of a novel intended primarily for children. For what is being ironically (and painfully so) figured in that detail is Hugo's exclusion from the formal wage relation, stressing that he is living a wageless life in the same sphere into which Méliès has also been thrown.

Wageless life has gained expanding structural ground in the post-1973 era, with exclusion from the wage relation defining the terms of social reproduction for more and more people, including children, not only in the advanced capitalist world but also across the planet. In "Wageless Life," Denning writes that after "mass unemployment" seemed to have become "a thing of the past" following the Great Depression in the 1930s, when, we should note, *Invention* and *Hugo* are set, "the Great Recession of the 1970s in Europe and North America marked the return of the specter of wageless life, now under the sign

of redundancy—the permanent shuttering of plants as entire regions underwent an Industrial Counterrevolution," with "rust belts [emerging] around
the globe" from the United States and the United Kingdom to India, South
Africa, Brazil, and South Korea.[43] What living wagelessly has meant in these
rust belts depends on where in the world a person is. In the industrializing
world of the latter countries, especially once "the growth of [manufacturing]
jobs stalled" in them in the 1970s, it has meant the material explosion and neoliberal normalization of an "informal sector" marked by high levels of "self-
employment," such as street vendors in South Africa who gather "fabric scraps
discarded by textile mills" to make quilt covers they then sell or "the thousands
of street children [in Egyptian cities] who gather and resell cigarette butts
(a pack a day otherwise costs half of a poor man's salary)."[44] In the advanced
capitalist world, wageless life has been dominated by the idea of unemployment steadily normalized across the metacycle of productive capital in the
long nineteenth and twentieth centuries.[45] In that world, it has covered those
who find themselves out of work in a variety of forms, with the most salient
ones for this chapter being what Aaron Benanav and John Clegg describe
as "the explosive growth of a low-wage service-sector [that has] partially offset
the decline in manufacturing employment," with those low wages themselves
problematically offset by unsustainable levels of personal debt among workers.
This debt is itself evidence for the attenuation of the formal wage relation in
the post-1973 era. Compounding this situation is the fact that unemployment
is more chronic and protracted in the advanced capitalist world than it used to
be, including for what Hugo is—a young person.[46]

The story of Méliès fairly clearly addresses the obsolescence of labor, his
plot making him a figuration of the outmoded in that he embodies the shift
from production to circulation work, from laboring in manufacturing to
getting by in services. Keyed more to the wageless subject than the obsolete
laborer, how the story of Hugo addresses the obsolescence of labor is different.
Hugo emerges as a figuration of the outmoded because he has affinities with
the child who must survive in the wake of the wage relation in the deindustrializing world where, like Hugo, he lives off of the scraps of the economy. Of
course, he figures that child, not to mention wageless life as such, in what is
by and large a comfortably sentimental form. Nonetheless, he still also figures
the more terminally insidious drive toward the obsolescence of labor embedded in capitalist history. "Over time," to return to Benanav and Clegg, "more
and more workers . . . will find that they are unable to insert themselves into
the reproduction process. In this the proletariat tendentially becomes an externality to the process of its own reproduction, a class of workers who are 'free'
not only of the means of reproduction, but also of work itself."[47] In the case
of Hugo, this externality appears when he collects paychecks he cannot cash
to sustain himself—an exclusion from the wage relation, moreover, which

novel and film picture through the clockwork device described earlier. In giving us drawings and shots of Hugo peering out from behind clocks he himself keeps synchronized, the novel and film ironically inscribe how out of sync this out-of-work subject is in the world in which he nonetheless must labor to get by. It is worth it to be unduly literal for a moment. These images communicate that he is *behind the times*, dominated by an economy from which he is excluded and of which he is simultaneously constitutive. They announce that he is outmoded in the capitalist present by giving us pictures of Hugo as a nonsynchronous subject getting propelled *out* of a *mode* of production—a mode that he cannot *not* inhabit. A ghost before he has even died, a subject of the past before he has even had a chance to be in the present, Hugo has fallen into history before he has even entered adulthood.

The obsolescence of labor is thus a powerfully determinant force in the double story that *Invention* and *Hugo* tell, with the close reading of their mutual narrative pointing back as well to how much that obsolescence underwrites the historical experience of reading by residual means. In Williams's conception of the residual, the means that express it can sometimes assume a resistant energy, stirring alternative imaginaries and oppositional forces.[48] Something like this resistant energy fuels reading by residual means. The hermeneutics of historical time it sparks by reemploying the products and people of the cinematic past attempts to remind us that they are worthy of writerly reuse and readerly attention, refuting the contempt with which we often behold the obsolete and the outmoded by revaluing both as the stuff of cultural production.[49] This resistant energy also fuels the double story of *Invention* and *Hugo*, which attempts to undo the obsolescence of labor of which Méliès and Hugo are figurations by comically emplotting their reemployment, restoring these two characters to work they want to do.

This comedy hinges upon the all-important device of the automaton in the novel and film. Throughout both *Invention* and *Hugo*, Hugo labors to repair the automaton his father left behind as a means of remaining connected to him. It is precisely this labor that results in the narrative intersection of Méliès and Hugo in the first place, with Hugo stealing parts from Méliès's toy booth in the hopes of fixing it, until the former filmmaker catches him. The automaton, therefore, is a technological device and a narrative device, this latter function reinforcing itself as the story progresses—for example, when it is eventually revealed that Méliès was the inventor of this particular automaton, which itself leads to the revelation that Méliès was a famous filmmaker. The former event occurs because Hugo discovers that the final part he requires to make the automaton work hangs around the neck of Isabelle, the niece of Méliès who has befriended Hugo throughout the story. Once that key is inserted, the automaton not only operates, but it also does what Hugo imagined it would: it writes. Or rather, it draws and signs. What it draws is the famous image of the moon with the rocket in its eye from *A Trip to the Moon*. What it signs is the name "Georges Méliès." Believing the automaton was going to produce a secret message from his father, the automaton instead sets in narrative motion the sequence of events that leads to the children learning that Papa Georges is Georges Méliès, meaning that a father—a cinematic papa—nonetheless does emerge from the device. In fact, by the end of the novel, Méliès will adopt Hugo, rescuing him from economic immiseration and intimate deprivation. In producing that drawing and signature, the automaton brings about a happy ending, engendering a family for Hugo once again.

In all of this, the automaton serves a classic function. Its purpose is akin to that of "the traditional birthmark in comedy, which permits," as Peter Brooks observes, "the final recognition and untying of knots."[50] In serving that function, this device renders the obsolescence of labor as comedy, irrealistically remaking that which all too realistically brings about that obsolescence, automation, into that which reverses it. Over and against the realism within which narratives of the obsolescence of labor often tragically unfold (just think of Frank Socotra's tragic death in season two of *The Wire*), *Invention* and *Hugo* operate according to the principles of what Northrop Frye calls "low mimetic comedy," in which "resolution . . . frequently involves a social promotion."[51] In both the novel and film, an automated device enables characters to find a renewed place in their narrative reality rather than what such devices have done since capitalism began: displace them. This is why Joshua Clover describes *Hugo* as belonging to a mode he calls "comedies of reemployment."[52] In a brief but insightful review of the film, entitled "Enjoy the Silents," which applies equally well to the novel, Clover arrives at this fitting characterization of the genre of *Hugo* by close reading the automaton: "But of course it is also an image of the assembly line, the container crane, the mechanical loom. Automation is what replaces living labor, increasing productivity but undermining the very source of surplus value until every process is nearly perfected, nearly everybody is out of work and the economy is in crisis. It is not cinema so much as industry *tout court* that is a self-reproducing, self-annihilating machine."[53] In this respect, the automaton, like Méliès and Hugo, is a figuration of the outmoded in that it figures the obsolescence of labor as it "pivot[s] around technology-driven unemployment"[54] in the post-1973 era, in fact, since at least the onset of the first Industrial Revolution. But while it may *figure* that material reality now and then alike, what it *emplots* is the opposite, providing novel and film with a narrative device by which both Méliès and Hugo end up reemployed, promoted from their fall into history and restored to the capitalist present.

We have seen how this reemployment works comically to the extent that Hugo regains a family. But how does it work more specifically as a comedy of reemployment that "end[s] with everybody in the right job"? In the case of Méliès, two concluding developments take place. As a result of the automaton-triggered revelation that he is *the* Georges Méliès, René Tabard not only gives him a job on the faculty at the Film Academy but also undertakes the effort to find and restore as many of his films as possible. In the penultimate scene of both *Invention* and *Hugo*, there is a public screening of his films—a night of viewing that draws both the diegetic attendees and the readers and viewers of the novel and film, respectively, into a commemorative constellation organized around the cinema of Méliès not unlike the one into which reading the residual draws us in Selznick's novel. Méliès may not be making movies anymore, then, but he is reinstated in collective memory as a moviemaker, the things he made and the knowledge he has interesting and useful to people of the present once again, as is emphasized by the fact that he will work as a teacher. What his pedagogy will look like is actually a lesson we learned earlier, in the scene where he recalls his rise and fall in that moment of metadiegetic narration in the novel and in the moment of extended analepsis in the film. This is, in both, also a moment of intergenerational transmission with regards to technological change. However, it reverses the popular trope of youth teaching the aged how to make sense of newfangled technologies that befuddle them, with Méliès instead instructing Hugo and Isabelle, as we have been by this book and movie, about past processes of production in which living labor played a starring role in much the way the black-and-white stills engage us in the technological forces and representational forms of the cinematic past. By the end of the novel and film, Méliès has regained a version of that role, fulfilling the fundamental requirement of the comedy of reemployment: being returned to the work you love even if its material conditions are gone for good.

Hugo is similarly reemployed by the end of the novel and film. At a party following the public screening of his films, Méliès engages in an act that affirms his prototypically comic paternity in the plot at this point when he gives Hugo a name derived from that of a recurring character in his films, Professor Alcofrisbas. The significance of renaming Hugo to the comedy of reemployment is clearest in the final chapter of the novel, cleverly entitled "Winding It Up." It is worth quoting the chapter in full:

> Time can play all sorts of tricks on you.
> In the blink of an eye, babies appear in carriages, coffins disappear into the ground, wars are won and lost, and children transform, like butterflies, into adults.
> That's what happened to me.
> Once upon a time, I was a boy named Hugo Cabret, and I desperately believed that a broken automaton would save my life. Now that my cocoon has fallen away and I have emerged as a magician named Professor Alcofrisbas, I can look back and see that I was right.

> The automaton my father discovered *did* save me.
>
> But now I have built a new automaton.
>
> I spent countless hours designing it. I made every gear myself, carefully cut every brass disk, and fashioned every last bit of machinery with my hands.
>
> When you wind it up, it can do something I'm sure no other automaton in the world can do. It can tell the incredible story of Georges Méliès, his wife, their goddaughter, and a beloved clock maker whose son grew up to be a magician.
>
> The complicated machinery inside my automaton can produce one hundred and fifty-eight different pictures, and it can write, letter by letter, twenty-six thousand one hundred and fifty-nine words.
>
> These words. (Selznick, 509–511)

A fairy tale of modernity if ever there was one, to use Nathalie op de Beeck's useful phrase for children's picture books, the closing chapter of *Invention* narrates a minibildung in which Hugo Cabret finds not merely a profession but also a profession he loves.[55] That profession is a bit of a moving target, since Hugo-cum-Professor Alcofrisbas appears to be magician, author, inventor, and manufacturer all-in-one. Regardless, what is striking is that in all of these roles, what he makes is a book that he imagines as an automaton. This is in keeping with the comedy of reemployment, with "Winding It Up" effectively promoting Hugo to the jobs he desires, a promotion his renaming has already suggested. And yet it promotes him at the same time that it invokes, through the recurring figure of the automaton, the very thing that makes for so many tragedies of unemployment in the late twentieth and early twenty-first centuries: automation, mechanization, and computerization.

This is nothing short of the dialectics of technological change in reverse—the comic undoing of the obsolescence of labor and, more deeply, the repressing of the effects of the moving contradiction of Capital itself circa 2000. As such, the turn to comedy in the double story of *Invention* and *Hugo* fulfills what, thirty years ago, Fredric Jameson said is the task of narrative as a "symbolic act, whereby real social contradictions, insurmountable in their own terms, find a purely formal resolution in the aesthetic realm,"[56] for the double story of the novel and film attempts to put to comic rest the dialectics of technological change by which the obsolescence of labor proceeds in line with the moving contradiction of Capital itself, which defines the mode in which we must work—like it or not. In *Invention* as in *Hugo*, to be rendered obsolete is eventually to be rescued and restored. To fall into history is no longer to be left behind in the past but to be comically returned to the present—just as inventing an automaton means having a job instead of losing one.

Reading after Reemployment

In "Subterranean Gratification: Reading after the Picaro," Matthew Garrett argues that a "fantasy of good reading" becomes "integral to bourgeois civilization" from the sixteenth century to the present. As it develops in the long *durée* between then and now, this fantasy, in which reading is "a weird object [that takes] shape between textual form and readerly actualization," pivots around the picaro. Taking the main character of the picaresque as central to the formation of the bourgeois subject's readerly self, Garrett writes:

> The adventures, the fortunes and misfortunes, the movement [of the picaro] have been brought inside the subject. The satisfactions of being sated after hunger, of being safe from danger, are embedded within the form and texture of good, careful, and pleasurable reading. But it is integral to this situation of reading that satiety and safety should appear only through the narration of (the reading of) their opposites. The comfort of the reader, the reader's comfortable distance from the adventures in the story, depends upon the representation of dispossession, want, and danger. The reader, of course, is never in danger, for . . . the reader's great freedom is its distance, protection, and irresponsible relationship to the protagonist in the story world.[57]

A similar form of good reading is at work in the reading by residual means that *The Invention of Hugo Cabret* develops, especially when that two-pronged activity is considered in light of the double story that both Selznick's novel and Scorsese's adaptation tell. Like the good reading that Garrett describes in "Subterranean Gratification," reading the residual demands care, an attention to the forces and forms reused across the constellation of black-and-white stills. That attention need not be fully conscious. After all, even the most careful reading involves an aesthetically complex ratio of the aware and the unaware, the sensory and the cognitive. But the hermeneutics of historical time that reading the residual invites is nonetheless based in a notion of the reader as a spectator who—as I have tried to do in this chapter—carefully deciphers and sensuously decrypts what is inscribed in and across the photographic pieces of the past reused and recombined in *Invention*. The hermeneutics that reading residually stirs is more concerned with pleasure than care, with a conception of reading as reemployment in which the reader enjoys setting still images into motion as film projectionists used to do once upon an economic time. Reading after reuse and recombination—reading after reemployment—thus allows us the cultural pleasures of the past without the economic pains of being behind the times in the present.

Even as it reveals those pains in the double story of Méliès and Hugo, the movement of that story also reinforces a comfortable distance from those pains in its comic efforts to reverse the obsolescence of labor that determines both that story and our moment in capitalist history. Reading by residual means thus finds a palliative counterpart in our protagonists' trajectory from being out of work and out of sync to being gainfully reemployed and economically resynchronized, such that, to borrow some language from Garrett, their "narrative movement is inflected into the reading subject."[58] This is to say, once again, that the narrative restoration of Méliès and Hugo not only to work but also to work they *want* to do keeps us at a comically comfortable distance from what their double story simultaneously figures: the material reality of falling into history that has destabilized the lives and labor of so many across capitalist history.

Despite the comic comforts of the double story of Méliès and Hugo, however, some of the contradictions of that fall persist—pressing at the seams, for instance, of *Invention* in the final chapter. Recall that the final chapter, playfully entitled "Winding It Up," weirdly turns reading a book into an automated act when Hugo-cum-Professor Alcofrisbas imagines *Invention* as an automaton he has built—imagines it as the figure for the very process that significantly propels obsolescence despite the comic reversal of that obsolescence over the course of the narrative. Even when it is narratively reversed, then, the obsolescence of labor is as much an inescapable fact for the reader-cum-spectator-cum-projectionist of the novel as it is in our time. The comic comforts of culture are always going to feel a bit cold in the face of material reality, especially when that reality has been so irrevocably altered by the dialectics of technological change since the 1970s—dialectics that are coming for more and more of the workforce in manufacturing and services alike.

In many respects, *Hugo* knows this better than *Invention*. While the film ends with reemployment just as the novel does, it contains a scene that the novel does not. Throughout *Invention*, Hugo imagines himself as a machine inside, pointing to how much the human, his body, and his sense of self have become mechanized across the deep time of capitalist history. But machines are good in *Invention*, ultimately granting young men futures that are no longer there, as in a sentence that occurs toward the end of the novel: "In that moment, the machinery of the world lined up. Somewhere a clock struck midnight, and Hugo's future seemed to fall perfectly into place" (Selznick, 508). What *Hugo* does with this dream of the mechanized self and the mechanically synchronized world producing a perfect future is turn it into a nightmare of automation. In a sequence that recalls the irrealist figuration of the obsolescence of labor that the Vitruvian Steam-bot exemplifies, Hugo traumatically dreams that he is being transformed into the automaton he prizes. *Hugo* thus makes explicit that the automaton is not only the very image of automation in this narrative but also that the automaton is a disturbingly fantastic figuration of the violent replacement of men by machines. In the end, Hugo's nightmare is not so much a reflection of the material reality of our time. It is an irrealist reminder that no cultural work can quell the technological impulse to free labor from its capacity to sustain itself by rendering it obsolete—as so many laborers have become already and as so many more will be in the decades to come.

3

Narrative by
Obstinate Means

———————————————————•

Thirty years I've been doing this. And I've seen a lot of other games come and go. It's kinda sad. Think about all those guys from *Asteroids*. Ooh, gone! *Centipede*? Who knows where that guy is? You know. Look, a steady arcade game is nothing to sneeze at. I'm *very* lucky. It's just—I gotta say—it becomes kind of hard to love your job when no one seems to like you for doing it.

—Ralph in *Wreck-It Ralph*

When the lost children of this as-yet immobile horde enter once again upon the battlefield, which has changed yet stayed the same, a new General Ludd will be at their head—leading them this time in an onslaught on the *machinery of permitted consumption*.

—Guy Debord, *The Society of the Spectacle*

A Ludic and Luddite Historicism

The classic opening to the films of the Walt Disney Company is all too familiar to our eyes and ears: the descent into a magical kingdom from a star-studded dawn above the clouds, the unmistakable musical section of "When You Wish upon a Star" playing as that descent into a royally colored world occurs. In the case of the 2012 film about video game characters, director Rich Moore's *Wreck-It Ralph*, a second opening from a division of Disney follows the classic one (figures 3.1 and 3.2). After that famous vista and tune fades, the logo of Walt Disney Animation Studios appears, Mickey Mouse front and center, as iconic as the song we've just heard. The Mickey Mouse that materializes is his 1928 incarnation from *Steamboat Willie*, one of the very early cartoon shorts that debuted this now universally recognizable character. But the Willie-cum-Mickey we see in the Walt Disney Animation Studios credit for *Wreck-It Ralph* looks like an early video game character, the square display elements that make up a bitmap pixelating him as he dances while steering the steamboat. The music to which he dances is as aurally pixelated to the ear as he is visually pixelated to the eye.

It lacks the classic quality of "When You Wish upon a Star," but it nonetheless recognizably evokes the sound design of early gaming: a series of overly discrete electronic beeps and digital beats meant to recall the soundscape of the arcade of "the late 1970s and early 1980s," which one scholar remembers as "an overwhelming onslaught of crashes, laser guns, synthesized speech, and electronic beeping music, all competing for our attention."[1]

Returning us to that less developed visual and aural moment in digital ludics, the Walt Disney Animation Studios credit of *Wreck-It* remediates the technological sensorium of early video games within what is already a remediation of an even earlier animated character. This credit is a retrograde motion into media history in which the technics of 1920s cartoons converge for a moment with the technics of 1980s gaming as we ready to watch a 2010s film made using cutting-edge computing techniques to represent video games new and old alike.[2] The Willie-cum-Mickey that precedes *Wreck-It* is thus a figure generated out of two mediums and three differing technological moments.

FIGURE 3.1 Opening credit from *Wreck-It Ralph*, directed by Rich Moore, Walt Disney Pictures, 2012, film still

FIGURE 3.2 Opening credit from *Wreck-It Ralph*, directed by Rich Moore, Walt Disney Pictures, 2012, film still

Asked to enjoy the playful dance of two pasts in the present, the spectator watches technological differences between early video games and early animation cutely, cleverly boogying at a later moment for both mediums. Out of that dance, an experience of historical time arises. In this, Willie-cum-Mickey prefigures the larger choreography by which historical experience not only appears but also disappears in *Wreck-It*.

In *Wreck-It*, the choreography by which historical experience appears and disappears has a thickly genealogical relationship to the ludic history of video games since the 1970s and the Luddite history of machine breaking since the 1810s in the narrative it unfolds. That narrative centers on Ralph, a video game character who is tired of being disliked by all the other video game characters, especially the ones in his own game, because he plays a bad guy in *Fix-It Felix, Jr.* So he travels outside of his game in search of the medals that good guys get. This quest causes serious trouble in his game in addition to two others, threatening their ongoing existence such that they risk being *unplugged* (a supercharged term for technological unemployment and economic ruin in the film) in the arcade where they are located. But that trouble also brings to light that Turbo, a character who long ago refused to be unplugged when more popular and more advanced games rendered him obsolete, has survived in the game *Sugar Rush* by pretending to be its ruler, King Candy, which he pulled off by hacking its code and altering its memory. The playfully zany story that Ralph sets in motion in his quest to be a good guy thus leads to the violently villainous backstory of the film's real bad guy, Turbo-cum-King Candy. His, in fact, is the story of what is one of the most obstinate creatures that capitalist history has known: the worker who refuses to go quietly into that obsolete night, stubbornly bucking the obsolescence of labor by destructively interfering with the machines that have arrived to remake and replace him.

In telling a story in which both products and people are rendered obsolete, *Wreck-It Ralph* is narrative by obstinate means. This is narrative in which historical experience erupts in a relationship to the deep time of Capital itself that is far more playfully destructive, far more ludic and Luddite in its historicism, than we have so far seen in prior chapters' analyses of how falling into history pushes and pulls culture by outmoded means into the irrealist forms it takes. As such, the film allows us to see how the past that provides that culture with the outmoded stuff for an experience of historical time has the potential not only to be reused, recombined, and reemployed, as in *The Invention of Hugo Cabret* and *Hugo*, but also to be narrated as a mischievous theater of destructive conflict in which obsolescence is confronted by obstinacy. However, before we get to that narrative—to the world the film describes, the characters it selects, and the story it tells—it is worth staying somewhat longer with the credits. They provide a suggestive preview to the ludic and Luddite historicism of *Wreck-It*, helping lay the groundwork for the narrative analysis to come, including the central concept of obstinacy that emerges through that analysis when it falls into a two-century history of machine breaking.

The temporal choreography and technological dance of the credits cannot be disaggregated from what is a realm of both diversion and demolition, or in Joseph Schumpeter's famous phrase, of "creative destruction": the horizon of temporal sensation rooted in the capitalist sphere of circulation in which new commodities regularly appear to replace older ones such that an experience of historical time rhythmically arises as those commodities come and go, especially as they fall into obsolescence.[3] A moment of obsolescence in the case of any good is also a moment of temporality in which whatever had been briefly sharpening the cutting edge of the present is blunted with historicity, becoming distressed and dated, especially if its passage into the commodified past is connected to some ongoing technological transformation operating on more protracted and less punctual cadences. Put differently, as commodities come and go, as they get created and then destroyed in the marketplace, they mediate past and future as a counterpoint of times. In this counterpoint, past and future too quickly turn into one another in *a* present that seems to be continually resetting itself as *the* present, even as that counterpoint can bring about a rhythmic experience of historical time keyed to the coming and going of commodities within a longer and slower genealogy of ongoing technological change. The Walt Disney Animation Studios credit is part of this horizon of temporal sensation, with its contrapuntal mediation unfolding within it in two different ways. First, the credit points to the accelerated resetting of the present in which historical time contracts, past and future recursively folding into one another. Second, it also points to how the rhythm of resetting belongs to deeper tempos of technological change than those rapid recursions immediately suggest, such that historical time surges, the past ludically extending itself into the present in the case of the credit, even violently splintering and pixelating it in the process.

To grasp the first dynamic, imagine the context in which a spectator originally encountered this credit: a movie theater, still the first front of cinematic release, even in light of the steady decline in attendance numbers at theaters since the middle of the twentieth century. Part of the much wider world of capitalist circulation, the theater is more than a place where we have come to see *Wreck-It*. It is a site where we will also see advertisements for films "coming soon," as previews state in an explicitly temporal idiom meant to solicit that future-oriented feeling of anticipation in the spectator for what is approaching in the marketplace. As Mary Ann Doane writes, "Trailers spatialize time, transform it into an object, by condensing and commodifying it, yet simultaneously leaving it open. As a commodity, the trailer is never quite enough to satisfy desire, and inserts itself within a chain of commodities leading not only to the film it advertises, but to the cinema itself and its continual regeneration of more objects of desire."[4] Such trailers would have immediately preceded the credits that themselves precede *Wreck-It*, the viewing of which, as Doane's account suggests, itself allows the spectator to realize what she anticipated—seeing *Wreck-It*—when she got to see the preview for it sometime in the very recent past.

This may be the only past the moviegoer really knows, at least once inside the movie theater, or so Theodor Adorno thought in 1947. In that year, when moviegoing was at an apex of eighty-two million tickets sold weekly, he caustically wrote that "every film [must] be seen in its first flush at the top Odeon" because "scarcely less than the hatred for the radical, overly modern composition is that for a film already three months old, to which the latest, in no way differing from it, is relentlessly preferred."[5] Following Adorno's characteristically misanthropic tone, if fascinatingly uncharacteristic analogy between modern art and mass culture, we can say that by the end of watching *Wreck-It* for its 101-minute duration, what was once coming soon is now already gone. A film is not immediately, if ever, obsolete in the way a machine will be, though a movie is often enough of its moment, a fashion that is, as the previews indicate, part of the fleet of films coming and going. And in some real sense, that moment is the 101 minutes it takes to watch *Wreck-It*—the film all used up by the time the spectator leaves the theater. What was in the future less than two hours before is now already in the past, attenuating the distinction between the two such that, in Adorno's terms, the "first flush of the Odeon" and the "film already three months old" are all we have—a reduced present of commodified time—when it comes to our temporal senses and our historical sensorium.

While such attenuations define the horizon of temporal sensation that concerns me in this chapter, it is equally determined here by accumulations of historical time, most perceptibly in the case of *Wreck-It* as a function of the dialectics of technological change propelled by the moving contradiction (again, "the drive to exploit labor-power and, simultaneously, to expel it from the production process" that impels the motion of capital.)[6] This is evident in the second way that the credit mediates the horizon of temporal sensation. In figuring different technological moments in the pixelated Willie-cum-Mickey, it perceptibly evokes a history of media shaped by technologies caught up in competitive relationships of varying dominance in the culture industry writ large. In Willie-cum-Mickey, the cinematic past is splintered by the digital past in a far more robustly computerized present for both moviegoing and gaming. That figure thus indexes the computerization of culture that in the case of *The Invention of Hugo Cabret* resulted in the turn to the material form of the print book and the matter of black-and-white film for its residual means. In the case of the Walt Disney Animation Studios credit, indeed, of *Wreck-It* overall, that figure captures the shift from analog to digital that has reshaped the ontology of the cinematic image as no longer based in an indexical relationship to reality rooted in the photographic but in a plastic style of computerized mimesis rooted in the animated.[7] In this, the credit indicates the obsolescence of analog media. It mediates the more rapid and recent circulation of films coming soon and already gone in any given three months of film history or any given duration of viewing, to use the brief intervals of time cited above, as part of a post-1970s period in the late twentieth and early twenty-first centuries shaped by the more slowly developing rhythms of the computerization of culture, themselves part of a longer *durée* of technological change that, as the steamboat that Willie-cum-Mickey sails shows in pointing towards eighteenth- and nineteenth-century revolutions in industry, precedes early animation as well.

The rhythms of that post-1970s period are also shaped by competition within the culture industry writ large, in which moviegoing has been significantly outstripped by gaming. Where the former has seen theatrical attendance decline steadily over the post-1945 era, having already flattened to much lower weekly numbers than at midcentury heights due to inroads made by television for many decades, the latter has seen its share of the market rise since the 1970s. In 2007, each second of every day that passed saw nine games purchased, and five hundred million downloads of *Angry Birds* had occurred by sometime during the making of *Wreck-It*. This technologically ongoing and economically competitive situation of creative destruction, in which the digital is superseding the analog and gaming is outflanking an already diminished practice of moviegoing, suggests how the horizon of temporal sensation described above is possessed of more conflicted historicity than we usually admit.[8] Thus in the Walt Disney Animation Studios credit preceding *Wreck-It*, the pixelated figuration of Willie-cum-Mickey is a visual and aural site for the accumulation of historical time in that it perceptibly alludes to both early animation and early gaming. That allusion puckishly evokes obsolete forms of both media for our eyes and ears alike and obdurately pulls the technological past into the present through those organs. As such, it points to Willie-cum-Mickey as a mass-cultural figuration of what Alan Liu has christened, flipping Schumpeter on his head, "destructive creativity."[9] The credit of *Wreck-It* is destructively creative in that the historical experience figured by it emerges out of the past and the present, meeting up in what is a simultaneously playful and violent encounter. The pixilation is the perfect expression of that play and that violence together.

The historical experience that the destructive creativity of the credit previews within the narrative of *Wreck-It* more broadly is, to return to terms introduced earlier, ludic and Luddite at its core, making Willie-cum-Mickey a prefiguration of how historical time appears and disappears along similarly spirited and pugnacious lines in the film itself. This is in significant part because *Wreck-It* is set in the horizon of temporal sensation, its storyworld constructed out of the destructively creative rhythms of commodities coming and going in the sphere of capitalist circulation. As I argue in the next section of the chapter, that horizon finds such a clear parallel in how *Wreck-It* describes its world that the film seems, in keeping with the first part of the dynamic just sketched, to *de*activate an experience of historical time. That apparent deactivation hinges on the fact that the film mines video games for its narrative: world, characters, and story. Both the deactivating of historicity and the mining of gaming would seem to suggest, moreover, that *Wreck-It* is not even a work of culture by outmoded means. Gaming is utterly current. The products of that culture industry are profitable and popular alike at the moment, and the people working in it are beneficiaries, if unequally exploited ones, of a labor market that has expanded in the contemporary period of capitalist history.

In keeping with the second half of the dynamic, however, what *re*activates an experience of historical time in the film is how it turns the horizon of temporal sensation out of which it constructs its world into the stuff of a story about work more generally. It emplots the rhythms of the marketplace as the technological and economic cadences by which *workers* come and go, almost childishly personifying the "product life cycle" cited in chapter 1 in which "the growth of sales of a product follows a systematic path from initial innovation through a series of stages: early development, growth, maturity, and obsolescence."[10] In *Wreck-It*, the video games of an arcade become characters doing the work of play, with an obstinate story about the obsolescence of labor emerging as a result. As I argue in the second half of this chapter, that story is obstinate because it sabotages the horizon of temporal sensation by turning it into an arena of tactical action when the memory of one early video game and its central figure, the aptly named *Turbo Time* and Turbo, respectively, seizes upon the narrative. That seizure generates an analeptic narrative in which we learn Turbo refused to be *unplugged*, again, the film's term for technological unemployment and economic ruin, when more advanced video games diminished his popularity and profitability, bringing his product life cycle to an end. The memory of Turbo's violent refusal allows an active experience of historical time to take narrative form through analepsis. It does so because that analepsis mediates the memory of machine breaking in the capitalist past, near and far alike, drawing on the destructively creative acts of industrial sabotage from the Luddites onward that are themselves obstinate in the sense that they involve displaced workers who refuse to become memories at the hands of machines.

History hardly ever meets this obstinate refusal to be replaced forgivingly, though sometimes labor and capital strike bargains in response to it. This is because Capital itself must keep moving, propelling more and more workers *in* our time *out* of our time by pushing them into service work and wageless life of the kind we saw figured in *Invention* and *Hugo*. However, in *Wreck-It* at least, the experience of historical time to which narrating that obstinacy gives rise does not, as it does in *Invention* and *Hugo*, provide Capital itself with room to move that is decreasingly there. Instead that experience reflects the friction that contradiction engenders in our time, creating an angry vision of the present obstinately splintered by the obsolete stuff of a ludic past. Pulling the film's spectators into history, that more obstinate experience also allows for a political imaginary in the face of the obsolescence of labor that *Invention* and *Hugo* do not because it lets the destructivity of the past into the play of culture more intensively, more angrily and anachronically. Split between a comic fantasy of full employment on the one side and a daemonic figuration of proletarian obstinacy on the other, that imaginary thus makes for a much darker comedy in which the present and the past remain merrily and mischievously out of sync.

The Play of the Post-1973 Past: Deactivating Historical Experience

Unlike many of the works in this book, *Wreck-It Ralph* addresses itself to an industry that was "born digital," as they like to say. Gaming both was and is technologically keyed to the computerization of culture and capital in the late twentieth century. Of course, video games themselves have a ludic genealogy in prior eras of play shaped by both the technological developments and economic arrangements of earlier times, with, aptly enough, the emergence of video games themselves occurring around that date, 1973, which is a major turning point in capitalist history.[11] The emergence of video games thus occurs at the start of an epoch that would see an intensification of the obsolescence of labor that points outward toward the repetitive history of obsolescence across the capitalist metacycle of the past two centuries. Of all the media in this book, however, gaming is most synchronized with the post-1973 era, arguably providing a training ground for the new forms of labor in that period, rather than holding players back in some stubborn fantasy of the return of kinds of work that are gone for good. In fact, this is one reason that it might be puzzling that *Wreck-It* counts as a work of culture by outmoded means. Over and against the attachment to the print book and the return to stop-motion animation in chapters 2 and 4, over and against the nineteenth-century Steam-bot and the coeval recollection of the strike and the steam train in chapters 1 and 5, gaming is at the cutting edge of our technological times. So how does *Wreck-It* end up telling a story about obsolescence, especially the obsolescence of labor, operating both within and against the contemporary era of capitalist history? Answers begin to emerge if we turn to the political economy of the video game industry, including both the products it circulates and the people it employs, in relationship not only to the wider post-1973 epoch but also to the narrower storyworld that *Wreck-It* develops in a video game arcade.

At the time of *Wreck-It Ralph*'s making, gaming was an industry on the move, having undergone meaningful growth since it arose in the 1970s through three successive phases: the arcade phase, the home console phase, and the mobile phase. The arcade phase began in 1972, just one year before the signal crisis of 1973 that led the way into a long downturn in the advanced capitalist world—looking back, an origin point that looks like a harbinger of the crisis that awaited the video game industry a decade later. Between the early 1970s and the early 1980s, gaming grew such that "in 1981, the home video game market tripled, and the arcade video game industry had an estimated income of $5–7 billion, with 24,000 full arcades, 400,000 street locations, and 1.5 million arcade video games in operation."[12] But then this apex of growth faltered and crashed. Beginning in 1982, profits diminished even as arcades kept opening. At the same time, "home video game sales dropped, as the market became oversaturated and glutted with cheap products that disappointed consumers who were coming to expect more," with profits tumbling by 35 percent in 1983.[13] This was seemingly isomorphic with larger trends in the advanced capitalist economies of the post-1973 era, in which, as Gopal Balakrishnan writes, "technological change . . . has, by and large, brought vast quantities of goods from countries with lower labor costs into world markets already weighed down by overproduction of their higher-cost equivalents, instead of fueling growth through the creation of whole new lines of production."[14]

In 1985, however, the gaming market corrected course. This was the year when the Nintendo Entertainment System was introduced and the home console phase of video games began. A double movement characterized this phase: on the one hand, the steady obsolescence of the arcade as a sphere of circulation in which gamers paid to play; on the other hand, the steady growth of the market in consoles purchased to play games at home.[15] The emergence of the arcade as an obsolete space—as an architecture of play that belongs to the technological past—would only be reinforced as products and profits shifted toward home consoles from the mid-1980s onward. That obsolescence was then fortified by the later shift away from those consoles and toward mobile gaming on smartphones in the 2010s in particular. The latter are currently leading the way to a squeeze on the former, setting at least a part of the video game industry up for at best a critical flattening and at worst a bottoming out.[16] Taken in aggregate, however, between 2009 and 2013, years during which *Wreck-It* was being made and released, sales of video games leaped by $5.3 billion from $10.1 billion to $15.4 billion, with one trade group reporting that the "real annual growth rate of the U.S. video game industry was 9.7 percent for the period from 2009–2012. During that same period, real growth for the U.S. economy as a whole was 2.4 percent," though it is worth noting that growth was not as good as it was in the previous three-year cycle based on numbers from the same trade group. The video game market looks similar in the United Kingdom, with both national economies witnessing gaming overtake other branches of the overall culture industry such as movies, television, and music.[17]

This market creates a sphere of circulation marked by products caught up in rapid life cycles of innovation and obsolescence, the next turning over the now at a swift pace. In fact, this market marches in sync with the economic and technological developments of the post-1973 period. As Balakrishnan puts it in a relevant passage, "Rather than leading to any 'New Economy' in the productive base, the innovations of this period of capitalism have powered transformations in the *Lebenswelt* of diversion and sociability, an expansion of discount and luxury shopping, but above all a heroic age of what was until recently called 'financial technology.' Internet and mobile phones, Walmart and Prada, Black-Scholes and subprime—such are the technological landmarks of the period."[18] The market for video games is a significant contemporary moment, in other words, within a horizon of temporal sensation filled with technological commodities that are coming soon and already gone: here, new consoles, innovative devices, and the updated games that go with them, not to mention all the stuff these new (or now or next) items consign to the past.

More than with movies coming soon, moreover, the rhythms of video game release are, as James Newman has explained, punctuated by "genealogical" tempos we have come to associate with successive lines of the same technological good in what is a fantasy that "whole new lines of production" are emerging when they are not. Only minimally differentiated, the marketing of these lines nonetheless stresses those consoles and devices as a new "generation" of digital commodities. In advancing on prior commodities, these new "generations" discursively and materially enforce both the perceptual and actual obsolescence of suddenly old software and hardware. They impose a break with the past that, if the hardware has actually changed, may be impossible to avoid for gamers. As Newman puts it, "One thing gamers know well is that revolutions are revolutions for just a short time."[19] Indicative of how inescapable a fact of life planned obsolescence has become, the willingness to accept the brevity of these genealogical revolutions—the knowledge that as a gamer one must deal with this reduction in and acceleration of turnover time in which future becomes past or, in the more cynical rhetoric above, the process of creative destruction turns now into next—points to the health of the gaming industry at the turn of the twenty-first century, regardless of whatever multitude of goods, not to mention spaces like the arcade, have been rendered obsolete as it has progressed toward its position of dominance in the culture industry writ large.

That progress has meant more than an abundance of products and profits but also the emergence of new forms of employment. The same trade-group report from which the numbers about the 2009–2012 sales figures above were drawn, for example, trumpets these facts: "The U.S. video game industry directly employs more than 42,000 people in 36 states," and those "employees received total compensation of over $4 billion in 2012," with that compensation averaging $94,747 per employee. Between 2009 and 2012, "direct employment in the U.S. game industry grew at an annual rate of nine percent," in contrast to less than 1 percent growth in the U.S. economy overall.[20] Given their source in a trade publication, these facts ought to be considered skeptically, however, since exploitation of employees in this industry has been reported, including excessively long hours expected as normal, potentially higher rates of mass layoffs than the national average, major gender gaps, antiunion ideologies, and problematic links to for-profit universities who advertise education for careers in gaming, often to the jobless and the unemployed. There are also the issues of exploitation that shape the manufacturing of video games globally, though those issues are sometimes "fixed" by mechanized means, with sixty thousand Foxconn jobs in electronics manufacturing recently becoming the work of robots.[21] None of these factors means that well-paying jobs have not been created as a result of the emergence of the video game industry since the 1970s. But at least four of them—the higher layoff rate, the for-profit targeting of the jobless and unemployed, the antiunion ideologies of the industry, and the role of robots in manufacturing—are indicative of how in the post-1973 era the obsolescence of labor becomes more and more materially legible, including in culture industries, by way of not only the intensified automation of manufacturing and the computerization of capital more generally but also the erosion of steady employment and the declining power of organized labor.

In her aptly titled essay "Coin-Drop Capitalism: Economic Lessons from the Video Game Arcade," Carly A. Kocurek argues that gaming, especially in the arcade phase, was a ludic training ground for the post-1973 era in which employment shifted "from an industrial, production-based economy to a service-based, consumer economy." This is the shift we saw in Georges Méliès's narrative in *The Invention of Hugo Cabret* and *Hugo*. But where his narrative emplotted the obsolete worker expelled from the labor of production into the servitude of retail, what Kocurek contends the rise of the arcade did was prepare youth, especially young men, for "a seemingly unprecedented level of economic risk [in contrast to their parents, who had lived through the postwar boom], faced both with decreases in their earning power and increases in unemployment caused by palpable economic instability." In this context, paying to play video games while young could mean being more ready to face "computerization as a major factor in a labor market" that was shedding industrial jobs for service work that was, in the 1980s, "becoming computerized for the first time."[22]

As Kocurek's account suggests, this "playbor force" must be considered in relationship to the complicated increase in productivity during the late twentieth and early twenty-first centuries as a result of the dialectics of technological change that computerization realizes.[23] This is a phenomenon that Marxist economic historians have described. Aaron Benanav and John Clegg, for example, observe that "computers not only have rapidly decreasing labor requirements (the microchips industry, restricted to only a few factories worldwide, is incredibly mechanized), they also tend to reduce labor requirements across the lines by rapidly increasing levels of automation. Thus rather than reviving a stagnant industrial sector and restoring expanded reproduction . . . the rise of the computer industry has contributed to deindustrialization and a diminished scale of accumulation." In this respect, computerization is a moment within a larger epoch in which capital has shifted its center of gravity—and its axis of vulnerability—from a manufacturing economy to a service economy, in no small part due to the moving contradiction of Capital itself by which labor is both "too much and too little" all at once.[24] The video game industry is part of this movement, the jobs created in it symptoms of the obsolescence of labor that gained material and discursive momentum as the post-1973 era reached the end of the twentieth century and veered into the twenty-first.

In light of this abbreviated history of the video game industry since the 1970s, it becomes clearer how mining gaming for the raw material of its narrative coordinates links *Wreck-It Ralph* to the obsolescence of labor that this book foregrounds as central to the appearance of historical time in culture by outmoded means. For example, the film clearly draws on the history of gaming for its storyworld, making a video game arcade the setting in which the action unfolds. It describes this setting in the prologue to the film just after the credits explored above. Over the course of that description, it inserts the spectator into this obsolete space, this architecture from the first phase of gaming that home consoles and then mobile games have creatively destroyed, pushing it into history. Despite the turn back to that space, despite our insertion into it, however, that description compellingly deactivates the experience of historical time that it brings to the surface of the screen visually and to our ears aurally.

The description begins immediately after Willie-cum-Mickey fades from the screen and *Wreck-It* cuts to a shot of three coin-operated arcade games: *Pac-Man*, *Fix-It Felix, Jr.*, and *Space Invaders*. *Fix-It* centers the shot, flanked on the left by *Pac-Man* and on the right by *Space Invaders*. *Fix-It* is a fictional game that resembles *Donkey Kong*, developed by the equally fictional company, Tobikomo, and fictionally released in 1982. The date is clearly meaningful, given that 1982 is the year in which the economic crash in gaming initiated the technological end of the arcade era. Looking down at the screen of *Fix-It* from our, if you will, arcadian point of view, *Wreck-It* cuts to a shot in which the screen of the game fills the movie screen, the angle of the shot progressing into the juvenile perspective that a gamer would have occupied as he looked down at the cabinet (figure 3.3). Visually and aurally echoing the Willie-cum-Mickey we just saw, the spectator-qua-gamer watches and hears *Fix-It* run in pixelated images and electronic sounds from the ludic past like those remediated in the Walt Disney Animation Studios credit. At the same time, the spectator-qua-gamer hears a voiceover begin in which Ralph, the title character of the movie we are watching, tells us about himself. As he gives that monologue, *Wreck-It* cuts back and forth between close-ups of the 1980s graphics that fill the screen of *Fix-It* and the point-of-view shot that puts the spectator in the position of the young gamer looking down at the screen of the game. That this is an obsolete position within an obsolete space is stressed by a caption, "30 YEARS AGO," telling us that we have been inserted into a specific moment in the history of gaming, dating the opening images of the film itself to around 1982 as Ralph speaks in voiceover circa 2012. A steady zoom away from the *Fix-It* cabinet then ensues as Ralph continues speaking. The zoom out and voiceover are simultaneous with a time-lapse sequence during which, as the camera expands the spatial dimension of the arcade in an increasingly wider shot, the history of this arcade gets described in an accelerated summary in which generations of games and gamers come and go.

This summary brings to mind the elegiac time-lapse sequence that narrates the decline of Georges Méliès in *Hugo*, which palpably emplotted the obsolescence of Méliès in and over time. In the prologue to *Wreck-It*, however,

FIGURE 3.3 *Wreck-It Ralph*, directed by Rich Moore, Walt Disney Pictures, 2012, film still

the time-lapse sequence is more descriptive than narrative. It illustrates a blurred succession of spectral commodities and ghostly figures appearing and disappearing, the past of one generation of games and gamers visually over-lapping with and turning into a future generation that just as quickly turns into and overlaps with another one—all without any sense of the decline into which the video game arcade, like Méliès's studio, has fallen. Indeed, the rhythm of turnover occurs at such a rapid rate, such a state of pure currency, that the exact timing of it is not available to perception. This imperceptible rhythm yields not a succession of identifiable moments but a pulsating dura-tion of temporal sensation—the arcade described in terms of time more than space. These pulsations are represented by flashing neon lights and digitized sounds in addition to the games and gamers appearing and disappearing, with the prologue traversing thirty years of gaming history in fewer than thirty seconds. The ludic storyworld of *Wreck-It*, then, seems less to be the obsolete space of the arcade and more an accumulation of undifferentiated moments, the diachronic differences of which are leveled in a historical blur. We can tell that time has passed, but we can't tell what any of those times are or were. When we arrive at the end of this description of the setting, two and a half minutes have passed since the credits started, one and a half minutes since the prologue began, and thirty seconds since the blur of history sped by, with a caption that informs us it is "TODAY"—the past described now synchro-nized with the present from which Ralph has been speaking in voiceover.

The film may hardly pause in this prologue, but we should in order to observe what we can see and hear in how it visually and aurally describes the arcade. The first observation to make concerns that arcadian point-of-view shot that puts us in the juvenile vantage point (or vintage point) of gamers from the 1970s and 1980s, when arcades were not yet the obsolete spaces that they are "TODAY." That perspective to some degree engages the mimetic fac-ulty as chapter 2 theorized it in arguing for the nonsensuous similarity between *The Invention of Hugo Cabret* and a black-and-white film moving through a projector as well as the nonsynchronous similarity between the reader of Brian Selznick's book and a projectionist cranking a film. Not dissimilarly, *Wreck-It* posits a nonsynchronous similarity between us and the now-gone arcade gamer, where "us" refers to an intergenerational series of possible spectators who have worked and played across the decades of the post-1973 epoch: the early millennial child for whom this film is primarily intended, that child's parent, whose associations with gaming may involve memories of arcades, and any spectator who chooses to watch the film. In *Invention*, such nonsynchronous similarity draws the mimetic faculty of the reader into an active experience of historical time by letting her play at being the past, evok-ing the accumulated knowledge and skills of workers that have fallen into his-tory. Such nonsynchronous similarity in *Wreck-It* also invites us to look with obsolete eyes, playing at being part of a past in which the skills of gaming first developed, readying gamers to be that playbor force equipped for an increasingly computerized job market in the decades to come.

There is, however, an important dissimilarity between *Invention* and *Wreck-It* when it comes to their mimetic modes. The arcadian point of view may mine and mime the ludic perspective of this technological past in the present of the film, the "30 YEARS AGO" of the arcade in the "TODAY" of viewing *Wreck-It*. However, that moment of perspectival mimesis across the phases of gaming history is actually part of a prologue that, in contrast to *Invention*, deactivates an experience of historical time—or that at least serves as a tantalizing description, however brief, of how that experience can get deactivated despite the possibility of its surfacing when the past builds up in the passé. In the prologue to *Wreck-It*, this experience gets deactivated because to whatever degree the mimetic faculty arises, it does so not in the name of what Walter Benjamin referred to as a mimetic mode of *behavior* in which a subject produces and perceives similarities, imitating that which is other to her. It arises instead as a mimetic mode of *representation* in which the prologue to the film takes as its goal the aim of describing the history of video games. The prologue *represents* a temporal experience more than it *realizes* one. It does not *produce* so much as *portray* a horizon of temporal sensation. Looking at a depiction of that horizon and a description of those sensations in the prologue, we at best *see* time moving, but at a rate too fast for us to genuinely *perceive* it come and go, except as a historical blur that appears to synchronize then and now, whatever pasts and futures that unfolded between "30 YEARS AGO" and "TODAY" disappearing as if they were all one present, as if they were one enduring moment of synchrony.

This synchronizing effect on the storyworld of the film expands once the prologue comes to an end. After establishing its wider storyworld as this horizon of temporal sensation in which times and technologies rapidly turn over, *Wreck-It* focuses the narrative coordinates of its spatial dimension still further. Following a sequence of preparatory shots after the caption announcing "TODAY," *Wreck-It* cuts to the arcadian point of view above *Fix-It Felix, Jr.* again but this time passes through the surface of the screen into what turns out to be, like an Amazon distribution center, a hidden abode of circulation. There the video games are interconnected, and the characters live lives beyond the work of play they do all day when they are being coin operated. In revealing that hidden world, *Wreck-It* takes the description of the space of the arcade in terms of imperceptible tempos approaching a moment of total synchrony one asymptotic step closer to that moment, for in that world, all video games look as if they were manufactured according to the technological possibilities of 2012. Whatever diachronic difference exists between them—say, the pixelated graphics of early 1980s video games over and against the more smoothly verisimilar imagery of 2010s video games—is not totally gone but partially smoothed out. We get genealogical ripples of diachronic difference, but these are confined to sonic echoes, verbal gestures, movement styles, and visual traces. For instance, such confinement occurs in a verbal gesture when a technologically older character such as Felix encounters the technologically newer character Calhoun of *Hero's Duty*. He finds himself erotically entranced by how high definition she is, a feminized fetish of the future in relation to the primitive past he encapsulates. But in this moment, the diachronic difference between Calhoun and Felix is more an element of what he says than what we see. This is not to say that what we see in the hidden abode of *Wreck-It* lacks diachronic difference altogether. For example, each game in this storyworld is its own little diegesis constructed using a shape language idiosyncratic to it. The diegesis of *Fix-It Felix, Jr.* is built out of "a square shape language to reflect the 8-bit pixel of early video games whereas the triangulation of the polygonal environments of first-person shooters informs *Hero's Duty*." The former results in "staccato" motion and "grid-like movement," in addition to an "asynchronous" quality to the timing of bodies in motion, when we are inside the specific diegesis of *Fix-It* within the world itself.[25] What synchronizes some of these diachronic differences across diegeses are shading and reflection techniques that make the visuality of *Wreck-It* more verisimilar writ large, especially when it comes to lighting in the film, which the director of lighting has stated is invested in a "quality" reality effect.[26] While genealogical ripples remain here and there, then, the storyworld of *Wreck-It* in general looks synchronized as the same moment in historical time.

Of course, this is the same moment in a historically true sense. The leveling of diachronic difference and the blur of temporal sensations emerge from an industry only four decades old, not from eras indelibly far-flung. The gaming industry may have progressed through arcade, home console, and mobile phases since the 1970s, making for vintages of technological development keyed to the shape of the market for games at an identifiable time. But these vintages belong to the same moment much more than if the film were trying to synchronize in its storyworld the Mesozoic Era and the Anthropocene, the Neolithic Period and the Industrial Revolution, or even the three Industrial Revolutions since the eighteenth and nineteenth centuries as if they were all the same moment. Even if the film had attempted such a storyworld, it would not necessarily be so strange, since *Wreck-It* is a product, as Fredric Jameson wrote in the early 1980s, "of that most complex of all cultural revolutions, late capitalism, in which all the earlier modes of production in one way or another structurally coexist."[27]

However, quoting Jameson at this point is really a way of arriving at the different, if related, point that the diachronic leveling and historical blur in the prologue to *Wreck-It*, the moment of synchrony that it makes its setting visually and aurally, also tells a historical truth in that it accords with what we know about temporality and historicity in the late twentieth and twenty-first centuries from the rich tradition of thinking on which *Out of Sync and Out of Work* is built. The horizon of temporal sensation that the prologue to *Wreck-It* describes, for instance, resembles nothing so much as the "end of temporality" that Jameson limns in his account of the film *Speed* (1994). "The bus [in *Speed*] has momentum, but," he stresses, "that is not really time or temporality; on the contrary, it is the representation of temporality, threatened at every moment with some ultimate present of the bomb blast that can never take place." We can also cite another major thinker in this tradition, Andreas Huyssen, for whom the description of the space of the arcade in the only barely temporal terms of Jameson's pure "momentum" would indicate how "the present of advanced consumer capitalism prevails over the past and the future, sucking both into an expanding synchronous space." As we look at the representation of that "synchronous space" in *Wreck-It*, Mary Ann Doane would further suggest the following in an argument isomorphic to those of Jameson and Huyssen: "What is at stake is the representability of time for a subject whose identity is more and more tightly sutured to abstract structures of temporality."[28]

The point, however, is not to offer up *Wreck-It* as more evidence of what we already know from the tradition these and other thinkers now represent. But nor would it be anything but an argument in bad faith to posit that *Wreck-It* does not participate in the tendencies around historicity and temporality that earlier thinkers have identified. And the key tendency in which the prologue to *Wreck-It* participates revolves around the representation and the representability of what a more recent scholar, Devin Fore, calls the "time of capital." As Fore demonstrates in his discussion of early twentieth-century political economists and industrial novelists, the representational problem that the time of capital generates is that the latter constitutes "an inorganic rhythm whose periods unfold independently of the living." For the novelists, "capital's temporal autonomy" was an especially acute concern because of the centrality of the individual human being in and over time to their chosen genre of representation. The time of capital is, in contrast, "time without a subject," its "temporality fundamentally incompatible with the rhythms of human existence," raising the representational problem of how the novel could "produce concrete representations of [the time of capital] without lapsing into undue anthropomorphizing."[29] How can works of culture produce representations of time *in* capital when the time *of* capital has left human beings behind, a question that almost necessarily precludes any human reader or mortal spectator ever being able to have an active experience of time *under* capital?

The answer that *Wreck-It* gives to this question is twofold. On the one hand, the prologue serves as a description of a form of capitalist time that moves so fast it is beyond the rate of human perception, visualizing an inhuman rhythm that we can at best glimpse but into which we cannot enter. The inhumanity of this time appears in the way in which goods and gamers—products and people at play—both appear and disappear at spectrally swift tempos passing the point of human perception. On the other hand, humanity returns, recurring nonetheless in that element of the prologue we have not yet addressed: Ralph's opening monologue. Time regains a subject in the monologue, the voiceover grounding the prologue, if not in a person, then in a personification: "Thirty years I've been doing this. And I've seen a lot of other games come and go. It's kinda sad. Think about all those guys from *Asteroids*. Ooh, gone! *Centipede*? Who knows where that guy is? You know. Look, a steady arcade game is nothing to sneeze at. I'm *very* lucky. It's just—I gotta say—it becomes kind of hard to love your job when no one seems to like you for doing it." Thus *Wreck-It*, to use Fore's verb, *rehumanizes* the time of capital it describes in the prologue by personifying the games it depicts as coming and going at an inhuman rate as human workers, some of whom have been rendered obsolete. In this, the deactivation of temporal experience in the prologue is less an effect it creates than a condition it must describe, representing how much the time of capital is, like it or not, caught up in rhythms beyond the human eye and ear except as pulsations of temporal sensation.

Those rhythms are just one moment within the time of capital, however, with obsolete labor returning as an anthropomorphic accumulation of historical time that can reopen and reengage the talent of temporality for the living. That reopening and reengagement is ultimately the reactivation of temporal experience by narrative means—not, as in *Invention* and *Hugo*, so as to comically overcome the obsolescence of labor but rather so as to demonically emplot that obsolescence in its obstinacy by drawing on a different kind of material than the video game industry: the memory of machine breaking from across the metacycle of productive capital of which the post-1973 period is the end point. In the process, *Wreck-It* gives rise to an experience of historical time marked by a political imaginary in which General Ludd discovers an obstinate afterlife in our moment. Before turning to how that afterlife is narrated in *Wreck-It*, however, we need to trace the nature of that obstinacy as it emerges from around 1811 onward in what are, all too often, acts of machine breaking that come too late in their destructive efforts to stupefy the obsolescence of labor that Capital itself consistently delivers to classes of workers across capitalist history.

An Obstinate History of Machine Breaking, 1811–2012

In October 1975, the spirit of machine breaking seized a group of unionized pressmen in the predawn hours before their contract expired with the *Washington Post*. In an act that was variously described as "'preplanned and synchronized,'" akin to that of airline hijackers and political assassins, and as "a moment of 'temporary insanity,'" akin to a psychotic episode, the pressmen beat a foreman and did serious damage to nine printing presses.[30] As a result, the publication of the *Post* was halted for a day, and a contentious strike ensued in which the pressmen involved were charged and tried, reporters crossed picket lines, and scabs and strike breakers were brought in. At issue for the machine-breaking pressmen were "work rules known as 'manning clauses.'" These clauses "require the company to pay a full shift's wages to printers who report for work, but who may have to be idle once the presses start running."[31] Hard won by the union over the years, these practices were viewed as increasingly "archaic" by management, since the technology of printing required no actual labor time from the pressmen during these idle periods.[32] And having foreseen a strike over the manning clauses, the *Post* had trained nonunion workers in secret since 1973 (there's that year again) so as to achieve, as general manager Mark J. Meagher put it in 1975, "general parity at the bargaining table."[33] It had also developed a "contingency plan" since 1973 (and again), which, according to the leftist publication *Fifth Estate*, included "the use of a recent technological device which enables the paper to be typeset and laid out by computers."[34] The *Post*'s preplanning in case of a strike thus made advances in printing-press technology not only an economic threat the union had to manage during collective bargaining for workers facing their technological obsolescence. Advance planning also turned technological innovation into a political weapon to be used against striking pressmen should bargaining break down. The *Post* met the spirit of machine breaking with the spirit of union breaking.

The conflict between these two spirits materialized just two years after 1973, making it tempting to locate it cleanly within the epoch that date is said to have initiated. However, this conflict—this moment of creative destruction and of equal and opposite destructive creativity—is really only legible within capitalist history as it cuts across the eighteenth, nineteenth, and twentieth centuries. For instance, the dialectics of technological change had been altering the quality of labor in the printing industry since the invention of the Linotype machine at end of the nineteenth century. While the expansion of the industry at that time had solved the problem of technological unemployment the Linotype threatened to create, labor still sought to protect itself from that threat. As the manning clauses suggest, over time, labor struck bargains in which their wages were protected despite the fact that aspects of their work continued to be rendered obsolete. In the case of the pressmen, that bargain appears to have had a great deal to do with the vibrant genealogy of craft-union structures in printing, which persisted longer into the twentieth century than in many other industries.[35] Nonetheless, the dialectics of technological change had already begun to erode those structures at an accelerating rate by the 1960s, with craftsmanship in areas such as the compositing room and the pressroom diminishing due to computerization as time wore on. For example, the conflict at the *Post* erupted in a decade during which "the number of composing room workers declined from about 14,500 to about 6,900 between 1970 and 1983, a 52% reduction in this single occupation!"[36] While pressroom workers experienced a less radical decline in this same period, the fight over the manning clauses at the *Post* was a sign of computerized things to come for them as well, for that fight was part of a "secular decline in the skill ratios of the three highly skilled occupational groups (linotypists, photoengravers, and pressroom workers)" in the newspaper industry between 1931 and 1980. Over those fifty years, with computers playing an emergent role in the 1960s and 1970s, there was a convergence toward the occupation that required the least skill in that period: mailroom worker.[37] Both the decline in employment and the deskilling of the still employed were part of the larger secular decline that has pulled increasing numbers of workers into its descent in the post-1973 era: the obsolescence of labor.

Machine breaking is the *locus classicus* by which workers protest the obsolescence of their labor. As a form of struggle, however, it has often been understood as formless and pointless due to the violence of its means of objecting to the idea that, as the Luddites most famously did between 1811 and 1813, "the triumph of mechanization was inevitable."[38] As a corrective to this view of the Luddites, along with the much longer tradition of wrecking that extends back to the seventeenth century, Eric Hobsbawm published "The Machine Breakers" in 1952. "It is perhaps time to reconsider the problem of machine-wrecking in the early industrial history of Britain and other countries," the essay begins, because "about this form of early working-class struggle misconceptions are still widely held."[39] Against those misconceptions, still popular today, Hobsbawm argues that this form of struggle has two major variants. First, machine breaking was one tactic among a variety that labor used to pursue "'collective bargaining by riot'" between the seventeenth and early nineteenth centuries.[40] In this form, laborers destroyed machines not because the machines threatened them with technological unemployment but as a political and economic means of achieving solidarity as workers and of putting pressure on employers to address, for instance, wage reductions. In this respect, says Hobsbawm, "wrecking was simply a technique of trade unionism in the period before, and during the early phases of, the Industrial Revolution."[41]

Although it also has a genealogy going back to the seventeenth century, the second form of machine breaking—the more important one in the context of this book—was more keyed to industrialization as productive capital began its late eighteenth-century ascent into the U.K.-U.S. metacycle that extends from 1830 to 1973.[42] This form was "generally regarded as the expression of working-class hostility to the new machines of the industrial revolution, especially labor-saving ones." But every machine was not a crucial front in General Ludd's war. As Hobsbawm writes, "Resistance to the machine was quite consciously resistance to the machine in the hands of the capitalist." He elaborates that the machine breaker "was concerned, not with technical progress in the abstract, but with the practical twin problems of preventing unemployment and maintaining the customary standard of life. . . . It was thus not to the machine as such that he objected, but to any threat to these—above all to the whole change in the social relations of production which threatened him."[43] It was not technological change as such that threatened the machine breaker but rather the dialectics of technological change motored by Capital itself that made a new type of equipment an object of protest. It was not the experience of historical time that technological change on its own can bring about through the emergence of new apparatuses but the threat of becoming historical time, of falling into history in an individual and communal crisis of reproduction, which motivated this second version of the form of struggle known as machine breaking.

This last point begins to indicate an important dimension of the historicity of this form of struggle, indeed, of the texture of historical time that the struggle against becoming historical time materializes in conflicts such as those in England between 1811 and 1813 or those at the *Post* in 1975. The temporality of machine breaking is, in a word, obstinate. This is not exactly how Hobsbawm describes it in "The Machine Breakers," however. He characterizes this form of struggle more by belatedness in relationship to the dialectics of technological change as they dovetail with economic growth. But that belatedness is at the core of the obstinacy in the end. In an important observation about the timing of machine breaking, Hobsbawm points out that "most machines tended to be introduced in times of rising prosperity, when employment was improving and opposition, not fully mobilized, could be for a time dissipated. *By the time distress recurred—the strategic moment for opposing the new devices was past.* New workers serving them had already been recruited, the old hand operatives stood outside, capable only of random destruction of their competitor, no longer of imposing themselves on the machine."[44] As the italicized sentence states—and as Hobsbawm's tactical use of the em dash instantiates by creating a pause, a delay, in that sentence—machine breaking is a form of struggle that erupts too late.

The moment of machine breaking is already past, a delayed recognition of and willful revolt against alterations to technologically mediated relations of production that have already seized upon reality, making for a new moment, a new present. Belated and current, anachronistic and contemporary, machine breaking is a tactic that obdurately challenges that new present by attempting to bring the dialectics of technological change to a standstill. It is a form of struggle that aims to stupefy the motion of Capital itself by sabotaging the machines that are one medium for its movement. This is not the standstill we saw in *Invention* and *Hugo* when that novel and film turn to the device of the automaton as a narrative means of comically overcoming the obsolescence of labor. What distinguishes the stupefaction of machine breaking from Selznick's novel and Scorsese's film is that, once it erupts, it lets struggle take daemonic form rather than repressing it as they do, fanning the inherent antagonisms of Capital itself as workers confront their technological and economic death by automated means too late. Thus the historicity of this form of struggle is obstinate because it is a stubbornly combative effort to belatedly stupefy the motion of Capital itself.

The account of obstinacy that Alexander Kluge and Oskar Negt give in their recently translated *History and Obstinacy* is more general than the one that machine breaking has so far yielded for us but nonetheless salient in telling ways. Focused on a wider range of obstinate acts within the capitalist mode of production, for them, obstinacy turns not simply on pushing back against capital but on pushing back due to the social fact that certain traits—and, I will add, techniques and technicians—have been forcibly shunted aside in a market economy that sees no profit to be made from them anymore. As a result, those traits, like the historical time that accumulates in Willie-cum-Mickey, build up. Idle and unused, they amass as so much obstinacy, forcibly removed but palpably remembered, for instance, due to institutions of collective experience such as organized labor that transmit traditions of craft techniques across generations of workers. As Devin Fore synthesizes their views in his beautiful introduction to *History and Obstinacy*, for Kluge and Negt, "capital's violent expropriation is countered by the subject with obstinacy, *Enteignung* with *Eigen-sinn*." "For every trait that is capitalized," Fore continues, "another is shunted aside. As a result, alongside the primary economy of labor traits established through the historical mode of production there emerges within the human subject a secondary, black-market economy, where . . . repressed and derealized traits take on an intransigent life of their own." Not unlike Benjamin's revolutionary energies of the outmoded in "Surrealism: The Last Snapshot of the European Intelligentsia," this obstinate black market constitutes "potential sources of revolutionary force" for proletarian subjects. This force makes "obstinacy the underside of history: for each entry in the valorized record of human culture . . . a countervailing act of obstinacy pushes back against the thrust of so-called progress; for each luminous vista cleared by instrumental reason, a dense scotoma of stupidity emerges to blight the view; for every trait that is singled out and capitalized, a resistant trait gathers force underground."[45] Importantly, this amassing of traits belongs to more than any given moment in which an act of obstinacy takes. shape as an event, since any such event, to borrow as Fore does from Fernand Braudel's 1958 polemic "History and the Social Sciences: The *Long Durée*," "brings together movements of different origins, of a different rhythm: today's time dates from yesterday, the day before yesterday, and all former times."[46] The obstinacies that Kluge and Negt imagine being politically activated in any given current event by any given collective of proletarian subjects thus sediment within and emerge out of "the temporality of the deep historical cycles that Braudel, in his theorization of the *longue durée*, designated as the time of the 'conjuncture'— the time of enduring *habitus* and collective institutions, which is located somewhere between the slow geographical pulse of structural history, on the one hand, and the 'microhistory' of individual biographies and political events, on the other."[47]

The historicity of machine breaking as obstinate, then, points in the first place to how this form of struggle aims in a constitutively delayed fashion to stupefy the motion of capitalist history as it is propelled by the dialectics of technological change toward the obsolescence of labor. What pausing over the important work of Kluge and Negt adds to our sense of that historicity is that any single moment of obstinate delay inherently belongs to a much longer *durée*. This is obvious if we return now to the moment of machine breaking at the *Washington Post* in October 1975. The moment itself was obstinate in that the pressmen, trying to hold onto the manning clauses, were acting out against the dialectics of technological change overtaking them as archaisms by sabotaging the *Post* machinery that had rendered their labor socially unnecessary some time back already. But that moment was also obstinate in its belatedness, which becomes visible if we consider what unfolded at the *Post* in 1975 from the perspective, in Braudel's terms, of two "former times."

The first time is that of the post-1945 era. As Robert Brenner has argued, "The 1950s was the true golden age for the American worker," if not the accord between labor and capital that is often projected onto that decade as a result of what is known as the "Treaty of Detroit."[48] The goldenness of this age stemmed from the boom in the advanced capitalist world that, on the one hand, wedded wage growth and productivity growth to remarkable effect for labor and capital alike but, on the other, did so at the cost of laying the groundwork for wages and productivity to critically part ways eventually. While a number of factors were involved in that parting, key among them was that productivity would come in not-insignificant part to depend on automation increasingly across the lines that propelled living labor out of production, indeed, that propelled Capital itself out of production by the time of the post-1973 period to which the moment of machine breaking at the *Post* also belongs. This was thus the very dynamic that Hobsbawm describes with reference to the early nineteenth century—that machines introduced in times of rising prosperity can mean that forms of struggle not just *around* those machines but *out-and-out against* them can come too late because, even if objections to technological change arise, antagonism is managed along the way to that belated and belligerent point of obstinacy. Like the Luddites in 1811–1813, the strategic moment for opposing new devices as such was past for the pressmen by 1975—as it would be for many laborers encountering proliferating devices that do the work they once did in the post-1973 era. Unlike the Luddites, it was not industrialization but deindustrialization that those laborers were confronting in that era, with automation having curtailed the manufacturing workforce radically since the 1970s.

The above, though, folds the events at the *Post* too singularly into the general political economy of the postwar boom, especially since the printing industry, and newspapers in particular, underwent a profit squeeze that drove them toward labor-saving innovations arguably earlier than other sectors in that era.[49] More important, however, is how that earlier drive toward automation indicates that the moment of machine breaking in 1975 belongs to a "former time" deeper than the post-1973 era as it arose out of the conditions of the post-1945 era. For as we have seen, the invention of the Linotype and the Monotype in the late nineteenth century initiated the transformations that would lead to the shedding of labor and the elimination of skills in the printing industry as the postwar boom unfolded. In powerful control over the labor process since 1852, "when the National Typographical Union became the first recognized union in the United States," "the introduction of the linotype, while ultimately accepted by labor, signaled the beginnings of a shift in the power relations within the industry. As hand compositors were gradually retrained as machine operators, they began to lose control of the skills which had previously made them so indispensable."[50]

It is beyond the scope of this chapter to delineate with the fine-grained detail of eloquent historiography this decrease in autonomy in the name of automation. Nonetheless, as the work of scholars of that history suggests, that decrease did set in motion a process of deskilling and displacing living labor that resembled the shunting aside of capacities that Kluge and Negt posit as the material condition for the creation of a black market of palpably repressed traits that, once sufficiently amassed, result in destructive acts of obstinacy in which proletarians rise up as a "dense scotoma of stupidity . . . to blight the view," as the pressmen did at the *Post* in 1975. The moment of machine breaking at the *Post*, in other words, belonged to a "former time" that Braudel might call an "unconscious history" across generations of organized labor in the printing industry that went further back than the changes that unfolded after 1945 on the way to the post-1973 period.[51]

We can speculate, then, that in the belated moment of machine breaking at the *Post*, those remembrances became resentments. Anxiously and angrily, they turned into the wellspring of an obstinate experience of historical time in which "an ongoing qualitative transformation of work and production, of social life more generally, and of forms of consciousness, values, and needs" that had unfolded since the end of the nineteenth century was countered, if not for the first time in 1975, then in a more definitively final form than prior struggles.[52] The remembrances and resentments of that transformation thus burst forth as obstinacy not only vis-à-vis the postwar years of rising prosperity in general but also more specifically vis-à-vis an unconscious history in the printing industry, in which the dialectics of technological change had steadily stripped techniques from technicians and technicians from technologies, shedding a craft tradition going back to Gutenberg almost entirely between the 1880s and the 1970s.

The moment of machine breaking at the *Post* in 1975 was determined by one last "former time": the *longue durée* of productive capital that began its descent around 1973. This moment of machine breaking repeated a parallel moment at the ascent of productive capital, which Joshua Clover contends went through a metacycle between 1830 and 1973. In his account of the transition into that metacycle in the late eighteenth and early nineteenth centuries, Clover argues that machine breaking then signaled the "swing" from struggle in the marketplace to struggle in the factory, because these were the decades in which capitalism was beginning the massive process of industrialization that would result in the shift from the sphere of circulation being the center of capital to the sphere of production being the core of capital for almost two centuries. In Clover's account, machine breaking was a transitional form of struggle "one foot in enclosure and food riots, one foot in factory legislation and struggles over the working day,"[53] making the belatedness Hobsbawm identified in this form a political and economic sign of a shift that found its obverse just under two centuries later at the *Post*. This is to say that the moment of machine breaking at the *Post* in 1975 was a sign of a related swing starting in the 1970s: the large-scale transformations of the post-1973 era in which the obsolescence of labor took on intensifying material, discursive, and cultural legibility by the end of the turn of the millennium. Seen from the perspective of the long *durée* of the metacycle of productive capital, then, the ransacking of the presses thus resonates with the memory of machine breaking, suggesting a mnemonic dimension to the obstinacy of that act of destruction. In repeating and reversing this mode of praxis across two centuries of productive capitalism, machine breakers of the post-1973 era—and David Noble has shown that the *Post* was hardly the only instance of this form of struggle in that era[54]—created an afterlife for wreckers long gone.

However, the best evidence for this afterlife, for the memory of machine breaking stubbornly resurging in our time, may not be the acts themselves but those who took the time to reclaim and recuperate the history of these acts across the late twentieth century and early twenty-first century such that they, like the obsolescence of labor, became increasingly legible. And we can begin by pointing to one of the texts with which this section began, Hobsbawm's

"The Machine Breakers" of 1952, and then move forward into the post-1945 era to E. P. Thompson's magisterially detailed *The Making of the English Working Class* (1963), and finally onto later works such as Noble's *Progress without People* (1995), Kirkpatrick Sale's *Rebels against the Future* (1995), and Peter Linebaugh's *Ned Ludd and Queen Mab* (2012).[55] While too much should not be made of such coincidences, the last was published in the same year that *Wreck-It* was released, not to mention in a material form—the paper pamphlet—clearly meant to be both physically and politically outmoded in its means. Just as the memory of machine breaking resurges in texts such as these, so too does the usage of words such as *Luddite, Luddites,* and *Luddism* swell from the 1960s forward, spiking in the mid-1980s and then again around 2000.[56] Confirming the increased legibility of the obsolescence of labor at the end of the twentieth century, the Luddites obstinately reenter the vocabulary of our time, the memory of machine breaking gaining a belated currency akin to the historicity of this form of struggle itself.

That belated currency can be seen in a rather surprising place for the memory of machine breaking to be conjured: Guy Debord's *The Society of the Spectacle*. Issued in 1967, just four years after the 1963 publication of *The Making of the English Working Class* and just six years before 1973, the uprisings of the 1960s and the 1810s comingle in thesis 115 in Debord's famous work. In that thesis, Debord speaks, we might say, as a situationist-cum-Luddite when he writes:

Signs of a new and growing tendency toward negation proliferate in the more economically advanced countries. The spectacular system reacts to these signs with incomprehension or attempts to misrepresent them, but they are sufficient proof that a new period has begun. After the failure of the working class's first subversive assault on capitalism, we are now witness to *the failure of capitalist abundance*. On the one hand, we see anti-union struggles of Western workers that have to be repressed (and repressed primarily by the unions themselves); at the same time rebellious tendencies among the young generate a protest that is still tentative and amorphous, yet already clearly embodies a rejection of the specialized sphere of the old politics, as well as of art and everyday life. These are two sides of the same coin, both signaling a new spontaneous struggle emerging under the sign of *criminality*, both portents of a second proletarian onslaught on class society. When the lost children of this as-yet immobile horde enter once again upon the battlefield, which has changed yet stayed the same, a new General Ludd will be at their head—leading them this time in an onslaught on the *machinery of permitted consumption*.[57]

The appearance of "a new General Ludd" is, to me, always a bit surprising here. But it really shouldn't be, for earlier, in thesis 45, Debord evidences full-blown awareness of how automation was a growing problem already in the post-1945 era when he writes that it "confronts the world of the commodity with a contradiction that it must somehow resolve: the same technical infrastructure that is capable of abolishing labor must at the same time preserve labor as a commodity." While in thesis 45 he grasps that this contradiction—which is the moving contradiction of Capital itself—is being managed in the advanced capitalist world through the "happy solution," as he ironically puts it, "in the growth of the tertiary or service sector," in thesis 115 he has come to realize that "the necessity of reintegrating newly redundant labor" may end up not being understood as necessary enough for reintegration to adequately take place.[58] As a result of that realization, he predicts a horde of lost children led by a new General Ludd engaging in out-and-out struggle—but interestingly, not in the sphere of production, not in factories, but in the sphere of circulation, as the phrase he italicizes, "*the machinery of permitted consumption*," suggests.

It turns out Debord's prediction was right. Sufficient integration of workers is failing, with "jobless recoveries" becoming more and more globally frequent since the late twentieth century in both the United States and Europe, such that, as David Harvey writes, "future prospects point in one direction: massive surpluses of potentially restive redundant populations."[59] And the childish horde of latter-day machine breakers Debord envisioned has in many respects arisen, some on the attack in the sphere of production, as with the pressmen at the *Washington Post* in 1975, still others in the restive form of rioters, blockaders, occupiers, and saboteurs in the sphere of circulation elsewhere in the advanced capitalist world, from Oakland to London. The horde to which we will attend in this chapter, however—especially the new General Ludd, who obstinately carries on the memory of machine breaking in the capitalist present—is to be found in *Wreck-It Ralph*.

The Obstinacy of the Obsolete: Reactivating Historical Experience

Prefigured in Debord's conjuring of a new General Ludd in *The Society of Spectacle*, Fredric Jameson has recently and rightly argued in *Valences of the Dialectic* that capitalism has created a new character that will necessarily appear in the stories we tell: the formerly employed. In setting up a call for better cognitive maps of "the abandoned populations of the postmodern world" that "re-create actants, agents, narrative characters, in a far more inclusive narrative about late capitalism," Jameson suggests that the formerly employed was a category already embedded in Marx's account of related actants and agents such as workers, the reserve army of the unemployed, and the unemployable. "The empty slot is already implicitly identified in *Capital*," writes Jameson,

which presciently includes a withering attack on pious notions of retraining in
its epic account of whole industries driven out of business: but it remained for
globalization to dramatize this category far more visibly by projecting it out
into visible geographical space. For the new category can be none other than
the *formerly employed*: that is to say, the working populations once active in vital
industries which have now ceased to function, and around whose idle factories
the veterans of dead labor live on with their families in enclaves not much more
hopeful than [refugee camps], particularly when it comes to dwellings and
foreclosures.[60]

In keeping with much of his earlier work, Jameson sees the formerly employed
as the effect of a spatial phenomenon—globalization—and it is as a spatial
phenomenon that this effect demands better cognitive maps, an idea he introduced most famously in *Postmodernism*. Jameson is correct that the emergence
of the formerly employed is in significant respects the result of transformations to space, for the character of the formerly employed he is conceptualizing arises in the faded and fading industrial cores of such countries as the
United Kingdom and the United States as a result of the movement of labor
"offshore." That figure of speech, however, tends to deflect attention from
how "offshoring" stems from the dialectics of technological change. What
drives firms and industries abroad is more than cheap labor: it is the need for
less of it as well as older blocs of capitalist production falling into obsolescence
due to newer blocs arising. In these newer blocs, more-efficient machines make
more products with fewer people.[61]

What culture by outmoded means draws out, however, is that this spatial
phenomenon is in equal measure a temporal one—that displacement is also
superannuation. It shows that the fall *out of* history that the formerly employed
have undergone, which for Jameson demands spatial thinking, is also a fall *into*
history, which for me demands temporal and historical thinking—in fact, thus
far, a series of historicisms variously intensive, hermeneutic, and now ludic and
Luddite in their modes.[62] The ludic and Luddite historicism of this chapter
gives us a way of thinking about *Wreck-It Ralph*, especially the personification
of games that is so key to the film's narrative. As Ralph's voiceover suggests,
this personification allows the film to rehumanize time despite the inhuman
deactivation of it that the prologue describes. This anthropomorphic reactivation of temporality depends, moreover, on the late capitalist story about the
obsolescence of labor that *Wreck-It* tells. *Wreck-It* tells that story through
the antagonist of the film, Turbo, who fills the empty slot that Jameson
describes as an outmoded video game who personifies the formerly employed
rendered obsolete by the dialectics of technological change, if here, as we shall
see, in the sphere of circulation. Turbo, moreover, personifies the obsolete

laborers who have, since the Luddites, revolted against innovations that leave them jobless. The antagonist of the film is thus the site of narrative by obstinate means—that is, of the story of a worker who refuses to be rendered obsolete. Evoking the usurpers and scapegoats of the comic mode as well, the story of this stubborn refusal in *Wreck-It* fictionally and historically mediates the memory of machine breaking traced above.[63] The effect of this mnemonic mediation by means of the antagonist in *Wreck-It* is, first, an experience of historical time shot through with obstinacy and, second, a political imaginary that blights the comedy of reemployment that *Invention* and *Hugo* happily represent, disfiguring it with death and destruction, stupidity and stubbornness. In this comic disfigurement, *Wreck-It*'s narrative by obstinate means registers more fully the diminished room that Capital itself now has to move than does *Invention* or *Hugo*, envisioning an irreal reality in which full employment is a fantasy and the formerly employed are killed off for rising up to protest their obsolescence.

This chapter has so far operated on two temporal and historical scales: one small and contemporary, one large and genealogical. On the one hand, it has devoted extensive attention to fewer than three minutes of a 101-minute film from 2012—and the first three at that. On the other hand, it has attended to a genealogy of machine breaking centuries old, the memory of which gains traction at the turn of the post-1973 era, from the pages of *The Society of the Spectacle* to the pressroom of the *Washington Post*. In between these two temporal and historical scales is the story that *Wreck-It* tells. As the title of the film makes clear, the narrative center of gravity is Ralph, who is the "bad guy" in the game *Fix-It Felix, Jr*. In this, the film already announces its interest in shifting attention toward the character space of antagonists, since in his game, Ralph wrecks things and Felix, who the gamer plays, fixes things, winning a medal when he does.[64] As the monologue shows, Ralph's problem is that he doesn't love his job because even after hours, when the arcade is closed and the games lead their social lives, no one likes the bad guys, excluding them as if their labor and their selves were identical. Ralph seeks to remedy this situation of professional and personal alienation by crossing into another game, *Hero's Duty*, to win a medal there. And while he does secure his reward, in the process he also inadvertently ends up in another game, *Sugar Rush*. He also mistakenly brings with him the antagonist of *Hero's Duty*, the cybug, described by Calhoun, the protagonist of *Hero's Duty*, as being like a virus, its only purpose eating, killing, and multiplying within whatever game it finds itself. Venturing into *Sugar Rush* to find the cybug and Ralph, respectively, Calhoun further explains to Felix that unless they eliminate the cybug in *Sugar Rush*, it will virally multiply until a horde of them consumes the entire arcade. Once it does, it will effectively expel the video game characters it does not kill into a condition of electronic homelessness, leaving behind a wrecked landscape in this hidden sphere of circulation not unlike the enclaves of the formerly employed living within the circumference of those, as Jameson puts it above, "vital industries which have now ceased to function." In fact, the film produces at least one extended vision of the formerly employed caught up in systemic joblessness and mass unemployment, a vision in which characters flee into a fatal landscape in which no industry at all seems to be functioning.

But the point right now is how the actions that Ralph takes as a disgruntled worker makes the unhappy laborer a destabilizing source of narrative as such. In his influential work on narrative, Paul Ricoeur states that "a story describes a series of actions and experiences by a number of characters. . . . These characters are represented either in situations that change or as they relate to changes to which they then react."[65] Ralph's actions above induce just such a situation of change, causing narrative to arise as a result, indeed, a narrative that is about rising up. *Wreck-It*, moreover, has its own name for the particular situation of change that Ralph catalyzes: "going Turbo." Throughout the early parts of the film, characters use this phrase to pathologize Ralph's desires not to be a bad guy and to win a medal as well as the actions he takes to fulfill those desires. While Ralph is insistent that his need to be appreciated both for the work he does as a bad guy and for the good guy he is beyond that labor is not equivalent to "going Turbo," it takes some time for the film to explain what this phrase means.

That explanation eventually takes the form of a cautionary tale that Felix tells to Calhoun as they search for Ralph and the cybug in *Sugar Rush*. The tale begins as metadiegetic narration, Felix narrating what it means to "go Turbo" to Calhoun in the form of dialogue, before Felix's narration is visualized as a flashback to which he provides a voiceover. In that voiceover, Felix explains that in the first days of the arcade, "*Turbo Time* was by far the most popular game. And Turbo—ugh—he loved the attention." He then goes on to describe the arrival of a new game, one more technologically advanced than *Turbo Time*. "So, when *Road Blasters* got plugged in and stole Turbo's thunder," Felix tells Calhoun, "boy was he jealous! So jealous that he abandoned his own game and tried to take over the new one. Turbo ended up putting both games and himself out of order. For good." Visually, the transition from metadiegetic narration to flashback and voiceover is a direct echo of the prologue of the film, except that now *Turbo Time* centers the shot, *Fix-It Felix, Jr.* on the left and *Pac-Man* on the right. Once again, the film zooms into the arcadian point of view that the young gamers depicted occupy until *Turbo Time*—and its primitive bitmap graphics—fill the screen, putting us in their position. At this point, however, the flashback parts ways with the prologue, especially visually. The arcadian point of view immediately takes on a dystopian quality because the shot ominously rotates to the right, producing a canted angle (figure 3.4). These uncomfortably rotating shots and queasily canted angles

FIGURE 3.4 *Wreck-It Ralph*, directed by Rich Moore, Walt Disney Pictures, 2012, film still

proliferate as the flashback progresses in almost gothic fashion, giving way to dramatic low- and high-angle shots that visually reinforce the cautionary nature of the dark tale Felix is telling about "going Turbo." The flashback further darkens this tale by remediating interlacing such that a less visually detailed, but more electronically textured, sequence of images moves before our eyes on-screen, haptically overlaying this analeptic movement backward in the narrative structure with so much technological historicity at the surface of the screen (figure 3.5).[66] Much as this cautionary tale takes us back in narrative time to the moment when Turbo found himself out of work, then, the interlacing pulls the image creatively and destructively—indeed, obstinately—out of sync with the digital present in visual time.

But about what is *Wreck-It* going to such narrative and visual lengths to be cautionary in having Felix tell this tale? Like the metadiegetic narration and analeptic expansion of that narration in *Invention* and *Hugo*, the story that

FIGURE 3.5 *Wreck-It Ralph*, directed by Rich Moore, Walt Disney Pictures, 2012, film still

Felix tells is, in the first place, a story about the obsolescence of labor. Unlike Selznick's novel and Scorsese's adaptation, however, the obsolete laborer takes the personified form of an outmoded game in *Wreck-It*. What this act of personification does is show that the analepsis in *Wreck-It* is a story about the obsolescence of labor specific to the post-1973 era. It does not narrate how the dialectics of technological change put people out of work in the sphere of production. Instead, it emplots how those same dialectics, figured in mediated form in the flashback through the personified rhythms of goods coming and going in the marketplace according to their life cycles, can envelop labor (or playbor) working in services in the heavily retail landscape of the sphere of circulation. Looked at from another historically specific angle related to this first one, the tale of Turbo also suggests how much the computerization of capital in the late twentieth and early twenty-first centuries has exacerbated the obsolescence of labor despite the jobs created in digital industries such as gaming, though these jobs are, again, paradoxically themselves symptoms of that obsolescence.

In these two senses, the analepsis is a narrative mediation of the obsolescence of labor akin to *Invention* and *Hugo*, if more directly keyed to the technological and economic configuration of the post-1973 conjuncture than those works. That analepsis is cautionary, in the second place, because the tale it tells pathologizes "going Turbo." The narrative and visual energies given over to making the analepsis dark and gothic, queasy and uncomfortable, are about cautioning against what Turbo does: rebel against the threat of unemployment as a result of a newer and "nower" machine that means he might end up unplugged due to a decline in popularity because of his less advanced technology. In this, Turbo is what Scott Bukatman, in his definitive work on animation, *The Poetics of Slumberland: Animated Spirits and the Animating Spirit*, calls a "*disobedient machine*," which is "the animated creation [that] turns its back on its creator to pursue its own agendas, fulfill its own desires, or perhaps just fail in its own way." Or we might think of Turbo as what Wendy Hui Kyong Chun christens a "daemonic medium" in *Programmed Visions: Software and Memory*, where she writes that "our media are daemonic: inhabited by invisible, orphaned processes that, perhaps like Socrates's *daimonion*, help us in our times of need."[67] Disobedient and daemonic alike, what Turbo's actions most clearly evoke are the acts of machine breakers past and present. This evocation leads to the analepsis sparking an obstinate experience of historical time that reactivates the temporality we saw deactivated in the prologue that this analepsis recalls and revises.

Clearly, Turbo is not an exact replica of the Luddites or the pressmen in the analepsis. But he is an irreal mimesis of them. He willfully but belatedly goes on the attack against a machine that has already rendered him obsolete in much the way that machine breakers stubbornly oppose new devices once the strategic moment to do so for their opposition to matter has passed. Indeed, he is so obstinately committed to his opposition that he is willing to put both himself and the employees of *Road Blasters* out of order. And while the flashback is a tale meant to warn against such obstinate behavior, in issuing that warning it can't help but mediate the memory of machine breaking much as it remediates the interlacing of earlier video technology, with the analeptic movement backward in narrative time and the retrograde motion in visual time only stressing the act of recollection for us in the cautionary tale that Felix tells. The memory of machine breaking is in this sense immanent to the fiction of the film itself, part of the history of *its* diegesis. And "going Turbo" is the phrase that encodes that memory in the film's diegetic field. But that fiction is also resonant with the memory of machine breaking that is part of the history of *our* diegesis now, with Turbo looking very much like the new General Ludd that Debord predicted would come to lead an assault on the machinery of permitted consumption, of which video games could not be a better example in our time.

This dual mediation of the memory of machine breaking at both fictional and historical levels is an important act of destructive creativity, for if the prologue deactivated time with a pulsating blur of temporal sensation, then this analepsis reactivates it with an obstinate act of historical resistance, producing a flashback in which the memory of Turbo's machine breaking visually and narratively yields an experience of historical time marked by obstinacy from fictional and historical directions alike. That experience takes up more and more narrative room—or, more fittingly, narrative time—as *Wreck-It* proceeds. It does so because of what Ricoeur says are the defining features of narrative beyond the changes that set a story going. In any given narrative, those changes eventually, he writes, "reveal hidden aspects of the situation and of the characters that engender a new predicament that calls for thinking, action, or both. The answer to this predicament advances the story to its conclusion."[68] The hidden aspect revealed in *Wreck-It* ultimately is that the character that rules over *Sugar Rush*, King Candy, is actually Turbo. Fascinatingly for our purposes, this revelation begins in another analeptic moment of narration, in which Ralph forces King Candy's servant, Sour Bill, to reveal why another character, Vanellope von Schweetz, appears on the console to the game as a racer but is forbidden from racing. Sour Bill explains that King Candy tried to delete Vanellope's code but that he doesn't know why because King Candy "literally locked up our memories."

The rest of the story thus seeks to remember King Candy's reasons for locking up their memories. It eventually is revealed that King Candy is Turbo, who, in a digital version of machine breaking, hacked *Sugar Rush* in the past so as to stay employed in the face of newer and nower generations of games that threatened to leave him forever out of order. He does so, however, at the cost of Vanellope, for by the end of the story we learn that she was the ruler of *Sugar Rush* when she is restored to her rightful place and her rightful job, the usurper having been removed in much the way that the comic mode, of which *Wreck-It* is an interesting instance, historically entails.[69] The gendered and generational dynamics here work to pathologize "going Turbo" only further, since Turbo-cum-King Candy takes work away from a young girl, trying to hold onto a past in which he was the most popular game, boys ruled the arcade, and men had the jobs. Paradoxically, however, this pathological characterization of "going Turbo" depends on zanily queering Turbo in his status as King Candy at the same time, as if machine breaking means you must be less of a man—which is to say, a homosexual man.[70] But what ultimately makes the machine breaker into less of a man in *Wreck-It* is how Turbo-cum-King Candy melds with one of the cybugs, turning into a grotesque medley of Turbo, King Candy, and the cybug itself (figure 3.6). In this multiplied position, he threatens to take over any and all games in the arcade. Become not just Debord's new General Ludd but also the horde of lost children Debord imagines him leading, Turbo-cum-King Candy threatens, in short, to wreck the marketplace of permitted consumption—perhaps even to creatively destroy Capital itself. Not surprisingly, therefore, he is killed off by the end of the film before he can destructively create a new world, perhaps one in which the push and pull of labor are no longer coercing us—and no longer plunging us into history.

Because it murders the machine breaker, because it kills off Turbo-cum-King Candy, *Wreck-It* is a much darker comedy of reemployment than *Invention* and *Hugo*. Like those works, *Wreck-It* restores characters to their rightful jobs and to righted relationships to their jobs. In classic comic form, Vanellope returns as the princess of *Sugar Rush*, and Ralph grasps that being a bad guy is just a job, not an identity, not to mention the fact that Calhoun and

FIGURE 3.6 *Wreck-It Ralph*, directed by Rich Moore, Walt Disney Pictures, 2012, film still

Felix marry, as so many seemingly mismatched heroes and heroines of comedy do by the end of their springtime adventures. But Turbo-cum-King Candy remains what Northrop Frye calls an "irreconcilable character" that the narrative expels, with those restored to their jobs benefitting from the death of he who protested when he feared he might lose his own. While such expulsion threatens, as Frye notes in his gloss on *The Merchant of Venice*, to come "as close as possible to upsetting the comic balance," there is, to compensate, the character of Q*Bert.[71] A character derived from the actual history of video games, Q*Bert is not unlike Hugo, living a wageless life in Grand Central Station—the hub where characters pass from one game to another in *Wreck-It*—because he has been unplugged, no longer sufficiently popular or technologically edgy to attract enough players, whatever the appeal of his androgynous cuteness may be (figure 3.7). In our first encounter with Q*Bert, for example, he is begging for food—and later he informs Felix that Ralph has "gone Turbo." Never rising up as Turbo-cum-King Candy does—in fact, turning Ralph in when it looks like he might have bucked the system—Q*Bert is rewarded for not protesting his obsolescence as a laborer with a place in the bonus levels of *Fix-It Felix, Jr.* along with other unplugged games (figure 3.8). This is a contradictory development, if one consistent with how, as Lauren Berlant and Sianne Ngai have recently observed, "the affective labor of the comedic as a socially lubricating mood commandeers comedy to enable the very contradictions and stresses to which it points."[72] It is contradictory because the presence of Turbo in *Road Blasters* is precisely what had put *Road Blasters* and *Turbo Time* out of order; it is comic because the mode seeks "to include as many people as possible in its final society."[73] The film further tries to explain away the contradiction by suggesting that the popularity with gamers this inclusion restores to *Fix-It* accords with the retro culture by which a commodity is, as the film puts it, "old but cool."

FIGURE 3.7 *Wreck-It Ralph*, directed by Rich Moore, Walt Disney Pictures, 2012, film still

FIGURE 3.8 *Wreck-It Ralph*, directed by Rich Moore, Walt Disney Pictures, 2012, film still

We might conclude, then, by saying that *Wreck-It Ralph* partakes of the vision that Christian Thorne has ascribed to retro culture in his powerful essay "The Revolutionary Energy of the Outmoded." "Underlying retro culture," writes Thorne, "is a vision of a world in which commodity production has come to a halt, in which objects have been handed down, not for our consumption, but for our care." *Wreck-It* applies this vision to people as much as products by comically reemploying as many displaced workers as possible in an attempt, pace Berlant and Ngai, to commandeer the contradiction that the caring reversal of Q*Bert's obsolescence brings to the surface. The trouble is that the comedy of reemployment can't take fully soothing charge of the contradiction because of the film's narrative by obstinate means, which brings *Wreck-It* closer to what Thorne further states is the darker side of retro culture's vision in its desire to bring commodity production to a halt. "The apocalypse," writes Thorne, "is retro culture's deepest fantasy, its enabling wish."[74]

But if the apocalypse enabling retro culture turns upon ending commodity production in the name of a new "relationship to objects *as something other than commodities*,"[75] as Thorne puts it, then narrative by obstinate means stubbornly confronts us with a political imaginary focused more on those whose labor it is to make and sell commodities that have not yet transcended their state as such. When the obstinacy of the obsolete asserts itself as the core of historical experience in *Wreck-It*, the film opens up a political imaginary that stubbornly cleaves to the contradiction its story wants to dispel through Q*Bert and Turbo-cum-King Candy. Despite the reemployment of one obsolete worker and the murder of the other, that contradiction stubbornly refuses to go away in our memory of this film given how much it mediates—how much it narratively falls into—a two-century history of machine breaking that is an obstinate history of attempts to stupefy the motion of Capital itself. Indeed, in the case of the viral horde that Turbo-cum-King Candy becomes in the end—and in light of how violently that horde threatens the world of

Wreck-It Ralph with a collective act of destructive creation that feels like it is potentially aimed at undoing Capital itself altogether—the innocent play of the arcade with which the film began gives obdurately vehement way to an apocalyptic refusal to submit to the rules of the workplace that arcade turns out to be. By the end of the film, then, the political imaginary of *Wreck-It* is split between, on the one hand, a comically retro fantasy of full employment (which is always a fantasy anyway) that restores the obsolete worker to capitalist labor and, on the other hand, a daemonic figuration of proletarian obstinacy in the memory of machine breaking that Turbo-cum-King Candy awakens for us as the children of capital today. As such, *Wreck-It* is closer to the irreal reality in which we find ourselves as such children in our time—the bizarre conjuncture in which full employment is more and more a ludic fantasy and the obsolete are increasingly restive, obstinately animated in their Luddite anger about being unplugged. That obstinacy is both a singular rage about the loss of a job someone needs to get by and a collective fury at Capital itself for pulling us into work out of which it aims to push us by outmoding so many again and again. It is the core of a historical experience in which something other than Capital itself might get destructively created.

4

Cinema by Dated Means

————————————————————●

I found myself watching the fur move, rather than watching the faces.
—A spectator on seeing *Fantastic Mr. Fox*

Those for whom a stagnating or declining wage can no longer acquire the market basket—much less the ever-vaster surplus population beyond the wage—have realized the truth of the age: that a visit to the paymaster, even armed and in company, no longer affords a remedy. For them the action will be elsewhere, more and more intensely. Which is by way of saying: the riots are coming.
—Joshua Clover, "World-Systems Riot"

Fascinating Fur, Phenomenological Historicism

What fascinated the spectator above in watching *Fantastic Mr. Fox* wasn't simply fur that moved but fur that boiled.[1] Of course, the fur in Wes Anderson's 2009 film does not literally boil, like water heated to the right temperature. Part of the vernacular of animators, "boiling" refers to "unwanted movement" that results from manual adjustments to puppets between frames in stop-motion animation and from "random fluctuations" in the quality of a line from frame to frame in hand-drawn animation.[2] Historically, boiling has been an undesirable effect, largely because of the asynchronous quality it introduces from frame to frame, which intensifies discontinuity. In this respect, boiling breaks with the ideals of classical filmmaking, disrupting the self-generating enclosure of story and storyworld, including the idea of characters as individuals (or "faces") for the spectator above. In so doing, the characters were no longer humanized creatures for him because they became man-made creations instead.[3] This effect further results from the fact that the boiling is a trace of the means of production, including the living labor, that went into the making of the film: of the tactile materials out of which the puppets were made and the analog adjustments performed by hand to the puppets in the shooting of *Fantastic*. In fact, during shooting, Anderson stubbornly insisted to the film crew that the already obstinately fussy fur of the puppets be allowed to boil despite industrial norms to the contrary, converting boiling into a technique in its own right. Anderson's direction in this regard worked to enhance the fascination with the fur that the spectator above experienced.

Nor was that spectator alone in his fascination. As reviews by Roger Ebert and A. O. Scott show, that fascination was a feeling textured by the datedness of the technologically obsolete—the very stuff that this book has been arguing is elemental to an experience of historical time in culture by outmoded means. Ebert, for example, describes an experience of technological time travel that also invokes the textures of *Fantastic*. Made in what Ebert considers "one of the oldest animation styles of all," he writes in his review that the puppets "live in a sometimes flat dimension; the cameras are happier sliding back and forth than moving in and out. The effect is sometimes like an old-fashioned slide projector. The landscapes and structures of this world are mannered and picture-booky. Yet the extraordinary faces are almost disturbingly human (for animals, of course). We venture into the UnCanny Valley, that No Man's Land dividing humans from the devised. Above all, their fur is so *real*. I've rarely seen such texture in a film."[4] Ebert arguably has the inverse reaction to the epigraphic spectator, since the faces seem human to him. But their humanity is extraordinary, disturbed, in his words, by the fur, making his reaction largely identical to the epigraphic spectator's in that the reality that counts is that of the fur.

Scott echoes Ebert, writing, "*Fantastic Mr. Fox* is proudly analog entertainment, making its handmade way into a marketplace glutted with digital goodies. Next to the three-dimensional, computer-generated creatures that swoop and soar off the screen these days, the furry talking animals on display here, with their matted pelts, jerky movements and porcelain eyes, might look a little quaint, like old-fashioned windup toys uneasily sharing the shelf with the latest video game platforms."[5] That reference to the "swoop and soar" of digital beings brings to mind films contemporaneous with *Fantastic* such as *Avatar* (2009), Episodes 1 to 3 of *Star Wars* (1999, 2002, 2005), the *X-Men* movies (2000–present), and *The Lord of the Rings* trilogy (2001, 2002, 2003), though we could go back to *Jurassic Park* (1993) and *Terminator 2: Judgment Day* (1991) as well. That reference also suggests the outrageously dynamic camera movements and screen tempos that have come to characterize such films—movements and tempos that themselves feel like the cinematic correlative of the doubling of computer speed every eighteen months.[6] Thus in addition to adjusting to the "scruffy looks" of *Fantastic*, Scott also observes that he needed to get used to the film's "stop-and-start rhythms."[7] We can see what Scott means by contrasting early shots of *Hugo* and *Fantastic*. At the beginning of *Hugo*, on the one hand, a virtual camera plunges from the sky above Paris into the train station in which the film is set in a move that takes seventy-five nonstop seconds over the course of which it gains increasing speed, displaying the attraction of digital 3-D spatially and temporally.[8] In *Fantastic*, on the other hand, one of Anderson's characteristic tracking shots, lasting roughly sixty seconds, moves from left to right in far flatter space and less smoothly onrushing time, its rhythm more staccato and its momentum more analog than the digital rush of *Hugo*, until it pauses for dialogue at the end of the shot.

In the case of Scott, the fascinating datedness of Anderson's film also evokes the obsolescence of laborers that are in less and less use in the digital age, specifically journalists who have seen technological change, especially computerization, transform their work.[9] Referring to Mr. Fox's job as a newspaper columnist in the film, Scott anxiously and jokingly writes, "In enchanted talking-animal fairyland, that is apparently a thriving profession, and those of us in journalism who soon may be stealing chickens out of desperation may envy Mr. Fox the luxury of doing it for love."[10] This is something of a misreading. It is explicitly suggested that Mr. Fox is neither thriving in his profession nor devotedly read by the community to which he belongs. And the thefts of fowl and other food goods are more necessary than Scott suggests on the basis of the film alone in his review, for these thefts are aspects of the plot that are a narrative mediation of the objective dynamics of our historical moment: the obsolescence of labor that is a legible feature of our moment and the related shift from strike to riot in that moment to which the epigraph from Joshua Clover points. For now, though, the point is that Scott's review shows that at least one spectator experienced the furry fascination of *Fantastic* in tandem with an anxiety of obsolescence that is all too real for workers as fact and force today. After all, in the same review in which he describes the dated delectations that *Fantastic* offers, Scott takes note of the shifting mediascape of journalism in which, as Richard Susskind and Daniel Susskind describe in their recent book on the technological transformations to which middle-class professionals can look forward, "the traditional newspaper business model is in crisis." Scott may not directly mention the algorithms that are now handling some of the reporting that humans used to cover.[11] But clearly the computerization to which the *Washington Post* pressmen objected in 1975 has, more than forty years later, caught up with journalists such as him.

This chapter locates the source of the spectators' experiences above in the cinema by dated means that *Fantastic* develops. In their datedness, those means create a historical experience in which the obsolete tech that spectators can physically see makes them sense the obsolescence of labor that is not truly visible in *Fantastic*. Like the labor time that invisibly congeals in the commodities we consume, the obsolete labor that went into the making of *Fantastic*, especially the "stop-motion labor time," as I call it, required in its production, underwrites the dated feeling of the film. To put the matter differently, the fascinating fur of *Fantastic* is indicative of a phenomenological historicism demanded in the cinematic viewing and critical analysis of Anderson's mass-cultural masterpiece (however noncanonical it may finally be, it remains a masterpiece). In the case of this film, the intensive anachronies of culture by outmoded means more specifically yield a '70s feeling in the fourth dimension of the film, its space-time built out of analog technologies that feel out of date in the digital moment of 2009 when *Fantastic* was released. Indeed, beyond the '70s and 2009, the datedness of *Fantastic* in relationship to the digital also involves a '30s feeling because it beautifully draws on the original *King Kong*, especially for the technique of boiling. With the '70s, 2009, and the '30s all in play in the experience of watching *Fantastic*, it becomes clear that the dated means of the film do not operate according to what Wai Chee Dimock has called "the jurisdiction of the number" in her critique of a historicism unduly beholden to the habit of assuming that a particular year—1973 is one we could invoke—is adequate to situating a novel or film in history, much less to demonstrating how time passes, especially as the passage of time occurs in culture.[12] Those means unfurl, instead, by way of a phenomenological historicism in which datedness is not chained to any single year or decade but rather stands for a historicity more unevenly developed out of the film, falling into any number of years and decades that it transmits as past in the present. Moreover, what the datedness ultimately transmits—and such subjectively affective and atmospheric verbs as *transmit, emit, evoke, hover, feel, sense, imbue, reverberate, texture,* and *allude* are central to the idiom of a close reading indebted to a phenomenological historicism—is the obsolescence of labor that has materially, discursively, and culturally intensified since circa 2000, especially so much beautiful feeling for the sphere of production that so many of us in the United States and United Kingdom now read as a thing of the past.

In light of the above, the close reading in this chapter turns significantly on the material form of *Fantastic*, with the first three sections of the chapter devoted to the analog technologies that emit a '70s feeling, the analog technique of boiling that textures the film with datedness, and the 1930s sources the film evokes and on which it drew in production. However, the story the film tells is also important and is the subject of the final section of the chapter. Initially focused on a midlife crisis in which Mr. Fox starts stealing chickens from the local farmers, Boggis, Bunce, and Bean, *Fantastic* develops into the story of two classes at war with one another: the animals, here so many middle-class professionals that figure a kind of middle-class proletariat, and Boggis, Bunce, and Bean, here the figures for local farmers-cum-agricultural industrialists-cum-multinational capitalists. That story is, importantly, shaped by the form of struggle that theorists of political culture have established is more and more dominant in the contemporary moment in light of the obsolescence of labor: the riot in the marketplace. To steal a phrase from Clover above, the riots are coming in *Fantastic Mr. Fox*. In fact, they arrive—but in a bourgeois form. As a result, the narrative content of the film exists in counterpoint to the dated means of its material form because the plot is mark-edly contemporary, telling a story in which a class of characters, to use the verb that replaces *fuck* in the film, *cusses with* capitalism in the sphere of circula-tion. In exploring the nonsynchronism of material form and narrative content in *Fantastic*, what emerges is how the contemporaneity of its plot turns upon the historicity of its means. Narrative currency goes hand in hand with dated means, making *Fantastic* an experience of historical time in which we must feel out the fact that the politics of the present cannot be easily separated from the conditions of the past.

That '70s Feeling

Beyond the year of its release, 2009, *Fantastic Mr. Fox* is a film that can be dated in a number of fashions. But the date—or the feeling of datedness—that predominates is a feeling of the '70s. That '70s feeling is common to Ander-son's films, imbuing them with quirkily nostalgic pleasures, especially for those us with childhoods that began in the technological and economic crucible of the 1970s. Most immediately, however, the feeling of datedness is born of the belated transition to digital production and projection in the film industry. This transition is inseparable from the emergence of the post-1973 era that forms the time and terrain of this book. However belated, indeed, however debated, the digital transition has itself been a crucible for cinematic experi-ence as the film industry has brought an end to the century-long era of ana-log filmmaking and moviegoing. "Cinema was the last medium in popular culture to go fully digital," David Bordwell has written, with the other major media of the culture industry—books, magazines, music, photography, gaming—computerizing their technical and transactional means at earlier dates over the past forty years.[13]

In addition to changing where we watch films, with theatrical moviegoing increasingly turning into the memory it is in *The Invention of Hugo Cabret* and *Hugo*, what this longer and wider moment of technological and economic obsolescence has meant is a transformation of our experience of the cinematic image. Where spectators used to experience that image as a species of photog-raphy, they now know that it is closer to a species of animation. For example, following Lev Manovich's influential work in *The Language of New Media*, John Belton writes, "Digital technology has transformed the photographic image into a truly 'plastic' object that can be molded and remolded into what-ever shape is desired.... Digital cinema has made the cinema a subset of anima-tion."[14] Where we used to perceive even a fictional film as the photochemical index of an irreducible historical moment crystallized in the space-time of the moving image on screen (an analogon of reality), we now know that we are looking at something more plastic and plasmatic, a more perfected painting created on a computer using binary code (a homologon of reality). Films such as *Avatar* and the *X-Men* series reflexively dramatize this shift in the means of cinematic production when human actors become digital beings in them and when the characters they play change their corporeal forms and species-beings in the storyworld itself. The means of projection, moreover, often ask us to experience this shift through technical innovations such as digital 3-D, as in *Hugo*, which uses 3-D to posit a relationship between the postclassical present and preclassical past of film aesthetics. But given the mainstream prominence of studios such as Pixar and genres such as the superhero film, it is hardly necessary to remind spectators that, to paraphrase Bordwell, film is now a file, especially given how much the infrastructure of "moviegoing" has taken significant leave of theaters in favor of streaming services.[15]

Not everyone, however, sees a significant shift in this delayed moment of obsolescence for the technical means of filmmaking and moviegoing, especially when it comes to how spectators experience the cinematic image. For example, in a markedly skeptical series of articles written over the decade from 2002 to 2012—the decade during which, as Bordwell has written, "the image of miles of film curled up tight on a platter or tangled on the floor" became "outdated," turning "analog cinema" into "a metaphor, or a *memento mori*"— Belton repeatedly claimed that nothing is really obsolete because the transition during this decade "is not a new experience for the audience."[16] Despite corporate proclamations that it constituted a revolution in the means of cinematic production and projection, Belton consistently argued that little transformative took hold.[17] Although Belton observed in 2002 that the shift to digital technologies "does indeed threaten to overthrow the dominance of 35mm film, which has been the chief format of the motion-picture industry for over one hundred years," he further pointed out that "all that the proponents of digital projection are claiming is that it is comparable to 35mm."[18] And in a 2008 essay about *Pleasantville*, the first major film in which what is known as the "digital intermediate" process was used, Belton further contended that digital cinema usually "mirrors the course of digital imaging technology which tends to simulate older, analogue, image-making conventions, not to create radically new perceptual modes."[19]

For Belton, the so-called digital revolution in the film industry is largely about "innovation for innovation's sake." This is the phrase with which David Harvey describes innovation as "a vast domain of ever-changing possibilities for sustaining or increasing profitability," regardless of whether anything genuinely new has actually been developed, much less allowed for any real accumulation or economic growth to occur.[20] This view of innovation clearly fuels Belton's cynicism, as when he starkly writes, "The digital revolution was and is all about economics—all about marketing new digital consumer products to a new generation of consumers."[21] The endgame is thus not a new cinematic experience but the creation of a market of "digital omnivores" in the 1980s, 1990s, and 2000s. These omnivores are the consumers of the various media—books, games, movies—all converging in digital devices on sale in the sphere of circulation at sometimes headily rotating rates of microinnovation.[22] What further substantiates Belton's economic critique is a point made by Bordwell: theater owners also find themselves forced to return to the sphere of circulation more often than when 35mm projectors were the fixed capital in which they were investing. The earlier projectors were not only cheaper, but they lived longer lives than digital projectors as well, for "built-in obsolescence," which we have seen pick up significantly after 1945 as a feature of capitalist production and circulation, means that digital projectors may only last three years. In this respect, the end of the film projectionist discussed in chapter 2 (and it's worth remembering that Anderson was a film projectionist once upon a time) has coincided with the acceleration of turnover times for the projectors that replaced them, with the latter obsolescing at an appreciably faster pace—if in a depreciating form—than the analog projectors that preceded them.[23] Belton's is thus a critique of both the perceptual and political economies of a digital revolution he takes to be false. To echo Theodor Adorno and Max Horkheimer, that new economy is largely a broken promise in Belton's eyes, cheating customers of the brand-new visual experiences it proffers as part of a larger strategy to get them to buy goods that don't live up to their marketed potential.[24]

Nonetheless, the feeling of datedness, even the simple feeling of furry fascination, that spectators experience in watching *Fantastic Mr. Fox* shows that something in both the perceptual and political economies of the present has changed for moviegoers. Otherwise, professional spectators like Ebert and Scott wouldn't notice how old-fashioned *Fantastic* feels. So if for Belton nothing new has arrived to punctuate perception in film history, then something older has in the case of *Fantastic Mr. Fox*. Like a willful child refusing to budge, this is a film that exhibits an obstinate attachment to analog tech, producing a feeling of datedness that in its most immediate sense depends on its date of release being 2009—for it is circa 2009 that the digital revolution essentially came to an end in the film industry, with the industry finally relinquishing its protracted attachment to analog means of production and projection. Between 2000 and 2010, digital screens multiplied by almost 1,200 times alone as more and more films were released globally in digital formats, jumping from 30 to 36,103 worldwide. And by 2011, the film industry, especially Hollywood, made clear that between 2012 and 2015, analog copies of films would no longer be distributed, even if, because a director preferred, a film had been shot on 35mm.[25] Although *Fantastic* was not shot on 35mm but with digital cameras, its temporal sensation is palpably analog and distinctively dated because of how it asserts its analog qualities in the very year that the digital transition was completing its ostensible revolution. Within the film itself, that sensation is in significant part the felt effect of aspects of its diegetic spaces and temporal structures—of the space-time of *Fantastic*. These mediate historical time by way of analog technologies explicitly dated vis-à-vis the digital, making for a structure of feeling that transmits what I am calling the '70s. This takes us beyond the year 2009 in dating *Fantastic*, though in transmitting that '70s feeling, *Fantastic* is not so much a work of the 1970s, when Anderson—born in 1969—was himself a kid. Instead, it is a work that arose in the afterlife of that decade as part of the late twentieth- and early twenty-first-century moment in which all the works explored in this book were made.

Consider the spaces of *Fantastic*. The mise-en-scène of this film is chock-full of analog tech that takes up space. The stuff of pawnshops and antique stores in everyday life, analog tech makes itself both seen and heard in the world of *Fantastic* far more powerfully than the digital devices that also occasionally appear there. In the opening scene of the film, for example, a long shot shows Mr. Fox (or Foxy) standing on a hill, casually exercising and blithely malingering, all the while enjoying "The Ballad of Davy Crocket" (1954) on his Walk-Sonic, an analog radio he wears on his belt. When the future Mrs. Fox (or Felicity) arrives, the camera cuts to a close-up of the Walk-Sonic. After this initial close-up, which serves no narrative function, the world of *Fantastic* becomes ever more analog. Although he owns a digital wristwatch, Mr. Fox is especially fond of analog listening and recording devices, since we later see him at home twice using his Tape-Sonic cassette player. When he visits the office of Badger, his lawyer, it is remarkably analog. In the foreground of the mise-en-scène, there is a Dicta-Sonic, a mechanical clock, and a rotary-dial landline on his desk. While Badger plays a song about the film's antagonists, Boggis, Bunce, and Bean, on the Dicta-Sonic, his secretary efficiently types away in the far background of the shot—with what looks like a Mac computer screen behind Badger turned on but crowded out by the analog tech that otherwise fills this space. This accumulation of analog tech in the animal spaces extends to the human spaces of the world of *Fantastic* as well, where, for instance, cathode ray and closed-circuit televisions are the broadcast media and surveillance equipment of choice for Boggis, Bunce, and Bean. These are not the gadgetry and goods of the digital omnivores that Belton insists are the market for digital cinema but the devices of an earlier generation of technological consumers, those who came of age in the 1960s, 1970s, and 1980s.

But the devices of a later technological and economic generation are also present. Mr. Fox's digital wristwatch looks like it could be from the later 1970s, but it equally could be of 1980s vintage, when such wristwatches achieved greater popularity as consumer novelties in the technological marketplace.[26] The other digital goods include the cell phone that belongs to Weasel, Mr. Fox's real estate agent; the Mac-like computer in Badger's office; and, at the end of the film, the digital successor of the analog Walk-Sonic that Ash, Mr. Fox's son, similarly wears on his waist. In the forms we see them here, the vintage of these is the final decade of the twentieth century and the first decade of the twenty-first. What to make of the uneven development of this world: saturated by analog tech but containing digital media both material to and marginal in its spaces? Given the preponderance of the former, the world of *Fantastic* is, despite Pierre Nora's claim that they have disappeared in contemporary life, a "*milieux de mémoire*" grounded in a technologically out-of-date infrastructure. It is an analog world nonsynchronous yet still contemporary with a digital mediascape that we know in reality has almost fully encroached upon its *milieux* but that is not much more than a technical trace in the film.[27] In this respect, the date of this world is less any particular decade or specific year than it is built out of obsolete stuff that gives off a feeling of the '70s more than referring to the 1970s directly.

To put this point differently, the '70s feeling is a function of the forty years that have opened up since the 1970s, with the dialectics of technological change by which the digital has overtaken the analog for successive generations being one form in which the film speaks to those decades. These intergenerational technics make *Fantastic* of a piece with other works in this book that, as we saw in *Invention* and *Hugo* especially, privilege past technology in relation to present technology. And while this preference for the obsolete, this will-to-obsolescence, is a feature of the diegesis in the film, it is also a quality of the theater, since the '70s feeling is an experience contingent on watching *Fantastic* for the first time in 2009. This is because the intended audience here is both adult and child. In 2009, adult spectators would have experienced the deeper and longer obsolescence of the analog by the digital themselves since the 1970s, perhaps having owned any number of the predigital gadgets and goods collected in the film. Meanwhile, younger viewers would be growing up in a technological world already largely digitized, in which the analog is becoming the generational memory of their parents and grandparents, even if it is still around in various material forms left over from the past. The nonsynchronous coexistence of analog and digital in the world of the film is thus a fourth dimension of the space of the theater itself in 2009, with the movie playing for parents and children who are generationally distinct. But it is equally cinema by dated means, precisely because it is insistently analog regardless of which spectator we consider. This analog dimension—which draws out the '70s—would only be stressed for spectators by that which Scott figuratively emphasizes when he juxtaposes windup toys and video games in his review: how *Fantastic* sits "uneasily" beside a film such as *Avatar*, also released in 2009 but one month apart.

Fantastic consistently makes comedy out of this simultaneity, if not out of the fact that *Fantastic Mr. Fox* and *Avatar* were playing in movie theaters at the same time. For example, where Weasel's cell phone has trouble getting a signal once the animals have collectively fled underground, the far more primitive and totally nonfunctional phone that the animals make out of a tin can and string improbably intercepts, in the same subterranean spaces, a high-frequency radio transmission that allows the animals to strategize in their struggle with the capitalist trio Boggis, Bunce, and Bean. That tin can is an example of how children's play embodies Walter Benjamin's mimetic faculty, with the film riffing on how the child plays at being on the phone by positing a nonsensuous similarity between tin can and phone. As with *Invention*, that play also has a nonsynchronous dimension here. Adding to the cleverly comic energies of the film writ large, the tin-can joke lovingly lampoons how we fetishize the latest gadget as the most powerful precisely because it is the latest, when here it is the lowest-tech option that works best. But what this joke also transmits is how the spaces of *Fantastic* are not only full of analog tech but also more receptive to them. Getting good reception in this world means *not* having a strong digital signal. It means having the wherewithal—indeed, the tenacity—to continue listening on an older means of transmission that not only is out of sync but was also out of work from the get-go. In all of this, the signal of this world is stubbornly analog, emitting the '70s on its nonsynchronous wavelengths.

Fantastic engenders a feeling of datedness not only in the diegetic spaces but also in the temporal structures of the film. Consider a striking montage that occurs at a climactic and suspenseful moment set in motion by a directive to synchronize watches. At this moment—which occurs just before the narrative conflict between humans and animals becomes fully polarized and mostly politicized—Mr. Fox directs his fellow creatures: "Synchronize your clocks. The time is now 9:45 a.m." This is quickly followed by another direction, though it sounds more like a quip: "Here, put these bandit hats on." The camera then cuts to the world aboveground, where the three human antagonists, Boggis, Bunce, and Bean, are awaiting Mr. Fox's arrival for a prearranged détente. Swiveling to the right, pausing with significance on a cobbler working—at what are audibly two distinct rhythms: one slower, one faster—before it pans up, the camera proceeds to give us an image of a traditional clock ticking above the exterior of the cobbler's shop. Finally, the film cuts to a montage of the now synchronized watches of the animals as story time progresses through three diegetic minutes in a span of ten seconds of discourse time. This progression has a recursive rhythm to it, alternating approximately every two seconds between an analog and a digital wristwatch—and then again, between an analog and a digital wristwatch—before bringing an end to this dilated moment that pauses the forward movement of narrative time. This rhythm does not deviate significantly from the norms of accelerated editing characteristic of postclassical cinema in contrast to prior moments in film history.[28] However, what decelerates things for the spectator is the compositional stasis of each analog point and digital counterpoint in the rhythm. With the watches all photographed in extreme close-up, these shots have a quality of still lives pausing in temporal succession, which nonetheless remind us of time's quantitative movement as the seconds and minutes visibly and audibly tick and beep over and over from frame to frame.

The alternation between analog and digital suggests, in the first place, a historical relationship of technological succession. The montage looks like a sequential progression from past to present, from a technics of timekeeping that is inferior to one that is superior, especially if we recall that digital watches are more accurate and more efficient than analog ones. What was once a technology we had to wind by hand has become a technology in which such winding is automated, a technical gesture in which we need no longer engage since digital watches do not require it. In this sense, the rhythmic alternation between analog and digital here constitutes a form of repeated stress that draws out this recursive progression as progress, a rout of the old by the new in the dialectics of technological change. This is a rout that the sound design of the montage amplifies since the beep-beep-beeping of the digital ones always follows the tick-tick-ticking of the analog watches. Accordingly, the temporal ordering of this montage suggests that we are in a historical era of technological succession in which the later technology is rendering the earlier one obsolete in a process of linear improvement from analog to digital. The digital supersedes the analog here, recursively transforming it into the palpable matter of historical time because the former dates the latter as an obsolete thing of the technological past.

But in an interesting inversion, it is actually the digital that looks palpably dated in the montage. The analog tech that appears so prominently throughout *Fantastic Mr. Fox* is in historical fact much closer to such a moment. More outdated than the digital, it is the diachronic echo of the '70s in 2009, especially in the various forms in which we see it in the mise-en-scène: the tape recorder and belt radio, displaced by the MP3 player; the cathode ray television, superannuated by high-definition flat screens; the typewriter, left behind by the computer; the landlines, forsaken in favor of cell phones. However, the digital wristwatches in the montage look much more like the products of technological fads of the recent past, especially the 1970s and 1980s, than the analog wristwatches, which possess a timeless aura of enduring utility and classic style. In this respect, what the montage projects is that the digital was itself already dated at one point. Indeed, it was destined to be so in the sphere of circulation due to those fads that correspond to the deeper and longer transformations that the dialectics of technological change enact in the sphere of production—indeed, to especially problematic effect in the post-1973 era. The recursive rhythm of this montage is readable, in other words, as the cycle of consumption as much as the line of succession. Read as both linear and cyclical, this montage is textured by, first, a rhythm produced simultaneously out of the slower-moving tempo of technological change by which the shift from analog to digital progresses over decades, in a line more recursive than straight that is tied to broader technological shifts. Second, and simultaneously, it is produced out of the faster-cycling recursions through which the tempo of that change materializes in technological fashions of their moment, which often assert that they are for all time. This montage is not one temporal thing but a structure that contains four temporal things that belong to not only two technological modes but also two interrelated rhythms of technological change, all of which brings about a feeling of datedness.

Of course, the mere fact of attending to wristwatches in this montage is itself a source of that feeling. As Aubrey Anable has written, "Smart phones are elaborate timepieces that have more or less made the wristwatch redundant" for many consumers.[29] By pausing plot to make the watches appear as nothing less than objects of auratic attention, the montage asks us to perceive the obsolete historicity that both analog and digital wristwatches materialize in a computerized era marked by the imperceptible rates at which processing speeds get insensibly swifter and the all-too-perceptibly rapid turnover time of "generations" of smartphones and their kin in the sphere of circulation. But it invites that perceptual act by way of an interplay of technologies (analog and digital; digital and analog) that is also an interplay of temporalities (dated and current; dated and timeless) mediated by a montage in which two rhythms, both of them effects of the dialectics of technological change, texture its rhythm with that dated structure of feeling I am calling the '70s. In this respect, *Fantastic* involves spectators in the opposite of what Fredric Jameson described as the waning of historical affect in his great work of 1991, *Postmodernism, or, The Cultural Logic of Late Capitalism*.[30] As a result of the recursively rhythmic buildup of obsolete stuff, what is happening in this is the *waxing* of historical affect. The object matter of *Fantastic* is the matter of historical time.

That the date of *Fantastic* is the '70s is hard to resist given my claim that the works in this book are all, at least in part, operating within an epoch that began around 1973. And in a few fleeting moments, we do—sort of—get a precise sense that the film ought to be dated to the 1970s. We learn that as an adolescent Mr. Fox was the most valuable player of the fox year in whack bat from '68 to '72—not, it is notable, from 1968 to 1972. The latter are roughly the years that Robert Brenner identifies as the economic passage from long boom to long downturn between the post-1945 and the post-1973 periods. "During the brief period between 1965 and 1973," Brenner demonstrates in *The Economics of Global Turbulence*, "the advanced capitalist world was suddenly projected from boom to crisis" because "profitability for the G-7 economies, taken individually and in aggregate, fell sharply, especially in manufacturing, initiating a long epoch of reduced rates of profit on capital stock." Due to intensive investment in fixed capital, "a long economic downturn thus began because the stereotypical process of adjustment—whereby firms suffering reduced profit rates cut back production and move into new lines, bringing supply and demand back into line and restoring average profitability—failed to take place." This failure to adjust led to critical—in the strong sense of propelling into crisis—amounts of redundant overcapacity and repetitive overproduction in the global market.[31] The dating of the film is too deliberately vague, especially with some of its gestures to "fox years," to contend that the film is referencing with any sort of precision the developments within this economic moment in which we passed into the post-1973 era. But that does not mean the moment doesn't hover on the horizon of *Fantastic*, especially within its political imaginary. We get, for instance, a cut-off reference to Mrs. Fox's days as an activist who marched with . . . we know not what protest movement, except that it hints at the upheavals of the real 1960s and 1970s, all of which are in some sense keyed to the economic shifts described above.[32]

However, in *Fantastic*, it is more the afterlife of that period of politics that reverberates, the ways in which the global upheavals of, say, 1968 remain an element of the imaginary of the post-1973 era. At the end of the film, for example, after the animals have joined together in a class struggle of sorts against Boggis, Bunce, and Bean, Mr. Fox and a wolf in the wild salute each other. They raise their fists high in a form that can't help but recall the famous Black Power salute at the '68 Olympics in Mexico City, not to mention a long and radical tradition associated with the defiantly raised fist. For so many reasons, it would be easy to dismiss Felicity's past and recoil from that raised fist as political pastiche, as a neutralization of the politics of difference, as a blind act of love and theft. But there is, as Jack Halberstam has argued, something wilder going on here, perhaps especially because this is a movie meant for overlapping generations—analog and digital alike—growing old and growing up circa 2000.[33] Just as the memory of moviegoing becomes a memory of making movies in *Invention* and *Hugo*, just as those memories are replaced in *Wreck-It Ralph* with a memory of machine breaking that the film ultimately erases, just as all of these are memories tethered to the historical time accumulating in these works, so too do certain economic and political memories subtend the '70s feeling that *Fantastic Mr. Fox* builds up in its datedness.

The Historicity in the Haptic

The political imaginary of *Fantastic Mr. Fox* requires more thought yet. But right now, take a moment to recall the antagonist of *Wreck-It Ralph*. As Turbo, he is all rage before he becomes a sore loser. As King Candy, he is sickly sweet and zanily queer, the past hiding in the plain sight of the present. And then, in the end, Turbo-cum-King Candy is psychotically grotesque, a hybrid monster that refuses to be unplugged. So the villain of *Wreck-It Ralph* is put down instead, eliminated and exorcised along with the memory of machine breaking he is keeping alive. These features of Turbo-cum-King Candy's figuration mean that he embodies the obstinacy of the obsolete. As his grotesque figuration and final elimination shows, Turbo-cum-King Candy is a scotoma of historical time blighting the view, becoming a visual monstrosity to erase from the system he tries to break.[34]

The obstinacy of the obsolete also shows up in *Fantastic Mr. Fox*. It sends its signal in the unduly powerful tin can phone. It shows its breaking power when it slows down the montage to make us look at the wristwatches. But as these instances suggest, it does not blight our view with the past in the process. Instead, as the montage in particular suggests, it beautifies the outmoded from the perspective of the present, turning accumulations of historical time into objects of auratic perception such that cinema by dated means produces a '70s feeling. But the key property of cinema by dated means resides in its most tangible element of material form: the boiling fur. When read closely as a haptic scotoma of tactile temporality, the boiling fur allows us to make visible in the next section that it is the obsolescence of labor that is the key tendency that *Fantastic* is mediating—or rather, evoking and transmitting, to be more phenomenological about it—in the experience of historical time it stirs.

All the spectators cited at the beginning of this chapter were fascinated by the rippling reality of the animal fur in *Fantastic Mr. Fox*. This fascination probably unfolded—it did for me—primarily in the series of close-ups in which this boiling is most evident. These close-ups are all counterparts to one another, just as they are a counterpart to the montage of analog and digital wristwatches in the quality of stasis it has. Here that stasis takes the form of a repeated shot fixedly directing the spectator's gaze in close-up or extreme close-up on the faces of the animals, sometimes in shot-reverse-shot, with the foxes predominating as the primary subjects. Like the close-ups of the wristwatches, these shots have a quality of duration due to their compositional stasis, as is emphasized when this durational effect takes place in the shot-reverse-shots, which should disrupt any real sense of duration because of cutting but instead textures that rhythm by fixedly alternating between furry face and furry face. Much as this alternation harkens back to the wristwatch montage, in these shots, a face looms large. Although watches have faces too, in these close-ups, the faces are characterized by the stirring of the fur rather than seconds passing in audibly abstract regularity. There is no immediately discernable uniformity to the rhythms of the fur, certainly not in the way that the montage yields itself up to more precise calculation, indeed, in which time is being synchronized before our eyes and is synchronizable in the storyworld itself. When the fur boils across frames and shots here, time instead takes on an asynchronous texture even as that texture requires the syncopated time being taken to materialize.

The haptic texture more specifically results from a tension between narrative content and material form in the series of close-ups. Consider figures 4.1 and 4.2, counterparts to each other. Both depict scenes of pathos between Felicity and Foxy in which wife and husband struggle to come to terms with the situation of danger in which he has put them by rejecting his respectable job as an occasionally read columnist in favor of so many criminal jobs stealing from Boggis, Bunce, and Bean—as he feels a fox should. In the first scene, Felicity partakes of her own animal side, slashing open a wound on her husband's face, telling him that unless he changes, his family, not to mention the larger community of animals in the film, will die because of his inability to transcend his foxiness as a means of dealing with what is, in a second code the film circulates, depicted as an existential crisis almost inevitable in a personified fox (*Am I fox, or am I person? Do I hunt and kill or earn money and raise sons?*). In the second scene, Foxy comes to truly recognize the danger that his crisis has unleashed in what is, he is beginning to see, not only *his* world but also a world that belongs to others—and for which Boggis, Bunce, and Bean have a careless disregard into which he threatens to fall should he not change.

FIGURE 4.1 *Fantastic Mr. Fox*, directed by Wes Anderson, Twentieth Century Fox, 2009, film still

FIGURE 4.2 *Fantastic Mr. Fox*, directed by Wes Anderson, Twentieth Century Fox, 2009, film still

Meanwhile, Felicity tells Foxy she should not have married him in the first place, though she does join in subsequent efforts to take down Boggis, Bunce, and Bean before they unmake the world of which she is a part, drawing on her activist past. Emotionally and narratively, these are scenes in which characters are movingly in conflict, caught up not only in the struggle of individuality and intimacy but also in the destiny of their community.

And yet such scenes are precisely the ones in which the characters stop being faces and start becoming fur—or at least these are moments that hold face and fur in dynamic tension, driving us toward narrative content and material form dividedly and simultaneously. In the first scene, this divided drive occurs as a result of the close-up strategy described above, which in this instance occurs in shot-reverse-shots, flatly and fixedly—even fixatedly—staged with a largely static camera such that the primary movement, the primal site of time, becomes the fur moving. The close-up strategy importantly converges with the mise-en-scène of the mineral deposit in which the scene unfolds. The mineral deposit sparkles with glinting light much as the fur ripples, illuminating—and functioning as luminous double for—the tactile effect that the boiling creates. In the second scene, again paralleling the first one, this close-up strategy is repeated and revised. Set in front of a waterfall, the background lighting actually reinforces the status of these two characters as personified figures by a formal device that simultaneously abstracts them as silhouettes. Thus instead of the light constituting an optical double for the boiling, as in the mineral deposit, what it does in front of the waterfall is flatten referential figure into abstract form. This is not a purely abstract move, however, with the extreme close-ups that follow the silhouettes drawing us not simply into so many lines undulating in syncopated time but also intensively into the fur in its asynchronous texture. The extreme close-ups constitute a haptic movement into tactility in all its intimate materiality. We are not required to move with the film into this tactile matter, as it generates the narrative option of staying within the equally intimate drama unfolding between Foxy and Felicity. Thus it is most accurate to say that *Fantastic* phase shifts back and forth between face and fur in these close-ups, however tempting it is to insist that it is impossible for the spectator not to be pulled into the haptic intensities flickering into being in and over time as tactile material on screen.

And these phase shifts do occur in and over time, even if we have not yet circled back to the matter of historical time. Instead, to draw on the richly detailed language of Matthew Fulkerson's *The First Sense: A Philosophical Study of Touch*, what we are in the midst of in these close-ups is temporal synesthesia, with visual time and haptic time decomposing into each other. This isn't decomposition in the sense of physical rot. It is, rather, decomposition in the sense of what Fulkerson calls "noise in the informational channel," which is akin to perceiving sentences as a series of letters instead of meaningful statements. But decomposition is more than the cognitive dissolution of denotative and connotative meaning. It is also deeply sensory, occurring, to turn to an example from Fulkerson, when a smudge on a movie screen distracts you from the narrative content, deforming the narrative hold of the diegesis with your senses. What the "noise" of that smudge does is make the spectator corporeally cognizant of the sense that film most actively engages: vision.[35]

But what the "noise" of formal devices and technical choices does in *Fantastic* is draw attention not to vision but to another sense: touch (or what Laura Marks has called *haptic visuality*). Those devices and choices turn *Fantastic* into a "tactual projection" in which vision becomes a synesthetic means of "inferring" the tactility of the objects on screen, but in a way that deconstructs vision. More specifically, it creates "haptic texture," which is organized around the "material properties" of the puppets themselves, especially the "largely intensive" feature of the stirring fur, by decomposing "visual texture," which is organized around "the geometric features of objects (largely spatial)," allowing us to comprehend them as faces, as characters in a world.[36] In fact, the typically flat staging of the puppets in close-up often reduces spatial relations such that the puppets are foregrounded. This doesn't mean we don't perceive them spatially at all, as much as the flattening intensifies the "space" taken up by haptic texture. In these moments, however, the space of that texture is the matter of time. Unlike vision, using touch to determine the geometry of an object is an act of perception that usually takes significant time, with haptic exploration needing to be sequential and lengthy to sense the spatial properties of, say, the basic physiognomy of a fox or the holistic fact of a man's face. In contrast, the time it takes touch to feel the "intensive" features of something—the coarseness of a fox's fur, the softness of a man's beard—is brief, quick. It's a glance more than a gaze.[37] But in *Fantastic*, the times of these senses cross in temporal synesthesia. Looking longer is what allows tactility to emerge in the close-ups, coarsening the surface of these moments as the visual texture of the image decomposes into so much haptic texture. Even further, looking longer allows the haptic texture itself to feel temporal, since the durational quality of the close-ups makes that texture asynchronous and enables the syncopated rhythm itself to appear.

In all of this tactility and temporality, the boiling fur of the animal puppets constitutes the most potent property of cinema by dated means. It is the material form through which historical time fascinatingly appears—through which it most fantastically accumulates—in *Fantastic Mr. Fox*. There is, in short, historicity in the haptic. That historicity builds up in the first instance, as we saw in the discussion of the space-time of the film in the prior section, because of the film's insistent attachment to analog tech and willful protraction of the industry's analog past. We can further draw out how the film protracts that past—even, if you will, renders itself obsolete—by considering the influences on the film most often mentioned by Anderson and the animators: *King Kong* (1933), *Roman de Renard* (1937), *Jason and the Argonauts* (1963), and *Rudolph the Red-Nosed Reindeer* (1964).[38] Just as the world of *Fantastic* is built from its stuff, the influences on the film constitute an extended allusion to analog tech, especially to the analog past of cinema and television that, at least in the case of *Rudolph*, still shows up every holiday season to mark the arrival of Christmas.

The most important influence for understanding the fur in the film is probably *King Kong*. *Kong* is repeatedly mentioned as the inspiration for turning the boiling into a technique in its own right in *Fantastic*. Enamored of the way fur moved in early feats of stop-motion animation such as *Kong*, Anderson asked his animators to do more than allow the boiling to occur. He wanted them to tangibly draw it out, to make it the *locus classicus* of animation as such (suggesting, in fact, that this is a film of the '30s as well). As the animators put it, the asynchronous fur gives the film "life," "beautifully [adding] a new dimension to stop-frame animation," especially in how it is lit, as in the mineral deposit explored above.[39] Ironically, perhaps even dialectically, that new dimension turns upon the old matter of the film. It is a techno-aesthetic past revived and reanimated, the boiling fur an analog scotoma that gorgeously blights the latest vista of computerized looking with its sensuous datedness.

How this scotoma achieves this effect becomes clearer if we compare *Fantastic* not to the original *Kong* but to Peter Jackson's 2005 remake. There the fur was designed to reflect the various ecologies and climates depicted in the film, with Kong sometimes being in cleaner and dirtier states but always with rough fur. While the fur achieves a high degree of verisimilitude, including a coarse texture—with 3 million to 3.5 million hairs being regenerated for every single shot on a per-frame basis—it is, to return to Ebert's description of watching the fur in *Fantastic*, more realist than real by way of comparison to Anderson's film.[40] What I mean by this realism is that where visual texture is maintained and dominant, haptic texture is generated but subordinate in Jackson's *Kong*. It rarely, if ever, threatens to overtake the narrative content with material form, to supersede the face with the fur—even in the extreme close-ups that introduce us, for instance, to Kong on Skull Island. The fur does attract attention, as in a scene where Ann's blowing hair visually rhymes with Kong's stirring fur at night as she sleeps in the crook of his arm, her lover pausing for a moment to take in this spectacle, providing an amazed stand-in for the film spectator being asked to feel wonder at the technological leaps forward from analog to digital enacted in this film. But when it does, it is so that Jackson's *Kong* can show itself overcoming the verisimilar limits of the original *Kong* with the potential of digital cinema to achieve a greater reality effect even in the most fantastic of situations, to advance beyond the imperfections that working with puppets, including the difficulty of boiling fur, inflicted upon filmmakers trying to depict such fantasy scenarios in 1933. In this, the 1933 *King Kong*, often considered a classic, becomes a dated wonder of the technological past instead—though of course, Jackson's *Kong* itself will probably look the same in fewer years than the decades it took to make the original *Kong* appear that way, since it's not at all clear that CGI (computer-generated imagery) creatures are always an improvement over stop-motion puppets.

That wondrous datedness, however, is the very element to which *Fantastic* attaches by way of the boiling, making of the film more than a singularly extended experiment with animation in Anderson's larger body of work. It is more strikingly akin to Selznick's *The Invention of Hugo Cabret*. Book and film turn to the residual and the dated for their material forms. In so doing, an active experience of historical time arises for readers and spectators—hermeneutically through readers turning pages in which the cinematic past is recombined and reemployed, phenomenologically through spectators watching undulating lines and textured fur they can almost feel. But the historicity in the haptic is more than residual in *Fantastic*. There is an emergent quality to the temporality of the boiling fur, an invented quality of technical newness beyond the innovative.[41] As already noted, the movement of fur from frame to frame and shot to shot is traditionally an effect that animators have attempted to control, as they tried to at first on the set of *Fantastic* until Anderson asked them not to do so. Instead, they not only allowed the fur the freedom to move on its own but also developed a repertoire of experimental techniques for encouraging more movement, from blowing on it to brushing it lightly in between shots so as to "give it a little bit of life."[42] The fur has always been wily and willful—doubly so, since controlling the boiling entails acts of labor that have become a normative dimension of stop-motion animation over time. The work of *Fantastic Mr. Fox* was to reject that labor by experimenting with other techniques for mobilizing the obstinacy of the fur.

An obstinate quality rooted in obsolete technics in *Fantastic*, this historically taboo effect creates a temporality simultaneously residual and emergent in its datedness, escaping into the digital present from the analog past as an accumulation of historical time with old and new dimensions alike—as a haptic scotoma of tactile temporality more beautiful than stupid. Released in the now of watching the fur shift and stir according to uneven tempos, this temporality rivets the spectator with what was *not* realized by earlier technological developments that later came to feel outdated—even if such realizations will not be the movie playing in each and every spectator's head. In liberating the fur from the industrial norms of stop motion by which animators have historically tried to contain it, boiling in *Fantastic* becomes what it is—and was: a fugitive temporality resistant to rationalization. "The fur will out!" we might exclaim.

Stop-Motion Labor Time

But what is outed when the fur refuses to stay still? The first answer to this question is that haptic scotoma of tactile temporality that gets animated rather than, as Turbo-cum-King Candy does, killed off. The second answer is living labor: more specifically, the temporal traces of the labor time that went into the material making of the film, including turning boiling into a technique in its own right. Given the dated quality of that technique, given it is predominantly residual even with its aura of emergence, what is therefore also outed is the film's investment in obsolete labor. We can bring that investment into view by looking at some of the outdated processes that occurred at the point of production for *Fantastic*, along with the conflicts over them. Even if one way living labor shows up is in the "life" with which the animators added further dimensionality to the fur's boiling on screen, those conflicts can't be seen there. This is of a piece with the phenomenological historicism of cinema by dated means. As a matter of method, however, that historicism entails describing those conflicts here so as to make legible what remains largely sensible in the experience of historical time *Fantastic* evokes: that the wellspring of that experience is the obsolescence of labor as it has intensified due to the dialectics of technological change circa 2000, especially the computerization of culture and capitalism.

A wide range of materials stresses the "handmade" quality of the film. The boiling discussed above clearly prompts such characterizations in some of these materials, since it holds before us the fact that the puppets and thus *Fantastic* are made things. One reporter, for example, speaks of Anderson "pursuing a more homespun, see-the-joins vision" akin to "the original 1930s *King Kong*."

The same reporter uses the adjective "handmade" later in the same article, while animators who worked on the film referred to it as "crafted" in a "European" manner that is "old-school" in its style. In interviews, Anderson tended to characterize that "European" manner as "primitive," noting that among contemporary animators, what he wanted for the look of the film was considered "bad form" because "you can see these objects that you recognize and you're very aware it's handmade."[43] The "handmade" characterization, however, is somewhat misleading, not unlike the two-page spread in the Rizzoli book *The Making of "Fantastic Mr. Fox"* that depicts Anderson in profile staring directly at one of the Mr. Fox puppets, the director's fingers grasping the protagonist's hands in a gesture that draws out and displaces the great quantities of labor—and labor time—that went into the film.[44] Despite the implication of this image, there is no simple sense in which *Fantastic* was "handmade" since the making of *Fantastic Mr. Fox* was really a process of craft subsumed to capital and indicative of the capitalist mode of production, especially as that mode has shaped filmmaking. For example, the cast and crew involved hundreds of workers in a complex division of labor. The labor of many of these workers required them to use their hands, since in stop-motion animation, puppets are physically and incrementally altered at a rate of one or two frames at a time to create the illusion of movement in painstaking acts of manual labor. But that labor also occurred within an advanced process that reflected fully developed norms of film production that have been in place for nearly a century, if in their own specific forms here, which ultimately did include digital technologies as well. The attention to the "handmade" nonetheless shows how uniquely suited stop-motion animation has become, especially in light of the digital transition in film and the computerization of culture in general, to telegraphing to spectators not only a heavily manual process of material making but also obsolete labor more broadly.

What is obsolete about the labor in this instance is how it depends on a residual form of technical knowledge, an older set of skills and processes decreasingly used due to advances. It also refers, crucially, to how using such knowledge after its sell-by date involves laborers in slower tempos palpably decelerated in relation to our just-in-time day and age. In fact, one recent film, *The Boxtrolls* (2014), ironically makes that slowness explicit in an accelerated time-lapse sequence at its end that displays the making of the film in a paratext that riffs on the process genre.[45] And the slowness of stop-motion labor time predominates in reporting done on the crew's experience of the making of *Fantastic*. "Everything is moving very, very, very slowly on each set," Anderson observed, even as a great deal was busily happening across the thirty filming units.[46] And there was good reason for this sense of slowness over the two-year period during which the film was made. One approximately 180-second shot took almost three months to film. That means about two to three seconds per day, with the animator Andy Biddle estimating that on average, the making of *Fantastic* amounted to four seconds of footage each day.[47] Stop-motion animation, then, tends at this point in the history of media to communicate obsolete labor in ways that often embody the tedious rhythms that labor involves. It appears in the digital moment as a backward industry, if also a quite beautiful and busy one in the case of *Fantastic*.

Such backwardness was enhanced by Anderson's requirement that animators actively use techniques, skills, and processes that the digital transition has rendered obsolete. Some of the animators enjoyed this requirement, while others found it burdensome. The *Los Angeles Times* reported the situation as follows:

> In keeping with the stylized nostalgia that looms large in almost all of his films, Anderson knew he was after a particular lo-fi aesthetic. And despite giant leaps forward in computer-generated imagery in recent years, he put CGI and green screen off-limits for [the film's] animators. Materials such as plastic wrap would stand-in for water, cotton balls would be puffs of smoke and green terry cloth, grass. Even though it was much more difficult for fabricators and animators, everything had to be shown "in camera" rather than added digitally later. As well, the writer-director [Anderson] stipulated that the animal puppets have real fur—long verboten in stop-motion circles for the material's discontinuous, blown-by-the-wind look on film.[48]

This return to analog techniques, skills, and processes was out of sync with digital norms in the early twenty-first-century animation industry, making cinema by dated means a feature of the production of *Fantastic* as much as a feature of the consumption of it. As in the space-time of the film explored earlier in the chapter, these dated means constituted an accumulation of historical time in the making of the movie not only because Anderson insisted on resurrecting superseded knowledge with regards to animating on the set of the film but also because the application of that knowledge involved the animators in slower rhythms *and* older technics of material making vis-à-vis computerized times.

The making of the film was not absolutely free of computers, however. The film was photographed using digital single-lens reflex cameras. Some CGI was required for the product to go to market in a finished state.[49] And strikingly, computers and computer networks played a role in a conflict on set that received unusually public attention in the press. Given both the time-consuming tedium associated with stop-motion and Anderson's general ignorance of the labor it entailed, he decided that he "didn't want to be at Three Mills Studios for two years." He instead worked from his Paris apartment for the year devoted to principal photography, which was possible because he had a real-time live feed that allowed him to watch the work being done on the thirty filming units. He also received dailies as digital files, returning them each day with emails detailing gestures for the puppets along with particulars about how he wanted the film to look. He would even add videos in which he performed scenes for the animators. Anderson, in short, directed *Fantastic* by email and iPhone, embracing a computerized mediascape—especially what we might call networked relations of production in communicating with his crew—even as he insisted on cinema by dated means as described above. Anderson's decision to direct remotely from Paris infuriated no one so much as director of photography Tristan Oliver, who vented his frustration to the *Los Angeles Times*: "It's not in the least bit normal," Oliver complained. "I've never worked on a picture where the director has been anywhere other than the studio floor!" His frustration elevating into anger, Oliver further told the *Times*: "I think he's a little sociopathic. I think he's a little O.C.D. Contact with people disturbs him. This way, he can spend an entire day locked inside an empty room with a computer. He's a bit like the Wizard of Oz. Behind the curtain." Oliver was not the only one of Anderson's "underlings," as the *Times* referred to them, to express consternation with Anderson. The director of animation Mark Gustafon had less invective for him, enjoying the challenges Anderson created aesthetically and technologically in cinema by dated means. But he too wearily noted that the director "made our lives miserable," even if he "probably shouldn't say that" to the *Times*.[50]

Not everyone on the set felt so negatively about Anderson's role in the making of *Fantastic*, nor is such networked labor so unusual in an era of visual effects created globally in forms that connect laborers across the compressed space-time of late-capitalist modernity. *Hugo* is a good example, since it involved a networked workflow that required dexterous coordination of humans and machines across various time zones. In addition to networked relations of production, the 75-second virtual move that opens *Hugo* took 150,000 hours to render on multiple powerful computers. To make sense of this detail, consider that if it had been rendered on only one computer, the opening shot would have not been completed until 2031.[51] Thus *Hugo* is a film in which the ratio of machine to human labor favors the former in a digitally superhuman form, a ratio that reverses itself by comparison in *Fantastic*. Here resides a potential crux of the "misery" some felt on the set of *Fantastic*. Frustrations arose at least in part because production involved the felt coexistence of the digital and the analog, which, moreover, had a temporal dimension to it relevant to the accumulation of historical time in the making of *Fantastic*.

To make this point, it is most helpful to look at the making of the film from the perspective of labor time, since the conflict above was arguably triggered by the asynchronous encounter of two technologically nonsynchronous kinds of labor time introduced by Anderson's absence. We have considered one of those kinds already, what earlier I called *stop-motion labor time*. Characterized by slowness, by an incremental tedium directly experienced by the crew working on the film, stop-motion labor time contrasts with the quality added to the production of *Fantastic* by Anderson's Parisian absence and networked presence—for networking relations of production means working long-distance is not a problem of time because computer networks enable instantaneous communication in real time. In an incisive account of this temporality, Mark McGurl describes real time as "the time of organizational command, minimizing the lag between command and execution, as between desire and fulfillment, and feeding the results back into the system without delay. . . . Always rushing forward, ever privileging action over reflection, the force of real time is felt more in the form than in the content of contemporary systems, and is difficult to get a handle on."[52] There was indeed significant content to Anderson's communications, which as the selected emails sprinkled throughout *The Making of "Fantastic Mr. Fox"* show, contained a high degree of thoughtful work and compelling direction that took, yes, real time to elaborate each day.[53] However, the real-time form in which that content was communicated signaled a quality of temporal force in the networked relations of production between director of film and film crew, which Anderson's ability to remotely watch the work of the latter in real time as well probably only intensified. Given Oliver's anger and Gustafson's weariness in response to Anderson's remote location and real-time labor, the director must have seemed the aesthetic incarnation of "technocratic impatience" that McGurl describes.[54]

At least since Marx's chapter on the working day in the first volume of *Capital*, we have known labor time is a key dimension of struggle in capitalist relations of production. This is not to equate Oliver and Gustafson's consternation with the far more excruciating and brutalizing misery that the chapter on the working day voices—or, for that matter, the way in which time exhaustingly dominates those working in the global visual effects industry today, which has expanded due to the ontological shift toward animation catalyzed by the digital transition in the film industry.[55] But the two kinds of labor time that congealed in the making of *Fantastic* are nonetheless indicative of how elemental historical time was to the cantankerous creation of this commodity, with stop-motion labor time and real-time labor time rubbing up against each other asynchronously. While this asynchronicity potentially added to the tension between director and crew, it definitely produced historical time as a felt element of the material and affective production of the film due to the contrast between the analog processes of then and the digital systems of now that overlapped in the making of the film.

We can speculate, then, that the anger and the anxiety that arose did so because in rescuing certain techniques and tempos from the stop-motion past, Anderson was also pushing his animators into history. His push to return to analog techniques, skills, and processes portended for them the fall that the film projectionist underwent and that the *Post* pressmen disputed. His demand that they revert to stop-motion labor time in an era of digital film-making and real-time networks may have made the animators feel as if they were being required to render *themselves* obsolete. However challenging and compelling the requirement, reviving so many "idled capacities" in the dated means central to the making of *Fantastic* is not unlike what reading *Invention* asks us to do by drawing on the residual means described in chapter 2.[56] Reading by residual means in significant part reemploys the obsolete worker who has fallen into history, conjuring the film projectionist in an experience of historical time that page turning in particular materializes. Similarly, cinema by dated means—or more specifically, the work that goes into cinema by dated means—resuscitates analog techniques, making the technicians behind *Fantastic* fall behind the digital times, forcing them into the technological past in order to fabricate the film.

The comparison will seem counterintuitive to some. While the work of film projectionists has faded, the work of animators has expanded, especially if we include the visual effects industry in our accounting. But such an expansion does nothing to undo the fact that the dialectics of technological change, which have enabled both of these developments, have tended across the post-1973 era toward "*the production of nonproduction*," with "empty factories and unemployed populations [piling] up side by side."[57] This is the scotoma with which the obsolescence of labor blights our view in the present, becoming ruinously legible in Rust Belt cities worldwide. While animators are not at the cutting edge of what is a thoroughly racialized vulnerability to that obsolescence, they nonetheless feel the moving contradiction of Capital itself that threatens all of us to varying degrees with the possibility that our work, too, will become socially unnecessary in the search for profit. "I did at one point think that [traditional stop-motion] might die out," one animator has commented, "but I've always seemed to have ended up with work. It seems to be a valuable way of making films." Another has said, "For awhile computer-generated movies sounded the death knell for stop-motion animation, but there are people like Nick Park . . . Tim Burton and Wes Anderson who have a passion for these older, hand-made techniques. . . . I think there has been a renaissance in stop-frame animation features the last few years. There are three stop-frame features at the moment [2009]. That would have been a dream 15 years ago. It wouldn't have happened. . . . Whether it's a fashion, I don't know, but it's good that people appreciate the difference."[58] Gainfully employed as both of these animators may currently be, the anxiety of obsolescence nonetheless hovers over their comments—and with good reason, in light of both circa 2000 developments such as the digital transition in the film industry and the obsolescence of labor intensifying. They express what Theodor Adorno cuttingly describes as a "fear of falling in spite of everything behind the *Zeitgeist*, of being cast on the refuse heap of discarded subjectivity."[59] In this, they are not so far from A. O. Scott's reaction to watching *Fantastic*, in which he jokingly expresses this fear of falling behind, quipping that, once they too are obsolete, journalists "may soon be stealing chickens out of desperation."

The obsolescence of labor is thus in play in both the making and the viewing of *Fantastic*. At the point of production, it appears as a return to specific forms of obsolete labor that paradoxically invokes the obsolescence of labor as a phenomenon of our time. It materializes as a refashioning and revalorization of skills, techniques, and processes that entail the deep involvement of living labor but that have been propelled out of production more and more by machines with computing power far beyond the capacity of almost any collective of human workers. It simultaneously invokes the possibility, built into the very motion of Capital itself, of ending up both out of sync and out of work. At the point of circulation and consumption, at those sites where we pay to watch the film, the obsolescence of labor appears as a phenomenological accumulation of historical time we actively experience in the boiling fur. And that experience occurs in relation to the '70s feeling that the film transmits within the horizon it opens up as its diegetic space and time—as its world. In that horizon, the fur figures and fights the obsolescence of labor that defines the deep time of capitalist history, the moving contradiction of Capital itself rippling in residual fits and emergent starts as historical time accumulates on-screen before our eyes, just as it did in and through the hands of the animators on set.

The Bourgeois Riot

We began with boiling fur. We end with the bourgeoisie rioting. Boiling and rioting, however, are historically misaligned, a nonsynchronism that plays itself out in the material form lagging behind the narrative content of *Fantastic*. Where the boiling is invested in revalorizing living labor at the point of production by turning back the clock to older skills that allow for a reinvention of animation, the rioting in the film takes place in spaces traditionally associated with the sphere of circulation (the marketplace, the town square) or transfigured as that sphere despite its associations with production (the factory farm). While in the economy writ large, production and circulation form a contradictory unity—with the value created in the former appearing as price and, hopefully, realized as profit in the latter—one side of this unity tends to dominate certain phases of capitalist history.

In the current phase, circulation predominates as the force field in which labor and capital seek to reproduce themselves. This is because, as Joshua Clover has argued, in the post-1973 era "capital has departed a diminished sphere of material production for profit-taking in circulation."[60] The most visible signs of this departure are the rise of speculative finance since the 1970s, with the most spectacularly recent episode of the effects of that shift being the sub-prime crisis, along with the movement of so much economic activity, including work, into the sphere of circulation—both of which have a direct bearing on *Fantastic*. Among both the effects and causes of the leap into circulation is the obsolescence of labor, that "production of nonproduction" in which "displaced workers discover that labor-saving automation has generalized itself across the various lines. Now unused labor piles up cheek by jowl with unused capacity."[61] But part of what makes labor obsolete in this situation is not simply that people no longer work, though many remain "unused." It is that the space of collective struggle shifts from factory to marketplace. There the participants do not participate as labor. There riots, not strikes, organize themselves—and they do so precisely because the strike, which as we shall see in the next chapter has undergone a massive decline in frequency in both the United States and United Kingdom since the 1970s ended, is so indelibly tied to that which is now increasingly automated across the world: labor in the sphere of production. This is a fact that can be seen in the data interpreted in important works from E. P. Thompson's classic essay "The Moral Economy of the English Crowd" to what will be the far more recent touchstones of this section, Clover's "World-Systems Riot" and *Riot. Strike. Riot: The New Era of Uprisings*.

For Clover, strikes are "production struggles" that wrestle over the wage and the conditions of work, that involve workers struggling from their standpoint as labor, and that interrupt the sphere of production through a variety of tactics. Riots, in contrast, are "circulation struggles" in which the price and availability of goods are what is being contested, in which participants are not held together in their status as laborers, in which the proletariat that emerges has "no necessary kinship but [shared] dispossession," and in which the sphere of circulation is subject to tactics of disruption and disorder.[62] As *Fantastic* progresses, the plot moves asymptotically toward the riot, though the word itself is never used, with terms like *job*, *master plan*, and *go-for-broke rescue mission* appearing instead. Nor will the argument from this point forward be that the film is "about" the riot as such or any particular riot—and there have been many globally—in the contemporary moment.[63] However, the economic fact of circulation is the contemporary motor of the plot of *Fantastic*, and the logic of the riot is what drives its narrative forward.

The plot of *Fantastic* begins with an inadvisable purchase. After a prologue in which Felicity reveals her pregnancy and Foxy agrees to take up a "different line of work," *Fantastic* cuts to a scene two fox-years later in which he sees a real estate advertisement for a "Classic Beech." He wants the Beech because it would mean moving out of his foxhole with Felicity and his son, Ash, for the roomier and airier possibilities of "tree living." After snipping and saving the ad, Foxy complains to Felicity, "I don't want to live in a hole any-more. It makes me feel poor." To which Felicity practically points out, "We *are* poor, but, we're happy," only to feel compelled to stress to her husband, "You know, foxes live in holes for a reason." Ignoring her advice, Foxy purchases the Beech, borrowing at 9.5 percent with no fixed rate, against the advice of Bad-ger, his lawyer. Not unlike Felicity's reminder that no matter how Foxy *feels*, the Fox family simply *is* poor, level-headed Badger points out how terrible the interest rate on Foxy's loan is. He shores up his advice by noting that the Beech is in the worst imaginable neighborhood for a fox because the factory farms of the antagonists of the film, Boggis, Bunce, and Bean, are clearly visible from its windows. Agricultural industrialists who not only make foodstuffs but also own an international chain of supermarkets, Boggis, Bunce, and Bean are capi-talist figures in *Fantastic*, apparently dominating a near totality of production and circulation in the world of the film—which is exactly part of the appeal for Foxy. Underneath his willfully bad purchase is a set of wily desires to cuss with capitalism as a wild animal, with his plotting against them beginning to hatch in the scene in which Stan Weasel, the real estate agent, shows him the Classic Beech.

Despite the view of those factory farms from the Classic Beech, which sug-gests Foxy's plotting will strike at the sphere of production, it is crucial that the film begins with an event that is nowhere in Dahl's novel but was unfolding everywhere in the first decade of the twenty-first century: subprime real estate purchases. The 9.5 percent variable rate points to the subprime real estate mar-ket that triggered the Great Recession in 2007–2008, years during which *Fan-tastic* was being made. That rate seems to have been surprisingly close to the average for adjustable interest rates on subprime mortgages over the course of the subprime boom and bust between 2000 and 2008, with the rate just below 9.5 percent in 2008 itself as well. Even if only roughly close to the exact rate, the presence of the 9.5 percent variable rate in the film clearly keys *Fan-tastic* to the vicissitudes of economic crisis in the early twenty-first century.[64] A subprime candidate buying property beyond his means, in full view of the more-than-propertied interests with whom he is readying to cuss, Foxy will later toss and turn at night over the plummeting value of the Classic Beech just before Boggis, Bunce, and Bean destroy his home. This anxiety is hard not to read as a gesture to foreclosure and eviction given the subprime subplot. Later in the film, he will also find himself surprised that his opossum sidekick, a handyman and minnow fisher named Kylie, has such a strong credit history that he has a platinum credit card, further suggesting the subprime purchasing power of Foxy.

These economic details tie *Fantastic* to the cruel optimism that Lauren Ber-lant has discussed as an affective structure of neoliberal culture in which the subjects of late capitalism strive for what they can no longer obtain without cost—here, home ownership. As in many of Berlant's examples, what drives Foxy is the *feeling* that he is poor and the *desire* for upward mobility—a poverty and a mobility literalized in the film when the Foxes move from a hole in the ground without any views to a tree aboveground with views—despite material conditions that militate against overcoming the former and realizing the latter. Even more significantly, the details make of Foxy a figure of bad credit, along the lines that Annie McClanahan has analyzed in her account of the character of credit scoring in contemporary cultural forms that mediate the debt crisis of the early twenty-first century.[65] But these details equally make one of the initial triggers for the plot of the film a market phenomenon that is itself an index of the post-1973 shift into the sphere of circulation such that the marketplace has become the locus where political struggle, especially rioting, unfolds more and more over the past four decades. Thus what the subprime subplot of *Fantastic* will find in the main plot of the movie is its subversive mirror: a series of raids on the factory farms of Boggis, Bunce, and Bean that, as the film progresses, begin to resemble circulation struggles of intensifying collectivity. These raids reflect and reject the profit taking in circulation to which Foxy subjects himself and his family when he agrees to the toxically variable 9.5 percent mortgage, with the looting that occurs during the raids progressively giving them the contours of the riot form as they become collective and communal.

It is important to this argument that the word *job* makes a significant appearance in the film, though it is subversively resignified in the process much as the raids on the farms themselves are subversive mirrors of the subprime subplot. After moving into the Classic Beech, Foxy secretly meets with Kylie and lays out his intention to return to stealing, describing his plan for a heist of Boggis's farm in what is also a reflexive allusion to those other heist films, Steven Soderbergh's *Ocean's* trilogy, in which George Clooney, the voice of Mr. Fox, also starred. Foxy explains to Kylie, "I used to do this professionally, and I was very successful at it. I had to get out of it for personal reasons, but I've decided to do one last big job on the sly. I'm bringing you in as my secretary and personal assistant." The *Oxford English Dictionary* (*OED*) documents the association of *job*, a word of uncertain origin, with a manifold of primarily legitimate and remunerated forms of labor: individual tasks for which payment is received, as in the odd jobs that Kylie does as a super; a form of regular employment, as in the real estate career that Stan Weasel pursues or the squirrel contractor who, with his crew, moves the Foxes into the Classic Beech; and lifelong professions, sometimes understood as vocations the payoff of which exceeds or lacks remuneration, as in the case of Badger and his wife, a lawyer and a doctor, or Felicity, painter and homemaker. These more economically and socially respectable meanings of the word *job* are evoked when Foxy ironically refers to Kylie as his secretary and personal assistant.

But when Foxy refers to "one last big job on the sly," he is employing *job* in its illegitimate and disreputable sense, which the *OED* lists among all the more remunerated forms listed already: "*Criminals' slang*: A crime, *esp.* one arranged beforehand, *spec.* a theft, a robbery." Or as Foxy tells Weasel, "I used to steal birds, but now I'm a newspaperman."

The "one last big job on the sly" turns out to be a "master plan" in three "phases" orchestrated around stealing foodstuffs from Boggis, Bunce, and Bean, respectively. This is a plan that is figured at first as the masculine midlife crisis with which Foxy deals by secretly refusing the domestication Felicity demanded when she became pregnant with their son Ash and made him change his line of work from thief to newspaperman. Mr. Fox's plotting is thus in part driven by the personal desires of a vulpine individual, which he will later confess to Felicity are initially motivated by a fecklessly selfish impulse to cuss with the factory farmers. In this impulse to cause havoc, to outwit and outfox those in power, he is entirely a creature of the tradition that whelped him, from the tales of Aesop that nursemaids once told to their charges in the ancient world, to the beast fable *Reynard the Fox* that circulated in medieval Europe, to the Roald Dahl children's novel of 1970 that Anderson remembers reading and owning as a boy.[66] But that tradition adapts in Anderson's film to the logic of the riot, if initially in a largely individualist and only minimally collective form. That this logic is in motion is most evident in that the "job" here precisely is to steal, bringing Foxy's plan in line with one of the central aspects of the riot form: looting. "Looting," as Clover writes, "is not the moment of falsehood but of truth echoing across centuries of riot: a version of price-setting in the marketplace, albeit at price zero."[67]

This is a truth that echoes in Foxy's master plan as well. Along with his nephew, Kristofferson, and Kylie, Foxy poaches chicken, geese, turkey, and cider that Boggis, Bunce, and Bean produce for market, mobilizing around not wages and work but products and prices—around, in fact, the joy of setting the price to zero. That this is the case is ironically evident when Foxy conceals his looting from Felicity by buying price tags at the five-and-dime to place on the goods he has stolen once he puts them in the pantry for her to find. That ironic move is part of a larger irony related to the logic of the riot here that returns us to the term *job* beyond Foxy's humorously subversive use of it in criminal counterpoint to the work of respectable remuneration as described above. The use of that slang to describe the raids on the farm only stresses a further aspect of the riot form enumerated by Clover: "Labor takes part, but not necessarily *as labor*," which is clearly the case for Foxy and Kylie.[68] Indeed, even the sphere of production, the factory farms where employees work (108, we are told) and where food is developed and manufactured (Bean has "invented a species" of turkeys and apples each, the film informs us), is turned into its circulatory twin in Foxy's plan. It is treated as a sphere of circulation from which the animals steal goods that are, as the fake price tags indicate, destined for the marketplace that is the space where looting typically takes place. The commodities they steal only further shore up this transfiguration of the sphere of production into the sphere of circulation: foodstuffs. From the eighteenth to the twentieth centuries, food, especially the price of food, has been a key source of struggle in the marketplace riot.[69]

However, while the stuff that Foxy and his partners in crime steal converges with the riot past and present, the group of subjects engaged in rioting diverges, even as it develops more collectively into something like a class as more and more animals are forced, as we shall see below, to cuss with Boggis, Bunce, and Bean over the course of film. These animals are not the "angry crowds" reacting to austerity that sociologists of late twentieth-century food riots have described. "Owing to the complexity of modern markets," two such influential sociologists write, "angry crowds fix responsibility [for the elimination of consumer protections and price increases in the market] on the retailer rather than the middleman—supermarkets, clothing, and appliance stores rather than grain merchants and speculators," as in the eighteenth century.[70] Nor are the animals members of the "surplus populations" that are often "the subject of the riot" in the "deindustrializing core" and the global periphery: in the former, for instance, African Americans ejected from employment at extraordinarily high levels in the United States, with black laborers often being the first to go when labor-saving innovations appear.[71] While some of the professions of these animals (e.g., journalist, lawyer, doctor, secretary) are up for technological grabs at the moment, especially around certain kinds of tasks, these characters are not represented as obsolete workers, certainly not in the way that Georges Méliès is in *Invention* and *Hugo* or Turbo-cum-King Candy and Q*Bert are in *Wreck-It*. All of them are gainfully employed, though, it is worth noting, largely in services not productive labor in manufacturing. Moreover, given Foxy's desire to purchase a home and his theft of commodities from Boggis, Bunce, and Bean, one class of subjects toward which he does point are those consumers that Jameson described in his 1977 essay "Class and Allegory in Contemporary Mass Culture": "For the citizens of some multinational stage of post-monopoly capitalism, the practical side of daily life is a test of ingenuity and a game of wits between the consumer and the giant faceless corporation." But forty years have passed since that influential essay was published. And the post-1973 period that Jameson saw coming elsewhere in his work has opened up in the interim as a period in which significant swaths of consumers have, as Clover's work shows, become rioters on a more comprehensive scale than the small acts of anticapitalist consumer rebellion that Jameson had in mind at the outset of that period.[72]

However, despite the fact that Foxy, his partners in crime, and the rest of the animals that ultimately join with him are, none of them, exactly any of this list of classes of subjects—the angry crowd protesting austerity, an African American underclass without work, an obsolete laborer expelled from production or circulation, or a lone consumer outfoxing a corporation—all of them do belong, it is striking, to the middle class. Newspaperman, real estate agent, painter and homemaker, pianist, lawyer, doctor, secretary, tailor, chef, perhaps even the credit-worthy handyman—this is the capacious realm of the contracting middle class, that weakly cohesive class of subjects that used to go by the name of the *bourgeoisie*.[73] As the plot of *Fantastic* progresses, in other words, the riot that comes is a bourgeois riot—a middle-class melee in which the participants do not take part as middle-class professionals so much as they pursue bourgeois forms of social reproduction by looting the sphere of circulation. For example, after Foxy's initial three raids on the Boggis, Bunce, and Bean factory farms, the trio of antagonists strike back, first purchasing tractors to dig out the Fox family, which destroys their new home in the process, and then detonating explosives and expanding their destruction such that all of the anthropomorphic animals get pulled into the struggle. Starving underground, the animals band together and steal all of the foodstuffs from the factory farms, along with, in a vivid detail that seems directly to evoke the looting of consumer electronics that mass-media coverage of riots enjoys depicting, a television. The end result of this more intensely collective act of looting is a middle-class dinner party: music playing, a feast laid out, all culminating in a toast in which Foxy celebrates, well, himself and how fantastic he is. Thus the threat of death for lack of food, the fear that the community will not be able to socially reproduce itself—in fact, that it will die out—ends in a mode of sociality that could not be more bourgeois in its sumptuous pleasures and conspicuous consumption.

William Godwin once wrote, "The conviviality of feast may lead to the depredation of riot."[74] And bourgeois conviviality does yet lead to further rioting in *Fantastic*, for Foxy and Felicity's nephew, Kristofferson, is taken hostage by Boggis, Bunce, and Bean because Ash, their son, sways him to try to steal back an item of value from the trio of antagonists after the animals steal all the foodstuffs and that television set. The point of this narrative development is that Foxy's bourgeois paternal ego comes at the cost of his nuclear family, though what results from that paternalistic egotism is an upping of both the riotous energies of the film and the bourgeois quality of those energies, since the former amplify so as to fix the family. On the one hand, the animals coordinate a go-for-broke rescue mission to save Kristofferson that begins with a détente in the town square in which the animals lead an all-out assault, this time not looting foodstuffs but setting ablaze the various stores in the square and detonating explosives in order to cuss things up. The struggle between the animals and the humans has turned fully to the sphere of circulation in a form that resembles the fires of the riot form. On the other hand, this riotous scene is meant to function as a decoy to save Kristofferson and reconstitute the family. Thus as the plot becomes more collectively riotous, the goals of the rioting characters become less and less so. According to Clover, part of the "depredation of riot" is that it "seeks to preserve nothing, to affirm nothing but for perhaps a shared antagonist, a shared misery, a shared negation."[75] Still living and laboring in the middle, even if not participating as labor in their battle with Boggis, Bunce, and Bean, the circulation struggle that steadily intensifies over the course of *Fantastic* is split between cussing with capitalism as that trio embodies it and making sure the family romance gets to tell its story all over again. None of this should come as a surprise, especially given how much the disappointing bourgeois father, caught in the trap of his own ego, figures in Anderson's versions of the family romance in other films such as *The Royal Tenenbaums* (2001). There is a lack of ideological surprise worth noting too. If Clover is right that the new era of uprisings is a time of riots, especially by racialized surplus populations, then what would make such rioting more palatable than attaching it to the affirmations of the bourgeoisie typically so happy to scold those who light the sphere of circulation up? In watching this movie, especially when it comes to signs of our times, many spectators undoubtedly find the middle-class melee far more pleasing than the explosive riot.

This reading suggests that what *Fantastic* does with the riot form is render it politically acceptable by making it the middle-class stuff of the family romance. However, this is too simplistic an account of the political imaginary of the film, for by the end of the film, the world of the animals has been destroyed as a result of the confrontation with Boggis, Bunce, and Bean. Not unlike the narrator of *Invisible Man*, we find them all, not just the Foxes, living in the sewers under the town square where they caused havoc, leading a diminished version of the lives they had before the blowout with the factory farmers and international merchants. Trapped in the sewers by Boggis, Bunce, and Bean, they are on the verge of starving until Foxy leads his family and Kylie to a manhole that allows them to steal into one of the trio's supermarkets, where row upon row of foodstuffs await their thieving. There they gather together enough food for all of the community trapped underground, Foxy giving a moving toast to their survival, a toast at some postindividualist distance from the egotistical one he delivered earlier. The scene is not entirely mournful though, playfully and preciously giving way to the animals dancing in the aisles of the supermarket where they plan to set the price to zero for the foreseeable future. Nonetheless, they remain enclosed, as the final shot of the film reminds us, cutting from the interior celebration at the discovery of a supply of sustenance to an exterior shot reminding us that they remain contained, a tremor of a commune trapped inside the sphere of circulation produced by Boggis, Bunce, and Bean.[76] If the plot of *Fantastic* began with a bad purchase, progressing to so much looting and rioting made palatable by its bourgeois motivations, then it ends with a baleful figuration of what comes of the middle class that decides to riot against Capital itself.

This ending, moreover, allows us to see the Black Power salute discussed earlier as more than empty expropriation. That salute is in a strong sense a displacement of African Americans struggling in the post-1973 era that Clover places at the center of the riot as a modality vital to the deindustrializing core in countries such as the United States and the United Kingdom. But it is also a moment of recognition of what, in the second epigraph to this chapter, Clover calls "the truth of the age": that a visit to the paymaster is less politically sensible than a struggle in the marketplace, including, potentially more and more intensely, for the bourgeoisie as well. In this, then, *Fantastic* multiplies as much as it displaces, suggesting "the shape of the double riot" most concretely telegraphed by the coexistence of the Occupy movement and riots over the deaths of young black men in the late twentieth and early twenty-first centuries. As Clover writes, "One riot arises from youth discovering that the routes that once promised a minimally secure formal integration into the economy are now foreclosed. The other arises from racialized surplus populations and violent state management thereof. The holders of empty promissory notes, and the holders of nothing at all." This doubling of the riot form in our moment makes for "these populations' increasingly shared terrain of struggle, their unfinished motion toward one another."[77] The scene in which Foxy and the wolf defiantly salute one another can be read as an image of this unfinished motion, as can the way in which the plot of *Fantastic* asymptotically moves toward the riot form without fully arriving at its depredations when it holds onto the middle-class family even as it pushes it into a life underground at the end of the film. The political imaginary here is thus tuned into the motion of contemporary history, with the story of the film propelled wildly forward by that motion.

In fact, that imaginary is even more compelling in the end because the currency of the film's narrative goes hand in hand with the datedness of its means, indicating that the experience of historical time that culture by outmoded means sparks need not be retrograde, need not be a rearguard disarming of the politics of obsolescence. In the comedies of reemployment that *Invention, Hugo,* and *Wreck-It* represent, the obsolescence of labor is reversed, with displaced workers regaining jobs. While *Wreck-It* makes this comic reversal more politically difficult to accept by invoking the memory of machine breaking, it nonetheless still seeks out the restoration of the obsolete worker, even producing a fantasy of full employment through Q*Bert to compensate us for the narrative death of Turbo-cum-King Candy. But in contrast to these works in which the narrative seeks to go back to how things used to be or to how the works imagine things ought to be, there is no going back in the story that *Fantastic* tells. At the end of Anderson's film, the animals and the humans—figures of a bourgeois proletariat and a capitalist class, respectively—are caught in an impasse of opposition with no apparent way out, much less a path back to the way things were. While this less-than-comic ending to the riotous story of *Fantastic* tunes it into the motion of contemporary history, the means of the film turn against that motion, trying to reinvest in the sphere of production that is the terrain neither of the story of the film nor of capitalism as it has developed over the post-1973 era.

But it is precisely in the way in which the means of the film lag behind the story it tells that we discover what is finally most politically interesting about *Fantastic*, for we can only imagine the politics of the present if we grasp—or in *Fantastic*, feel—the conditions of the past, an imaginative and phenomenological leap that the lag between narrative content and material form in Anderson's film enables by allowing present and past to evocatively coexist, like the digital and the analog, in the same work. The experience of historical time that cinema by dated means transmits in *Fantastic* and the political imaginary emplotted by the contemporary story it tells, in other words, work in tandem to show that present-day struggles cannot be disentangled from what has fallen into history—from the fact that the motion of contemporary history is backward as well as forward. In this respect, all politics are politics of obsolescence, with those that unfold in the riotous actions of the animals in *Fantastic* specifically turning on the obsolescence of labor that has shifted struggle from the factory to the marketplace in the post-1973 era. The most telling moment from the film in this regard is when the animals make sure their watches are perfectly synchronized in readying to do battle with the

FIGURE 4.3 *Fantastic Mr. Fox*, directed by Wes Anderson, Twentieth Century Fox, 2009, film still

capitalist antagonists of *Fantastic* (figure 4.3). In that moment, a bourgeois group of anachronic things from the past, materially beautiful to behold in their datedness, synchronize for the more proletarian purpose of struggle in the marketplace against Boggis, Bunce, and Bean according to the conditions of the present. Overly masculinized as it may be, moments such as this one make the political imaginary of *Fantastic* interesting and invigorating precisely because they telegraph how much the obsolete cannot be left behind as we labor to imagine struggle within the motion of contemporary history.[78] But imagining struggle points in the direction of a historicism different from the phenomenological one of this chapter. How imagining struggle is—and must be—animated by the past as much as the present is the subject of the final and concluding chapter, which allies itself with the imaginative historicism of a novel that wagers on politics by obsolete means.

5

Politics by
Obsolete Means

————————————————————•

There was an image on endless repeat last summer. A conflagration, the charcoal
shell of a local landmark, a well-known carpet shop. This was the first of a series of
disturbances that spread over successive nights around London and the country.
Britons saw loop after loop of images of buildings on fire, smashed glass, streets in
raucous refusal. Youths taking TVs, clothes, carpets, food from broken-open
shops, sometimes with dizzy exuberance, sometimes with what looked like thoughtful care.
—China Miéville, *London's Overthrow*

It is common for the wages train to be delayed. A day or two and there are only
grumbles, but sometimes as long as a week goes without money. Three times when
this happens there is a strike. By some chaos of democracy the track-layers put down
their tools and block the train until they have shekels in their pockets. They are
nonplussed by their own mass, by their numbers. Hundreds of muscled men, the
tall green brawn of the cactacae emerging from them. The prostitutes, the surgeons,
clerks, scholars, off scouts, and hunters come to watch them.
—China Miéville, *Iron Council*

Resuming the Strike on the Riot Side of History

China Miéville knows that we are on the riot side of history. This knowledge is
evident in both his nonfiction writing and the interviews he has given since the
burgeoning of riots globally over the last decade. For example, he has described
the 2011 London riots over the death of Mark Duggan at the hands of police
as "epochal." He sees those riots as part of a broader realization not only that
the police help violently maintain the lines of race and class in capitalism
but also "of the role of the police in relationship to Wall Street." This is a role
that the Occupy movement, which "marks a sea change" coeval with the riots
for Miéville, has drawn out as its activists lodge their protests in New York

City and London squares that were "once public, these days only [pretend] to be, and that if you ask nicely."[1]

This jab against the policing of and politesse around once open squares comes from Miéville's 2012 experiment in the situationist genre of psycho-geography, *London's Overthrow*. An effort to imagine a counterpublic by textual means in Miéville's typically irrealist style, *London's Overthrow* marks the contemporaneity of rioting and occupying in the historical present. After describing Occupy LSX earlier, he spends a number of pages meditating on the riots inspired by Duggan's death in "Tottenham, north of London, [an] area of extraordinary ethnic diversity and local pride, and one troubled by unemployment, poverty, poor housing." In what is a weird—or as he might say, "socially irreal"—effect of the trajectory of *Out of Sync and Out of Work*, he gives us images of actual rioters on television that evoke the animated and anachronic subjects lighting up the town square in *Fantastic Mr. Fox*. "There was an image on endless repeat last summer," Miéville writes. "A conflagration, the charcoal shell of a local landmark, a well-known carpet shop. This was the first of a series of disturbances that spread over successive nights around London and the country. Britons saw loop after loop of images of buildings on fire, smashed glass, streets in raucous refusal. Youths taking TVs, clothes, carpets, food from broken-open shops, sometimes with dizzy exuberance, sometimes with what looked like thoughtful care."[2] Nor is this loop without a past. Countering the "endless repeat" with historical awareness, Miéville is careful to observe that such exuberance and care has punctuated London with a political rhythm of rioting since the 1980s. In his accounting, that rhythm has culminated in events such as the Tottenham riots and is related to Occupy LSX. Alongside both, Miéville observes, there were austerity protests—for instance, one catalyzed by a strike over pension cuts at University College London Hospital. In addition to striking nurses and radiographers, this protest united farther-flung allies, such as the Communist Party of Iran and advocates for gay Africans seeking political asylum, who joined together in the wake of the Labour Party's rightward march and the ascendance of the Conservatives with the support of the Liberal Democrats in the United Kingdom at the turn of the millennium.[3]

In *London's Overthrow*, Miéville locates these riots, occupations, strikes, and protests in what was the capital of the long nineteenth century in the United Kingdom prior to the hegemonic rise of the United States as the capitalist core of the long twentieth century. As references to the wider world in interviews he has done often show, he views these moments of action as part of a much larger psychogeographic totality of struggle in the current era, one locus of which *London's Overthrow* maps.[4] Like all of the works in this book, moreover, *London's Overthrow*—and more significantly for us, the 2004 novel *Iron Council*—also belongs to the metacycle of U.K. and U.S. political and economic hegemony from the late eighteenth century onward in which productive capital reigned but that began to convulse around 1973. The multiple forms of struggle in *London's Overthrow* are signs of that convulsion, aligning the text with our moment as an outcome of that metacycle. *Iron Council*, however, looks back to the two-century metacycle that birthed our moment when it comes to struggle, imaginatively resuming the strike on the riot side of history. As such, the historical experience sparked by Miéville's novel revolves around the strike as an obsolete form of anticapitalist struggle.

Inseparable from the obsolescence of labor, the turn toward riot and away from strike is a contemporary transformation in the form of struggle that the bourgeois riot in *Fantastic* confronted narratively. The reading of *Fantastic*, moreover, implied a sharp break between strike and riot not unlike the periods that structure the title of Joshua Clover's *Riot. Strike. Riot: The New Era of Uprisings*. But in that powerful study, a touchstone of the reading of *Fantastic*, Clover does take note of the coexistence of overlapping forms of struggle that Miéville himself observes in describing the psychogeographic uprising of multiple forms of political intervention in the months of November–December 2011 that *London's Overthrow* details. This is not to say that what Miéville sees is exactly what Clover sees, even as the latter brings race riot, austerity protest, and the Occupy movement under the larger category of circulation struggle being conceptualized in *Riot. Strike. Riot* in a way that resonates with *London's Overthrow*. But much as he takes into account the uneven development of differing forms of struggle, Clover is more resolutely committed than Miéville to insisting that the strike is a thing of the past. Indeed, to characterize that insistence with an earlier concept, Clover can be generatively obstinate about the fact that the material conditions of the strike have so thoroughly faded on the riot side of history—such that anyone resuming this form of struggle, theoretically or practically, can sometimes seem like they are blind to a historical absence without any vital presence anymore.

But imagining begins in absence every day.[5] In the case of the strike, the absence is caused by the obsolescence of labor in our time, which has also made the strike into politics by obsolete means by dispersing millions of workers from the collective concentration that the sphere of production once ensured in the United States and the United Kingdom. We can conceptualize the obsolete in this respect as being itself a material condition for imagining struggle; as constituting that which is historically absent but needs to be thought of as coexisting with that which is historically present, retaining actuality as, in the example of the strike, a memory of militancy with imaginative traction even now; and, in the specific case of this chapter, as representing those forms of strife that have seen the dialectics of technological change outmode the standpoint of labor by which they once built mass and momentum but that have not yet made that standpoint inactive as historical experience. In its status as obsolete, then, that standpoint is both in and out of sync with the present much as the strike arguably is.[6]

These are the terms on which Miéville gives nonsynchronous pride of narrative place to the strike in *Iron Council*, with that novel wagering on an imaginative historicism that falls into the obsolete such that historical experience arises in reading it. This is possible because, as Elaine Scarry has conclusively defined it in *The Body in Pain: The Making and Unmaking of the World*, "imagining is an intentional object without an experienceable state," but such that experience is dialectically set going because "imagination is only experienced in the images it produces."[7] That "only" is too conclusive in light of the more materialist conception of the obsolete above, reflecting the fundamentally ahistorical nature of Scarry's work in *The Body in Pain*. However, in *Iron Council*, the experience that imaginatively arises involves falling into history in response to a moment—our moment—that emerges out of a much longer *durée* that has run its course such that the standpoint of labor no longer proffers what it used to but the images of which we recall and resume nonetheless for their political possibility.

Understanding how this imaginative historicism works, especially when it comes to imagining struggle, depends on three elements. First, *Iron* builds a world at a slant to the present, drawing on a reserve army of images of obsolete technologies and far-flung times from across the metacycle of productive capital that detail a world both in and out of sync with our own. This world building depends on a second element, a political economy of plot that allows the imaginative historicism of *Iron* to intelligently unify these technologies and temporalities not as directly experienceable in our reality but as a historical irreality at an imaginative angle to our own. That narrative intelligence, third and finally, proceeds from the standpoint of labor in *Iron*, with the strike over the construction of a transcontinental railroad in particular allowing it to amass images of workers in a chronologically complex figuration such that politics by obsolete means produce a historical experience not only active but also activist. That experience might not yield, for some, a political imaginary proper to the present. But the impropriety and untimeliness of that imaginary—the obsolescence of it—is the historical experience with which we must close, for in progressing from the least to the most political of works across *Out of Sync and Out of Work*, politics by obsolete means stands as the necessary endpoint if we are to keep faith with what it means to fall into history not only as a matter of culture and critique but also, at the close, as a matter of the struggles that push and pull at all of us across the deep time of capitalism.

The Obsolescence of the Strike

Intensive, hermeneutic, ludic and Luddite, phenomenological, and now, imaginative: these are the historicisms that have galvanized historical experience by so many outmoded means across *Out of Sync and Out of Work*. At the close of the book, imagining is the key to that experience. To borrow a phrase from *Iron Council*, the "old language" of the strike is central to the act of imagining, part of a larger idiom of obsolete images that engenders the irreal horizon of that novel.[8] But what makes the strike an old language, historically speaking? Why is the strike politics by obsolete means in our moment? As with so much in these pages, the obsolescence of labor is central to the obsolescence of the strike—and to the problems and possibilities of imagining struggle under obsolete conditions.

Like the obsolescence of labor, the obsolescence of the strike has been intensively legible in both of the successively superannuating cores of the metacycle of productive capital, the United States and the United Kingdom, across the post-1973 period. As we saw in the close reading of *Fantastic*, a strike is a production struggle and a riot is a circulation struggle. According to Clover, the former organizes itself around wages and working conditions, with labor disrupting the sphere of production through a range of tactics grounded in that standpoint. While labor may participate in a circulation struggle, theirs is a far less constitutive role because what the riotous subjects are usually contesting are the prices and availability of goods in the sphere of circulation, not the wage relation and working conditions. Both forms of struggle nonetheless pivot around the question of reproduction. This is the question of where "human beings . . . reproduce themselves and their livelihoods," which is itself the question of where capital reproduces itself. And as we heard Clover argue, the sphere of circulation has become the locus of reproduction for both in the post-1973 period, in which people and markets have relied "not on rising wages (which in the UK and the United States have stagnated since the late 1970s) but on aspiration, plentiful cheap credit, and access to cheap commodities."[9] As Annie McClanahan writes, "The result is a mode of accumulation characterized by precarious, short-term, typically nonunionized service work supplemented by debt and driven by a form of financial capital so mobile and liquid that it can outmaneuver any form of organization designed to resist it."[10] This mode, and the questions of political organization it forces us to confront, stems in no small part from the obsolescence of labor as it has built up over decades and centuries due to the dialectics of technological change that have been in vertiginous motion since the very start of the metacycle of productive capital, steadily enveloping more and more people and changing the work they do—that is, if they can find work at all.

The deindustrializing shift from production to circulation in the "twilit core" of the United Kingdom and the United States has been a determining resource for the experience of historical time in the post-1973 era, with the obsolescence of labor functioning as a major wellspring of versions of that experience as more irregular periods of employment and more precarious tempos of reproduction have become more and more common.[11] The larger experience of historical time that these locally instantiate has a political dimension as well because struggle has also shifted from production to circulation at significant levels. Clover has documented "the collapse toward zero of strikes involving more than 1,000 workers beginning in the late seventies" in the United States. As he further shows, "in the United States after 1981, only three years exceed 10 million cumulative days idle from strike actions, with several years below 1 million. From 1947 to 1981, the figure exceeds 10 million every single year, averaging more than twice that."[12] Clover provides one of the single most sustained theorizations and periodizations of strike and riot together that we currently have. But he is not unique in writing about the decline of the strike, including in relationship to the shift toward the riot. In the U.K. context that more immediately bears on *Iron Council*, Paul Gilroy has discussed the convergence of the early 1980s defeat of strikers and, if not the victory, then the surge of rioters at that time as an elemental prehistory to changes to the political culture of the late twentieth- and early twenty-first-century United Kingdom.[13]

Miéville shares a psychogeographic sense of this history in *London's Overthrow*. This is a history that shows how the political is a function of mutations in the economic. Born in 1972, Miéville is attuned to this history across the post-1973 period as it made the obsolescence of the strike politically legible with intensifying visibility (much as working in industries such as publishing, bookselling, film projecting, filmmaking, and animation has made the obsolescence of labor culturally legible to Scorsese, Selznick, Moore, and Anderson). Over the course of his post-1973 lifetime, Miéville witnessed a steady erosion of support for the material interests of the working classes from not only the Conservative Party of Margaret Thatcher in the 1970s and 1980s but also the Labour Party of Tony Blair in the late 1990s and early 2000s, which gave way to a coalition of Conservatives and Liberal Democrats with the election of David Cameron in 2010. Miéville was not insensitive to the neoliberal shifts of these successive rulers.[14] He campaigned to be elected to the House of Commons in 2001 as the candidate for the Socialist Alliance Party in Regents Park and Kensington North. He yielded only 459 votes over and against the 20,247 votes won by the Labour Party candidate, with the Labour Party also overpowering other parties in the general election that year. Along with figures such as the director Ken Loach, he has since been part of the formation of Left Unity, which aims to be an alternative to what it views as the Labour Party's abdication of the working classes in a time of deepening inequality and injustice, advocating socialist, feminist, environmentalist, and antiracist politics.[15]

Given his sensitivity to the psychogeography of political action in *London's Overthrow*, it is no leap to suggest that in the midst of this "rightward march," especially of the so-called Labour Party, Miéville perceived the obsolescence of the strike. Like a locomotive picking up steam, the obsolescence of the strike gathered momentum from the mid-1970s to the mid-2000s. He would have been a child when a series of strikes convulsed the country in the second half of the 1970s, eventually helping enable Thatcher's election. He would have been approaching adolescence during the famous and failed miners' strike of 1984, which he recalls as bringing about an atmosphere "of a massive retrenchment, of a sense that nothing matters."[16] His early years as an author would have been during the late 1990s and early 2000s when the Labour Party regained power, declaring itself "New Labour," though for many, "neo-labourism is a variant of neoliberalism."[17] Despite a flourishing of strikes in the United Kingdom and the United States in the 1970s, the efficacy of the British strike was in decline by the mid-1980s, only worsening in the decades to follow. As Susan Watkins observed in 2004, "Days lost in strikes have fallen from 27 million in 1984, through an annual average of 620,000 under [Conservative Prime Minister John] Major, to a record low of 368,000 during Labour's first term [between 1997 and 2001]."[18] On the basis of this brief history of neoliberalism from the perspective of Miéville, then, the rise of that political and economic ideology is one factor in the decline of the strike. And there is certainly no question that neoliberalism, especially the neoliberal state, contributed to its diminished efficacy. In the wider and longer history of the strike, the state has often played a significant mediating role, one that here takes the form of increasing antagonism toward labor. Thatcher incited and defeated the striking miners in 1984, cutting down such collective actions by 90 percent by the time she left office. And later, under Blair, "with very few exceptions—Bob Crow, the railway workers' leader, is one—union bosses have rallied to Downing Street's side every time it mattered," putting down potential strikes of varying kinds.[19]

However, that decline must be grasped as a political effect of the obsolescence of labor that intensified in lockstep with the developments above, especially if we conceive of the United Kingdom as part of the larger totality of the long twentieth century for which the United States has been the epicenter—and of the United Kingdom and the United States as forming an even longer "metacycle of productive capital in the west from about 1830 to 1973," if one "rife with volatility, crises, recessions, and one transfer between hegemonic powers."[20] That transfer was the one from the United Kingdom to the United States at the end of the long nineteenth century. However, as in the United States, the post-1973 period has been especially volatile for the

United Kingdom. While, again as in the United States, the groundwork was laid after World War II, the last third of the twentieth century involved more and more "technological fixes." These fixes have been met with resistance and unrest, even obstinacy of the sort we saw in chapter 3, though they did in many cases unfix labor, freeing some people of skilled work and liberating still others from jobs altogether, especially in manufacturing. Recall that in the longer *durée*, the rate of employment growth in U.K. manufacturing has tended to decline unevenly since the 1840s, even though the absolute number of workers employed in manufacturing increased from that same period until the early 1960s. At that point, however, absolute numbers began a precipitous fall from around fifty million people working in the sphere of production in 1961 to less than twenty million in 1991. Many of those put out of work in the sphere of production have found work in the sphere of circulation. And in the foreseeable future of the next two decades, jobs in the former sphere will continue to be more highly susceptible to further fixes because they "are vulnerable to advances in robotics technology." But work in the latter sphere will not escape this vulnerability in that same future. It too will be drawn into the dialectics of technological change that tendentially bring about the obsolescence of labor in capitalist history such that growing income inequality and explosive class polarization become, we might say, even more automated features of capitalist life than they essentially already are.[21]

As a result of those dialectics, what has become intensively unfixed in our time is the concentration of similarly situated workers in the sphere of production where they have both mass and momentum and thus a collective standpoint of labor from which to struggle at the very point where commodities are made. It is this standpoint that is now obsolete as a result of technological change dispersing labor into service work or no work at all, where what Jason E. Smith describes as "a tendential material density of the class" is undermined as the political basis for struggle within and against capitalism. Following Beverly Silver and James Boggs, Smith writes in "Nowhere to Go: Automation, Then and Now": "Comparable skill levels, wages, and working conditions prevail in massive plant facilities bringing together thousands of workers at each individual site. The workers' movement itself was one product and reflection of this convergent material unity of the capitalist mode of production: if worker struggles of the nineteenth century in part impelled the development of forces of production . . . the generalization of this development across lines of production in the early twentieth century shaped class into a compact and militant mass." But the cycling history of automation that Smith also posits, in which the obsolescence of labor intensifies rhythmically every few decades, dematerializes that mass as the twentieth century moves, making labor militancy ever more obsolete, making such a standpoint ever more a memory. The shift into services that accompanies this obsolescence only further exaggerates this process of political dematerialization. "Workers who find themselves stranded in low-wage service occupations in retail or hospitality," Smith observes, belong to "workplaces [that] are often dispersed and small in comparison with the great industrial concentrations of the past, and they have little fixed capital to idle."[22]

In light of the obsolescence of labor enveloping more and more work in the United States and United Kingdom, then, it is entirely appropriate to speak of the obsolescence of the strike. The strike is a *techné* of political struggle that the moving contradiction of Capital itself has rendered obsolete much as it has expelled higher and higher levels of labor out of production as a result of so many technological fixes. Of course, the obsolescence of the strike is not the end of the strike altogether. As Clover rightly observes of this situation, "It is inevitable that a growing percentage of the vanishingly few strikes will be in circulation, and that labor actions will shift toward circulation struggles, as a practical matter." This practical matter is inseparable from what I take to be one of Clover's most acutely moving insights: "People will struggle where they are."[23] This practical matter is, moreover, entirely visible in a text such as *London's Overthrow* in which people join together to strike *and* riot *and* protest *and* occupy. But even there, Miéville describes a strike not in its classic location as a result of the mass and momentum of the factory as a site of struggle but as one involving allies much more far flung, such as nurses and radiographers alongside communist and queer allies of color at University College London. While Clover's *Riot. Strike. Riot* and Miéville's *London's Overthrow* reveal leftists imagining struggle much more on the riot side of history where circulation struggles predominate, the obsolescence of the strike in our time has nonetheless also triggered the problem of imagining struggle at the end of the metacycle of productive capital, as labor and conflicts between labor and capital both reach a limit that the decline of the strike-weapon nonetheless makes legible. This is the problem that *Iron Council* confronts with an imaginative historicism. But before turning to the novel, it is worth charting more fully how the obsolescence of the strike has created a problem of political imagination discursively as much as culturally first, especially among leftists perplexed about how to imagine struggle circa 2000, when *Iron Council* was released.

An excellent example of such leftist discourse can be found in a long essay that Susan Watkins wrote for the *New Left Review*, "A Weightless Hegemony: New Labour's Role in the Neoliberal Order." Part of the value of turning to Watkins's essay is that it was published in 2004, the same year that *Iron Council* came out. The essay's subtitle points to Watkins's critique of New Labour as she traces the rightward shift of electoral politics in the United Kingdom, especially with the reelection of Tony Blair in 2001. But the essay is most interesting to us because in it Watkins relates that shift to the obsolescence of labor by drawing attention to the effects of deindustrialization on U.K. politics. For instance, she observes that despite Blair's win in 2001, "the hard-core Labour vote . . . stayed at home. . . . Turnout fell 44 percent in the blighted constituencies around the Tyneside shipyards, the bleak Glaswegian council estates, and the semi-derelict terraces of Salford and central Leeds; below 35 percent in the ruined zones of Liverpool's docklands."[24] This attenuated participation of key voting blocs in the 2001 election, including in afflicted areas such as shipyards and docklands transformed by the dialectics of technological change and affected by the obsolescence of labor in the late twentieth century, finds a political cousin in the decline of the strike in the United Kingdom charted earlier. Watkins pays frustrated attention to this decline in the statistics quoted from her above, along with expressing disappointment at the complicity of major unions in disarming strikes and mass protests under the rule of New Labour at the militarized turn of the millennium.[25] Among many other factors in this essay, including an explicitly historical concern with the shift from factories to finance of which the obsolescence of labor is both an effect and a cause in the post-1973 era, these contribute to a frustrated sense of political impasse in "A Weightless Hegemony," leading Watkins to conclude that "it is an anachronism to think that the performance of rival parties competing within the field of neoliberal politics can be distinguished."[26]

The problem with which this diagnosis leaves Watkins is the problem of imagining struggle, which she articulates in one of the concluding passages of "A Weightless Hegemony":

> [The] democratic capture [of the left] is unimaginable today. Furthermore, there is scant evidence of a new radical trade unionism on the march in Britain. Although labour markets are tight, days lost to industrial action remain at record lows. After twenty years of neoliberalism, the British working class has been transformed—above all, through the deindustrialization of its heartlands. Its capacities for collective action have visibly waned. Disciplined stands against New Labour have been increasingly minoritarian and defensive; if hard fought, as with the firemen. Other sectors have become more atomized, financialized—as home owners and future pensioners—and relatively better off. The potential for concerted social action has yet to be revealed.[27]

As the stress on deindustrialization suggests, the obsolescence of labor in the post-1973 era emerges in the above passage as, to borrow some language from Hannah Arendt, a gap between past and future. For Watkins, that gap operates as a political opening at which the historical experiences set in motion by that epoch, especially as it congealed in 2004, become the urgent matter of imagining struggle. Grappling with the politics of her immediate moment in terms of the decades that preceded 2004, Watkins inserts herself into the gap between past and future such that "A Weightless Hegemony" can be read as, in Arendt's words, a "thought-event" that "splits up the time continuum into forces which then, because they are focused on the particle or body that gives them their direction, begin fighting with each other and acting upon man."[28] This splitting of time, in which past and future forcibly meet, revolves around that which to Watkins is "unimaginable": actions that are collective and concerted, with the forms such actions take having both "visibly waned" (past) and "yet to be revealed" (future).

As Watkins's concern with the decreasing number of strikes and their material suppression within the neoliberal political field suggests throughout "A Weightless Hegemony," the past for her is the strike and the agents of that past organized labor. Signs of the future are there at times in her essay, as when she brings up "the short-lived fuel protests of 2000," which were, notably, really struggles over the price and availability of goods in the sphere of circulation.[29] Despite such struggles, however, that future remains unclear to her. We can speculate that she could not yet fully see the rise of rioting and occupying, not to mention the growth of other forms of circulation struggle, already taking shape in 2004, which Miéville, Clover, Gilroy, and others would all describe in the decade and more since the publication of "A Weightless Hegemony." But the point of this comparison is not to argue for a failure of imagination on her part but to insist on a different set of insights that shift the register of ones that we have already heard. This is a shift that moves us from space to time: people struggle *when* they are as much as *where* they are. Moreover, people *imagine* struggle when they are as much as where they are.

With regard to this *when*, the gap between past and future in "A Weightless Hegemony" is thus less Watkins's simple present in 2004 than an experience of historical time in which that present in that year emerges as a political moment for our moment. It is a historical opening in which the obsolescence of the strike is that which makes that political moment imaginable—an imagination-event, to adapt Arendt. The strike is thus recalled within the political imaginary of "A Weightless Hegemony" despite the fact that it is a form of struggle no longer proper to *where* we find ourselves—but that is capable of being resumed within the fourth dimension of *when* we find ourselves. Into this moment, perhaps even as a moment, *Iron Council* enters, for the politics by obsolete means by which Miéville's novel imagines struggle, especially the strike, nonsynchronously embodies that moment in a variety of ways, pursuing an imaginative historicism the experience of which is not only active but also activist in the face of Capital itself.

Imaginative Historicism and Imagining Struggle

Iron Council is the third novel in a trilogy that Miéville published at the turn of the millennium, with all three of these fictional works animated by an imaginative historicism that builds worlds and tells stories by mining the fourth dimension of capitalist history where prior times and past technologies accumulate as a source for historical experience at some later date than their originating moment. Preceded by *Perdido Street Station* (2000) and *The Scar* (2002), *Iron* is set in the fictional world of Bas-Lag. The gravitational center of that world is the capitalist city-state of New Crobuzon, which is, as a character states in *Iron*, "the strongest state in Bas-Lag" (Miéville, 332). In *Perdido*, another character describes New Crobuzon as a center of "science and industry that moves and moves here like nowhere else."[30] Together, all three of the novels make clear that the political and economic hegemony of New Crobuzon in Bas-Lag entails class conflict between labor and capital over wages and work; a carceral state that biologically and mechanically "Remakes" criminals for the purposes of corporal punishment of the most corporeal sort, with the "Remade" often being forced into unpaid labor as a captive population; a polyglot culture in a city troubled by violently contentious race relations between humans and other humanoid sentient species known broadly as "xenians," who have been drawn to this moving center of industrial activity in part due to the city-state's imperial and mercantile efforts to expand its reach and open new markets; and a wider, often war-torn world in which New Crobuzon, while dominant, is not the only alternative—even if within the city-state itself, dissidents, the various factions of which come together as a counterpublic known as "the Caucus," find themselves suppressed by a parliament voted into power without universal suffrage and maintaining its unrepresentative rule by means of a militarized police force known as the "militia."

This is the global picture taken of the world built in the Bas-Lag trilogy. As Christian Thorne elegantly writes about *Perdido*, the city-state of New Crobuzon is "clearly modeled on nineteenth-century London, as though it were describing Tolkien's Middle Earth a thousand years down the line, as though Endor had continued along its long-durée history, through its own capitalist industrial, bureaucratic, and imperial revolutions, so that the elves had become barristers and the orcs had become navvies and so on," with "no scene, however action-packed, that does not at the same time serve the novel's sociology."[31] What Thorne is registering here about Bas-Lag and New Crobuzon is that which has been a feature of every work of culture by outmoded means: its mimetic irreality, its aesthetic pursuit not of resemblance and verisimilitude but of the relational affinities that the children of capital chase and enjoy. More specifically, both wider world and city-state in the Bas-Lag trilogy exist in nonsensuous similarity to the nineteenth century we know—indeed, to the metacycle of productive capital that stretches from the late eighteenth to the late twentieth centuries. While it has an affinity with that metacycle, moreover, it is also out of sync with it. Its nonsensuous similarity to that metacycle is also a nonsynchronous one, as the dating of the events of the novel, the *when* of this narrative, suggests. The strike takes place about twenty-five years in the past of the novel, sometime in the eighteenth century of the world depicted in *Iron*. However, the present of the novel is the early nineteenth century of that world, with an initial event in the novel being very precisely dated: "On the sixth day, Fishday, the 17th of Chet 1805, they reached a village" (Miéville, 15). The calendrical language here is familiar and unfamiliar at the same time, the diction of dating at a slant to our own. So-called 1805 telegraphs the nineteenth century, but that historical telegraphy falls out of sync with the irrealist references to "Fishday" and "Chet." In this, it is not unlike *Fantastic*. Recall that the date of Anderson's film is the '70s, which is suggested by the brief reference to Mr. Fox being the most valuable whack bat player from '68 to '72, not 1968 to 1972. Similarly, the "1805" of *Iron* is not the 1805 of the nineteenth century. However, where *Fantastic* embodies a phenomenological historicism in its datedness, *Iron* pursues an imaginative historicism in turning back the clock. When it does, *Iron* draws on the metacycle of productive capital writ large as a repertoire of obsolete technological imagery out of which it builds its world—or more precisely, an image of its world. That image is an effect of the irreality function and mimetic faculty so central to culture by outmoded means, involving the reader of *Iron* in so much "creative miscognition" when it reworks the past to produce an irreal image of our present and its past.[32]

Consider the obsolete technologies that *Iron* inventively appropriates and creatively adapts from the metacycle of productive capital. For the most part, these evoke the first and second Industrial Revolutions. But they do so at a slant, the images of them often out of sync with the forces of technological production in the actual 1805. In *Iron*, for example, characters use blunderbusses and ride dirigibles. Respectively, still in use as both a weapon and a word in the real 1805, the former refers to a firearm from the early modern period that was rendered obsolete by advances in weaponry as the first Industrial Revolution progressed, with the word *blunderbuss* itself fading, according to the *OED*, by the end of the nineteenth century. The word *dirigible*, however, gains etymological traction at that very moment because it refers to airships that arose during the second Industrial Revolution, which airplanes eventually superseded by the middle of the twentieth century. Cameras, which emerged in the middle of the real nineteenth century, are used throughout *Iron*, including in the flashback to the late 1700s of the novel. The creative miscognition of all this imaginative historicism is intensified by the process of photographic reproduction invoked as common in *Iron*, the heliotype, which was not invented until the late nineteenth century in the United States. Alternative versions of real technologies from the late nineteenth century also appear, as with the voxiterator. Fascinatingly used for entertainment, anthropological research, political action, occult practices, and communication across the novel, the voxiterator is a phonographic device into which characters insert wax tubes with grooves in order to play back prerecorded sound. And of course, there is the steam train at the imaginative center of the novel, which is primarily depicted in the flashback to the 1700s. The imagined 1700s and the actual 1700s converge to some degree in this respect, since steam technology was perfected in actuality around this time, allowing for the emergence of the locomotive in the early 1800s. But despite such convergences between technological fiction and technological fact—the printing press and the newspaper are also central media to the novel, as they were in the real 1700s and 1800s—what reigns supreme is an imaginative historicism that allows us to experience the world of *Iron*, to make a mental picture of the historical irreality of that world, through this repertoire of images of obsolete technologies.[33]

Such historicism is a form of imaginative labor at which literature specifically and culture generally excel. This is the argument that Fredric Jameson makes in *Valences of the Dialectic*, where he contends that "the literary text . . . seems to jumble [distinct temporalities] pell-mell together in an immense omnibus of time frames whose random and multiple intersections are regulated only by emplotment, and accessible only to . . . narrative intelligence rather than abstract reason." Conceptualizing the literary work as "what makes of multiple discords a single discordant concordance," Jameson usefully concludes that "reading is then the momentary and ephemeral act of unification in which we hold multiple dimensions of time together for a glimpse that cannot [otherwise] prolong itself."[34] Like many of the other works in this book, *Iron* (not to mention *Perdido Street Station* and *The Scar*) is just such a pell-mell jumble of time frames pulled from the multiple technologies that the metacycle of productive capital invented but then left behind as so many ephemeral technical paths (the heliotype) and pathways we followed for much longer periods (the camera, the steam train, the printing press), as so many abandoned technologies (the dirigible) and alternative technics we fantasize still (the voxiterator). Brought together as an obsolete omnibus of technological and temporal details visible in the world of *Iron*, they are imaginatively experienceable in our reading as a historical irreality that is not unlike—but is still not directly experienceable as—the metacyclical history that has led to our own moment today.

The historical experience that imagining realizes in *Iron*, moreover, depends on the unifying power of emplotment to which Jameson refers above. Ever the defender of the idea that we cannot not tell stories, Jameson posits emplotment as the site of a narrative intelligence that enables us to imaginatively unify a discordant concordance of technological and temporal details akin to the obsolete omnibus of them in Miéville's novel. That omnibus of imagery needs, then, to be viewed in relationship to the narrative situation of *Iron*, a situation that makes a political economy of plot a central feature of the imaginative historicism the novel mobilizes such that the irreality of its world and the reality of our own possess affinities.

Early in *Iron*, for example, we learn that the narrative situation is interestingly one not so unlike—but nonetheless importantly not identical to—the deindustrialized reality in which the obsolescence of labor comes to define and destabilize the post-1973 era. Thus while the novel takes the metacycle writ large as its imaginative time and territory, it more specifically describes a moment of "long recession" in New Crobuzon. As if to evoke what Robert Brenner calls the "long downturn" and Joshua Clover the "long crisis" of capitalist history since 1973, *Iron* locates us in a time of "stagnant" economy that "slumped and slumped" as the city-state's "emergence into mercantilism" goes not only "unrewarded" but also "punished" (Miéville, 78, 79). The source of that punishment is a war with Tesh, a state that the novel depicts by barely depicting it at all as a means of indicating its alterity (otherness being one of Miéville's great and essential themes throughout his fiction). Although there is the suggestion that New Crobuzon's economic expansion is one reason ("As the long recession had bitten, years before, merchant ships from New Crobuzon had started returning to dock reporting piratical manoeuvres against them, sudden brigandry from unknown ships. The city's exploration and its trade were under attack" [Miéville, 78]), when and why the war began is unclear to the citizens of New Crobuzon, a point the novel makes to amplify the unrepresentable unknowability of the hostile Teshi others ("There was a *rumour* that through *long-disused* channels, Tesh's *secret and hidden* ambassador had told the Mayor [of New Crobuzon] that their two states were at war" [Miéville, 79, emphases mine]). But while Tesh and its reasons for declaring war are unknown, the effects of the military conflict on New Crobuzon are clear. The novel significantly emphasizes the negative impact for capital and labor alike as the city-state undergoes a protracted economic crisis compounded by the war blocking the circulation of goods and supercharged by class antagonisms when the sphere of production finds itself immobilized, with no fixes in sight.

"New Crobuzon was stretched out, pulled taut," concludes an early section of the novel that sounds like it could be a description of our reality in capitalist history now: markets drying up abroad for the commodities made in the city-state; new goods not making it into the city-state in turn; industry being suspended as some guilds and unions get "outlawed," drawing out Caucus dissidents; dissidence spurring oppressive responses from both New Crobuzon and the pro-state political group known as the New Quillers; and unemployment spreading, with the production of military equipment and weaponry only offering "something of a recovery"—and a cruelly competitive one at that (Miéville, 79–80). Evoking that mode of photography that turns Rust Belt factories across the globe into what Dora Apel calls "beautiful terrible ruins,"[35] an ironically lovely passage in the second half of the novel figures the economic crisis in *Iron* in postindustrial form: "An apocalypse landscape of long-deserted slag and stagnant shipyards, where the keels of vessels poked from their internment in shallow waters. No one salvaged these sculptures in rust," in this place "where dirigibles were once built" (Miéville, 303). It is unclear if these ships and shipyards are defunct as a direct result of the war with Tesh or the war in combination with the longer recession. But one way or another, they are the ruins of a New Crobuzon that is no longer moving and moving but is convulsing and collapsing in productive crisis for lack of markets in which to circulate its wares. Despite beautifully ruinous sentences such as the ones about the shipyard, however, the point of the novel is not to produce a representation of deindustrialized reality on the order of the portraits of man and machine from *Closing* that we considered in chapter 1. Instead, through its description of productive crisis and its depictions of formerly vital industry, the novel establishes a political economy of plot in which affinities between *Iron*'s historical irreality and our historical reality can be imagined. This political economy of plot provides a narrative situation in which we imagine more than a historical irreality made out of the repertoire of images but also one at a slant to our own, such that the imaginative historicism of *Iron* does the work of materially relating that irreality to our reality.

A political economy of plot, we might say, is a materialist approach to telling a story in which imagery of the kind described in the narrative situation above is ultimately set into motion among characters struggling in and over time, allowing readers to more fully imagine a fictional world where the actions unfolding have historical affinities to those in our own reality. The imagery so far, however, sets that situation into primarily economic motion for us. But there is also political movement within that situation, making the imaginative historicism of *Iron Council* a matter of politics as much as economics, especially in terms of emplotment. "No day passed," we read about halfway through the novel, "without a strike or riot: the numbers of the unemployed were growing, there were attacks on xenians by Quillers and on Quillers by xenians and dissidents" (Miéville, 314). Thus against the backdrop of economic collapse at home and warfare abroad, *Iron* alternates in the present of the narrative between two political storylines from part to part of this ten-part novel, with a third storyline—that of the strike—set in the past of the narrative. In the first plot, set outside the city-state of New Crobuzon and focalized by Cutter, a gay shopkeeper skeptical of the Caucus, a group of similarly disaffected Caucus members go in search of the Iron Council, that coalition of workers, prostitutes, and criminals that successfully struck against the Transcontinental Railroad Trust a quarter century in the past of the narrative. Once they find it, the Councillors decide to return to New Crobuzon because the "air of strikes and insurrection" (Miéville, 318) caused by economic crisis in the city-state could be, they determine, an opportune moment for revolution on a mass scale. It will turn out not to be the right time for revolution. In the second plot, set inside the city and focalized by a radicalized day laborer named Ori, who is equally skeptical of the Caucus, a group of anarchists engages in thefts of wealth, killings of the rich, and liberations of the incarcerated along the way to the larger aim of assassinating the mayor of New Crobuzon. Ori believes the assassination will catalyze revolution in light of the insurrectionist atmosphere, though he, too, will turn out to be wrong. A mass uprising does unfold in the city-state, giving birth to the New Crobuzon Collective. But the successful assassination of the mayor has little to do with it in the end—and like the Paris Commune to which it alludes, the New Crobuzon Collective ultimately falls. Each of these plots indicates how much *Iron* is a narrative caught up in the question of imagining political struggle in light of a moment of economic crisis.

The imaginative historicism of *Iron* thus involves a political economy of plot in which we imagine a historical irreality in economic relation to (rather than as a representation of) our own reality but also in which we imagine what it means to struggle in that irreality. As the plot summary above indicates, that struggle takes many forms here, different types of action and activism coexisting with one another in the story that *Iron* tells. But what is striking is how much the standpoint of labor persists and, at times, predominates within that plot. We are asked to imagine that which is increasingly obsolete as that which organizes struggle in the story and orients the point of view of the storytelling itself, to take as still central an image of the political rooted in work that is out of work—an image of struggle grounded in a standpoint of labor that is out of sync in our own time. The plot summary clearly suggests the complexity of this standpoint here, since both Cutter and Ori are skeptical of the Caucus, which in the novel foregrounds labor politically. However, the degree to which the standpoint of labor persists narratively—indeed, as a powerfully obsolete image for us to experience—is nowhere more evident than in the strike that takes up more mass in and gives more momentum to *Iron Council* than the plotlines above.

The strike occurs in the section of the novel set a quarter of a century in the past of the narrative present of 1805. Entitled "Anamnesis: The Perpetual Train," this section is the longest, taking up about 150 pages. In many respects, "Anamnesis" is a proletarian bildungsroman, a genre that typically "treat[s] working-class protagonists in the process of acquiring militant or revolutionary class consciousness."[36] The protagonists that acquire such consciousness in "Anamnesis," especially in their statuses as and sympathies for laborers, are

Judah Low and Ann-Hari; indeed, elsewhere in the novel, Cutter and Ori are also going through their own versions of proletarian bildung. Named after the sixteenth- and seventeenth-century European rabbi Judah Loew ben Bezalel, Judah develops class consciousness over the course of "Anamnesis" as a result of his intense identification with the workers building a railroad across the continent of Bas-Lag under horrific conditions. In the process of becoming a powerful golemist, Judah works in a variety of jobs, from research scout for the Transcontinental Railroad Trust to tracklayer for the same, all of which have radicalizing effects on him. Befriended and beloved by Judah, Ann-Hari is a prostitute radicalized in a not dissimilar way. Her militancy, however, arises as much among the prostitutes who service the railroad workers as it does due to her outrage over the exploitation of the latter, not to mention her horror at the Remade prisoners forced to labor for free. In their double bildung, Judah and Ann-Hari have pivotal roles in "Anamnesis," the former as the main focalizing character of the section, the latter as a charismatic figure that emerges as a leader in the strike.

All of the characters cited so far—Judah (golemist, scout, and tracklayer), Ann-Hari (prostitute), Cutter (shopkeeper), and Ori (day laborer)—suggest the novel's sense of the manifold of labor that keeps an economy going, including, lest we forget, the free labor of the unfree Remade. The kinds of jobs performed in the character system reveal, moreover, a proletariat multiplied in the novel beyond "the whole men, the free workers, the aristocracy of this labour" (Miéville, 166) that have often been taken, as the allusion to the famous notion of a labor aristocracy in this phrase reminds us, to embody the proletariat as such.[37] Recalling the attention to the assorted jobs the animals have in *Fantastic*, *Iron* is thus a novel narrated from the standpoint of labor. Most of its central figures are repeatedly identified with the work they do, as in an early passage in which we simultaneously learn the names and jobs of a series of characters for the first time.

To the contemporary reader, however, many of these characters' ways of making a living are obsolete. They do work that has been, like the temporal omnibus of dirigibles, blunderbusses, heliotypes, and steam train discussed earlier, superannuated by the dialectics of technological change as the latter progressed through the metacycle of productive capital that *Iron* invokes: "Words came out of Cutter in a loud involuntary chant: 'Ihona's a loom worker. Drey's a machinist. Elsie's out of work. Big Pomeroy's a clerk. Fejh a dockworker. I'm a shopman. We're with the Caucus. We're looking for my friend. And we're looking for the Iron Council'" (Miéville, 19). Some of these superannuated jobs even embody the obsolescence of labor more broadly. Recalling the Luddites of the early 1800s, loom workers are long gone. At the other end of the metacycle, the late twentieth century has witnessed containerization decimate the employment of dockworkers conjured here. This is thus a character system not only built out of a multiplied proletariat but also to a high degree imagined out of an obsolete proletariat, involving classes of labor both out of sync and out of work.

While *Iron*'s attention to how characters make their living (or can't, as in Elsie's situation of unemployment) is akin to *Fantastic*, the standpoint of labor from which the novel proceeds envelops the forms of struggle it imagines far more than in Anderson's animated film, especially the strike the novel emplots in "Anamnesis." In this, it is unlike *Fantastic*, since there the logic of the riot that the animals embrace in their struggle against Boggis, Bunce, and Bean is significantly disaggregated from their status as middle-class professionals, their respectable, remunerated jobs transformed, as we saw, into a disrespectable, criminal "job" in the sphere of circulation. Indeed, although trains—and transportation more generally—occupy a liminal position in between circulation and production, *Iron* imagines the strike as a struggle in the latter sphere. Consider the following scene from "Anamnesis":

> It is common for the wages train to be delayed. A day or two and there are only grumbles, but sometimes as long as a week goes without money. Three times when this happens there is a strike. By some chaos of democracy the track-layers put down their tools and block the train until they have shekels in their pockets. They are nonplussed by their own mass, by their numbers. Hundreds of muscled men, the tall green brawn of the cactacae emerging from them. The prostitutes, the surgeons, clerks, scholars, off scouts, and hunters come to watch them.
>
> Judah stands among them, ashudder with excitement. He is unlocked by this, and is briefly at one with the thing inside him. An *intervention*, he thinks. (Miéville, 221)

Instead of the looting and lighting up we saw in *Fantastic*, the focus here falls on what is central to the strike: the wage relation. And the reaction of the tracklayers here is one of the most iconic acts that conflict over that relation has historically taken in the strike: the downing of tools. And finally, the downers of tools are the subjects that have been symbolically central to the imagination of the strike: a multitude of brawny and muscular men. This scene comes into focus through Judah, moreover, whose "unlocking" in the above passage suggests the larger proletarian bildung through which he is going in "Anamnesis." But more important for our purposes, he stands in for the collective of other workers who watch the strike, focalizing an imaginative experience by way of a classically, if unduly gendered, image of worker solidarity and labor struggle for the multiplied proletariat to which *Iron Council* is attuned.

Iron will go on to unsettle this gendered image of the production struggle by means of the multiplied proletariat only watching in this passage. For eventually, a great many of the latter become involved in a mass strike in which the muscled men join with prostitutes who refuse to have sex with them when they can't pay because of delayed wages ("No pay no lay" is their mutual slogan), and the Remade prisoners rise up with the workers and whores after one of their own is beaten for refusing to scab ("going fReemade," in a phrase that recalls "going Turbo"). Crucially, this mass strike is successful, forcing the hand of the Transcontinental Railroad Trust when it comes to wages. However, a sequence of events unfolds in which a far more elaborated version of the downing of tools in the scene above takes place. This multiplied proletariat goes a revolutionary step farther, seizing the steam train and the railway tracks themselves in order to light out for territory where neither the forces of the Trust nor the militia of New Crobuzon can easily find them. This allows them to become "new people," as the reader discovers, once, in the 1805 storyline focalized by Cutter, he and his group of disaffected Caucus members, along with an older Judah, finally locate the Iron Council. At first irritated and disappointed by their "cashless economy," which he sees as so much "affectation," Cutter eventually changes his mind: "It took him days to know that he was wrong. Something was very not the same. The painting was different, and the ploughing, knife-grinding, bookkeeping. *These are new people*, he thought. *They ain't the same as me.* Cutter was terribly troubled" (Miéville, 346). It is almost as if he were looking in this moment at what Jodi Dean calls the "signifying stress" of the "communist horizon" in the post-1989 geopolitical landscape, with the mass strike that the novel narrates giving way to a communal mode of life and labor alien to the child of New Crobuzon capital.[38]

Given the obsolescence of the strike, an obsolescence to which Miéville was witness, what are we to make of this revolutionary resumption of it in *Iron Council?* When the logic of riot is operative even in films as arguably precious as *Fantastic*, what are we to do with the logic of return in a novel as overtly political—more overtly than any work so far—as *Iron?* We can move toward an answer by turning back to the efforts to theorize political struggle in the present, especially in light of the obsolescence of labor, which we have encountered throughout this book. In chapter 3, we heard David Harvey point to the restive masses of redundant workers in the global economy now. He links those masses to the dialectics of technological change that brought about the "miserable history of rearguard action fought against deindustrialization in the 1970s and 1980s," even as he acknowledges that such "rearguard action[s]" must continue to be mobilized because the contradiction of Capital itself "morphs into a contradiction that necessarily gets internalized within anti-capitalist politics." In that same chapter, we heard Guy Debord predict in 1967's *The Society of the Spectacle* the coming of a new General Ludd who would attack the "*machinery of permitted consumption.*" While that chapter found this new General Ludd in *Wreck-It Ralph*, the horde he leads has also banded together in reality, as Jasper Bernes effectively describes in his 2013 essay "Logistics, Counterlogistics, and the Communist Prospect." Bernes writes of twenty thousand blockaders at the port of Oakland, California, in November 2011, silencing just such machinery. "As an interface between production and consumption," he observes of the blockade, "between the United States and its overseas trading partners, between hundreds of thousands of workers and the various forms of circulating capital they engage, the quieted machinery of the port quickly became an emblem for the complex totality of capitalist production it seemed both to eclipse and to reveal." The riots in the marketplace discussed in chapter 4 provide further evidence of the historical shift of struggle away from production and toward circulation. And Clover's analysis of the riot form finds a parallel in Annie McClanahan's praise of the politics of sabotage, especially those who have joined together as collectives refusing to pay student debt or to take home foreclosures lying down.[39]

Despite struggle moving out of production and into circulation, despite the growing shift of action and activism away from factory and into marketplace, however, the strike and other modes of industrial organizing keyed to the sphere of production, such as the vanguard party, remain prominent figures in the imagination of struggle. This is not surprising, given that over the course of the metacycle of productive capital, the strike in particular became, as Clover writes, "the leading figure for social antagonism."[40] One of the problems for many of the thinkers cited above is that this figure persists as the one by which tactics and strategies continue to be imagined by many activists, theorists, activists-cum-theorists, and theorists-cum-activists—despite the obsolescence of the strike. And given that this obsolescence springs from the obsolescence of labor in the "old capitalist core[s], [their] industrial basis hollowed from within according to the exigencies of competition-driven development," it is incumbent upon activists and theorists alike to grasp that, as Aaron Benanav and Clover contend in an essay that critiques Dean's polemic in *The Communist Horizon*, a "changed capital-labor relation will give rise to new forms of organization. We should not criticize present-day struggles in the name of idealized reconstructions from the past." This claim, interestingly, implies its flipside: we can and perhaps should criticize idealized reconstructions from the past in the name of present-day struggles that those reconstructions threaten to eclipse.[41] And what is the story of the strike in *Iron Council* but such an idealized reconstruction, vulnerable to the critique that in imagining struggle it falls prey to a retrograde nostalgia because it falls out of sync with the conditions of the present? Constructing a character system grounded in superannuated work, narratively resuming and politically remembering the strike so prominently despite its obsolescence and idealizing this form of struggle as that which brings about a new people, Miéville's novel is arguably marred by an embarrassingly anachronistic investment in politics by obsolete means.

As with all of the means in *Out of Sync and Out of Work*, however, these too have their own pressingly temporal work to do in relation to our moment due to how they are part of the novel's overall imaginative historicism, complicating any sense that this is a text disfigured by its obsolete means for imagining struggle. Consider that the story of the strike in the 1700s of *Iron* unfolds in an extended analepsis called "Anamnesis," the title of which refers to a Greek term that means *recollection* (not to mention a Greek philosophical tradition that tries to unpack the fertile relationship between learning and remembering).[42] *Iron* is not simply idealizing the struggles of the past in this regard but recollecting those struggles as memories, with the past narratively pressing into the present of the novel. This narrative pressure from the past is only reinforced by that fact that this anamnesis of the late 1700s is emplotted in the present tense, while 1805, the present of the narrative, is recounted in the past tense. While the center of narrative gravity of *Iron* is nonsynchronous with both *its* present and *our* present, therefore, the novel temporally and historically marks this nonsynchronism, drawing attention to how the analeptic story of the strike is a memory of militancy—a still-active memory but a memory, an anamnesis, nonetheless.

Consider still further that this militantly nonsynchronous story culminates in the strikers seizing a steam train. Evocative of Marx's famous line, "Revolutions are the locomotive of history," the seizure of the steam train more directly alludes to a statement from the Russian avant-garde figure Vladimir Khlebnikov. Miéville takes the epigraph for the novel from Khlebnikov's *Proposals*: "Erect portable moving monuments on the platforms of trains" (Miéville, n.p.).[43] As we saw earlier, however, the steam-powered locomotive is also part and parcel of the metacyclical moment that the novel generates through the omnibus of obsolete technologies that helps to shape the time of this work of culture. By the end of "Anamnesis," moreover, the steam train has become the very figure of the strike itself. For the strikers in the novel, it is the technology that they claim as their own in a new way: "Their wealth and history is embedded in the train. They are a town moving. It is their moment in iron and grease. They control it. Iron Council. The motion of the council begins." "It is," the novel further recollects, "the same motion that has brought them so far" in constructing the transcontinental railroad, "and it is utterly new" (Miéville, 261). But the Iron Council in motion is also utterly old, especially for the reader of *Iron*. For that reader, the steam train that creates that motion is a superseded technology of transportation that nonsynchronously embodies the novel's politics by obsolete means, a figuration of the outmoded that in its technological obsolescence materializes how out of sync this resumed and remembered strike is in our time. But in resuming and remembering, it also allows for an activist experience of historical time that makes our era visible as a moment to us. The story of the strike, then, unifies *Iron Council* such that—as children of capital ourselves reading Miéville's novel now—we can actively experience our era as itself a moment of historical time. We can experience it as a moment in which we imagine struggle at the inflection point when the past keeps arriving in the present, however obsolete the means provided are.

The Lightning-Like Zig-Zag of History

This book began by falling into history. Throughout, this is a fall with which I have sought to keep faith by attending to the chronologically complex experiences of historical time that culture by outmoded means generates in our time and across the deep time of capitalism due to the obsolescence of labor that has propelled Capital itself for centuries. In the course of tracing the historical experience stirred up by the variously outmoded, residual, obstinate, dated, and obsolete means of the images, films, and novels discussed in these pages, what has emerged is how the work of culture is also the work of politics. What has emerged, in short, is the lightning-like zig-zag of history that is part of any fall into history, whether cultural, critical, or capitalist.

The phrase "lightning-like zig-zag" occurs in Rosa Luxemburg's remarkable essay of 1906, "The Mass Strike," a dazzling account of the 1905 Russian Revolution on theoretical, stylistic, and historiographical levels. In fact, to read that essay today is to be drawn into the historical experience of 1905 conceptually and cognitively—indeed, to be drawn into what it means for capitalist history to unfurl and unfold. "Certainly there are great contradictions," Luxemburg admits, "but they are not contradictions due to our reasoning, but contradictions due to capitalist development." She then proceeds to articulate a vision of history on the basis of the contradictory fact of capitalist development:

> It does not proceed in a beautiful straight line but in a lightning-like zig-zag. Just as the capitalist countries represent the most varied stages of development, so within each country the different layers of the same working class are represented. But history does not wait patiently till backward countries and the most advanced layers have joined together so that the whole mass can move symmetrically forward like a compact column. It brings the best prepared parts to explosion as soon as conditions there are ripe for it, and then in the storm of the revolutionary period, lost ground is recovered, unequal things are equalized, and the whole pace of social progress changed at one stroke to the double-quick.[44]

Variously out of sync with itself at some moments and fully synchronized at others, enabling politics by multiple means, history for Luxemburg moves according to many tempos. At certain times, past and present align to leap into a revolutionary future; at others, the obsolete and the contemporary proceed in crosscurrents that keep past and present in a juggernaut of temporal tension. Both of these, then, are the lightning-like zig-zags of history in political motion.

That motion is ultimately what culture by outmoded means makes palpable in the forms it adopts, the stories it tells, the movies it dates, and the irrealities it imagines, for the moments of historical experience that Joey Marsocci's Vitruvian Steam-bot, Brian Selznick's *The Invention of Hugo Cabret*, Martin Scorsese's *Hugo*, Rich Moore's *Wreck-It Ralph*, Wes Anderson's *Fantastic Mr. Fox*, and China Miéville's *Iron Council* create have all ultimately been moments of struggle in every instance, if in differing ways. The Vitruvian Steam-bot is an artifact of the struggle by which machine overtakes man in capitalist history again and again, with Selznick's novel and, even more, Scorsese's adaptation revealing the nightmare of automation that fuels that history. The moment of struggle that *Wreck-It* weaves into its ludic and Luddite historicism is the memory of machine breaking with which workers have resisted that nightmare, the obstinacy of the obsolete that carries within its core an impulse to destructively create a new mode beyond the one in which, like gravity, the push and pull of labor compels us. While the obsolescence of labor is a horizon we can sense if not see in *Fantastic*, the bourgeois riot that is the climax of that film situates the politics of the present in a haptic phenomenology of the past. And as the strike that organizes *Iron* has revealed, imagining struggle necessarily means pursuing politics by obsolete means, because all politics are the politics of obsolescence, rooted in standpoints the resumption of which need not be so much rearguard nostalgia but, rather, memories of militancy that our imaginations demand. With this cluster of irrealist works having unexpectedly revealed how being out of sync and out of work means staying in touch with history—how it involves remaining painfully and playfully inside of it, persisting creatively and destructively within it—what they finally bring to light is not only how contemporary culture incites historical experience still but also how urgently culture can do that temporal work, drawing us into the politics of our time by embracing the lightning-like zig-zag by which history moves.

Acknowledgments

Many, many people allowed me to write this book by being interlocutors of multiple sorts: friends, family, colleagues, and students. They all deserve the deepest of thanks for their roles in making it come into being—and for putting up with me while it did.

The idea for this book was born during my time as a postdoctoral fellow at the Massachusetts Institute of Technology, especially among the literature faculty, a generous and rigorous group of people to whom I will be forever grateful for helping me reimagine my academic self. I am also grateful to the other Mellon postdoctoral fellows in the humanities, among whom I would single out Amaranth Borsuk for the intellectual and aesthetic pleasures of her company. The book itself was written at the University of Rochester. There I have had the privilege of being junior faculty in the Department of English, though my colleagues across the humanities—especially in art and art history, visual and cultural studies, and film and media studies—have provided ongoing support and community. I have been guided by two superb chairs in the Department of English, John Michael and Rosemary Kegl. The latter saw me through a number of critical moments in which her help was both thorough and caring. The respective directors of film and media studies, Sharon Willis and Jason Middleton, have also been great supporters along the way, as have the respective directors of the graduate program in visual and cultural studies, Joan Saab and Rachel Haidu. My home department and these programs are filled with wonderful faculty and inspiring students. I wish also to acknowledge the support of two deans, Gloria Culver and Peter Lennie, who responded swiftly when matters mundane and pressing alike arose. I wish to thank Gloria in particular for a subvention that helped defray the costs of the permissions for images in this book. I could not have done better than the University of Rochester as the place to begin my career.

A funded leave as an external faculty fellow at the Susan and Donald Newhouse Center for the Humanities at Wellesley College was also pivotal in the writing of this book, giving me the time and space I needed to develop it. I want to thank Carol Dougherty, director at the time, for bringing me to the Newhouse Center. In addition to being a brilliant interlocutor and great colleague, Carol has a knack for knowing who to bring together to enable the kinds of interdisciplinary dialogue one truly wants at a humanities center. I especially benefitted from the insights of Arthur Bahr, Cristelle Baskins, Brigid Cohen, Brenna Greer, Lianne Habinek, Jane Kamensky, and Pauline de Tholozany over the course of my year at the Newhouse Center.

Among the many other individuals who inflected elements of this book through conversations casual or intense—especially by answering questions and making suggestions small and large, by collaborating with me on other projects, by providing research assistance, by getting me to come out and play or providing ongoing emotional support, or by reading sections of the book at various stages—I want to single out: Nico Baumbach, Joshua Clover, Amy Elias, Andy Elwell, Kathleen Fear, Patrick Keating, James Longenbach, Jason Middleton, Shankar Raman, Joshua Romphf, Jens Schlueter, Brian Selznick, David Serlin, Tracy Stuber, and Ezra Tawil. If I am forgetting anyone, my apologies, but you are in here. I also want to thank audiences at the American Comparative Literature Association, the Association for the Study of the Arts of the Present, and the Modernist Studies Association. I also appreciate all of those artists and publishers that granted me permission to reproduce their work in the book.

The editors and staff at Rutgers, especially Lisa Banning, have all been pragmatic, insightful, and timely—exemplifying how academic publishing should proceed in a communicative and clear way. Heather Hicks and Annie McClanahan, whom I later learned were the two anonymous readers of the manuscript, improved it immeasurably. They both truly saw the book—and helped me to see it more powerfully as well.

A number of other people—friends, family, and fellow faculty alike—are simply so woven into the texture of my personal and professional life that I'm not sure where their influence on the writing of this book begins and ends. Nothing I have written could have been completed without the support of my mother, Nancy Burges, and the rest of my family, especially my grandmother, Shirley Fray, and my aunt, Ann Burges, provided indelibly valued backup. While not biologically related to me, Dirk Dixon is the brother I never had. And my dog, Anya, has been there through it all, offering quiet comfort and sunny walks. Throughout this process, Mary Kiely and Marie Sergent have been the best therapists I could ask for.

Finally, on a daily and weekly basis while writing it, I found the friendship, discussions, and community that I needed for this book to exist in Arthur Bahr, Alan Brock, Lisa Cerami, Josh Dubler, Rachel Haidu, Heather Houser, Nathan Johnson, and Paul Torcello. I dedicate this book to all of them in honor of what they bring to my life, knowing that what they give me deserves far more appreciation than any acknowledgment in print can hope to offer in return.

Notes

Introduction

1   Richard P. Feynman, *Six Easy Pieces: Essentials of Physics Explained by Its Most Brilliant Teacher* (New York: Basic Books, 1995), 95–96. Feynman's chapter on the theory of gravitation helped in the writing of this paragraph, especially with the idiom of attraction, pulling, and even the prepositions "to" and "toward." So too did some less authoritative readings about why objects fall in online physics resources and various encyclopedias, which would point the curious reader toward the more complex distinctions between Newton's and Einstein's theories of gravity. These included entries of "free fall," "gravity," and related matters at Wikipedia, the Physics Classroom, and the Physics Hypertextbook. The last was particularly helpful in arriving at the statements regarding an object ascending already being in descent (see http://physics.info/falling/ in particular).

2   The passage that I have in mind, discussed at greater length in chapter 1, occurs in *Grundrisse: Foundations of the Critique of Political Economy* (Rough Draft), trans. Martin Nicolaus (New York: Penguin, 1973), 706.

3   No reader should take the analogy being developed here to mean that I take capitalism to be a natural phenomenon. Our mode of production is resolutely historical—but it is also an objective structure that, like gravity, doesn't care whether I believe in it or not. One way or another, it is there, in motion, setting the terms of how I get by. It is also worth noting that Marx himself was fond of all sorts of analogies to natural and scientific processes without his thereby undermining the fundamental historicity of Capital itself.

4   On wanting to work as an effect of a structure that demands I work, see Vivek Chibber, "Rescuing Class from the Cultural Turn," *Catalyst* 1, no. 1 (2017): 35–36, from which I also borrow the phrase "structural coercion" (36). For a more extended and far more theoretical consideration of how we are socially dominated by labor in capitalism, with time playing a key role as an external force in that domination, see Moishe Postone, *Time, Labor, and Social Domination: A Reinterpretation of Marx's Critical Theory* (New York: Cambridge University Press, 1993).

5   Dora Apel, *Beautiful Terrible Ruins: Detroit and the Anxiety of Decline* (New Brunswick, N.J.: Rutgers University Press, 2015).

6   Robert Brenner, *The Economics of Global Turbulence: The Advanced Capitalist Economies from Long Boom to Long Downturn, 1945–2005* (New York: Verso, 2006); Karl Marx, *Capital: A Critique of Political Economy*, vol. 3, trans. David Fernbach (New York: Penguin, 1981), 317–375; Robert J. Gordon, *The Rise and Fall of American Growth: The U.S. Standard of Living since the Civil War* (Princeton, N.J.: Princeton University Press, 2016), 2, 7, 566–604; Jason E. Smith, "Nowhere to Go: Automation, Then and Now (Part Two)," *Brooklyn Rail*, April 1, 2017,

http://brooklynrail.org/2017/04/field-notes/Nowhere-to-Go-Automation-Then -and-Now-Part-Two, my emphasis.

7 The best accounts of these phenomena are to be found in Joshua Clover, *1989: Bob Dylan Didn't Have This to Sing About* (Berkeley: University of California Press, 2009); Ursula Heise, *Chronoschisms: Time, Narrative, and Postmodernism* (New York: Cambridge University Press, 1997); and Fredric Jameson, *Postmodernism, or, The Cultural Logic of Late Capitalism* (Durham, N.C.: Duke University Press, 1991) and "The End of Temporality," *Critical Inquiry* 29, no. 4 (2003): 695–718.

8 As of the first half of 2017, the unemployment rate is hovering around 4.5 percent. However, the civilian labor force participation rate in the same period indicates a much higher percentage of potential laborers not working at all or enough: around 20 percent. See U.S. Bureau of Labor Statistics, Civilian Unemployment Rate [UNRATE], June 24, 2017, retrieved from FRED (Federal Reserve Bank of St. Louis), https://fred.stlouisfed.org/series/UNRATE; and U.S. Bureau of Labor Statistics, Civilian Labor Force Participation Rate: 25 to 54 years [LNU01300060], June 24, 2017, retrieved from FRED, https://fred.stlouisfed.org/ series/LNU01300060. For essays that help frame these numbers in relationship to the increasing precarity of the late twentieth- and earlier twenty-first-century workforces, especially in the U.S. context, see Aaron Benanav, "Precarity Rising," *Viewpoint Magazine*, June 15, 2015, https://www.viewpointmag.com/2015/06/ 15/precarity-rising/; and Smith, "Automation, Then and Now (Part Two)." The overdetermined importance of 1973 is clear not only in the economic scholarship already cited but also in the writings of influential thinkers working on the politics and culture—and the politics of culture—in the contemporary period. In *Riot. Strike. Riot: The New Era of Uprisings* (New York: Verso, 2016), for example, Joshua Clover makes much of this date, acknowledging that, "inevitably, '1973' is a metonym for changes too capacious for a single year to contain" (131). I address this metonym at greater length in chapter 1.

9 Jason E. Smith, "Nowhere to Go: Automation, Then and Now (Part One)," *Brooklyn Rail*, March 1, 2017, http://brooklynrail.org/2017/03/field-notes/Nowhere -to-Go.

10 I borrow the phrase "manias of the moment" from Jennifer L. Fleissner, *Women, Compulsion, Modernity: The Moment of American Naturalism* (Chicago: University of Chicago Press, 2004), chapter 3.

11 On the contours of this metacycle, see Clover, *Riot. Strike. Riot*, 17–21. The phrase "long metacycle of productive capital" occurs on page 107. On the long nineteenth and twentieth centuries, see Giovanni Arrighi, *The Long Twentieth Century: Money, Power and the Origin of Our Times* (New York: Verso, 2009).

12 For one of single most comprehensive accounts of what she calls this "materialist pedagogy," see Susan Buck-Morss's *The Dialectics of Seeing: Walter Benjamin and the Arcades Project* (Cambridge, Mass.: MIT Press, 1989).

13 Kristin Ross, *Communal Luxury: The Political Imaginary of the Paris Commune* (New York: Verso, 2015), 2.

14 Wai Chee Dimock, *Through Other Continents: American Literature across Deep Time* (Princeton, N.J.: Princeton University Press, 2006), 2, 3–4. For a contemporaneous approach related to Dimock's but more indebted to a cross of Benjamin and Arrighi, see Ian Baucom, *Specters of the Atlantic: Finance Capital, Slavery, and the Philosophy of History* (Durham, N.C.: Duke University Press, 2005).

15 Fredric Jameson, *The Political Unconscious: Narrative as a Socially Symbolic Act* (Ithaca, N.Y.: Cornell University Press, 1981), 96, 95.

16 Thanks to an incisive and insightful reader's report from Annie McClanahan for language that led to both this and a later sentence in the introduction.

17 "A fidelity to the lost cause of reading dialectically," writes Lesjak, "is the only way to keep faith with history" (264), in Carolyn Lesjak, "Reading Dialectically," *Criticism* 55, no. 2 (2013): 233–277.

Chapter 1 Culture by Outmoded Means

1 Carl Benedikt Frey and Michael A. Osborne, "The Future of Employment: How Susceptible Are Jobs to Computerizaton?" Oxford Martin School, Program on the Impacts of Future Technology and Department of Engineering Science, University of Oxford, Oxford, United Kingdom, September 17, 2013, https://www.oxfordmartin.ox.ac.uk/downloads/academic/The_Future_of_Employment.pdf; and "Agiletown: The Relentless March of Technology and London's Response," London Futures, *Deloitte*, 2014, http://www2.deloitte.com/content/dam/Deloitte/uk/Documents/uk-futures/london-futures-agiletown.pdf.

2 Hal Foster, *Compulsive Beauty* (Cambridge, Mass.: MIT Press, 1993), 159.

3 See the entry for "Joey Marsocci" at the International Movie Database (http://www.imdb.com/name/nm3215574/) and the website for Grymm Studios (http://www.grymmstudios.com).

4 For a related genealogy of the aesthetics of obsolescence in modernity, see Mark Goble's wonderful essay "Obsolescence," in *A New Vocabulary for Global Modernism*, ed. Eric Hayot and Rebecca L. Walkowitz (New York: Columbia University Press, 2016), 146–168.

5 Bill Bamberger and Cathy N. Davidson, *Closing: The Life and Death of an American Factory* (New York: W. W. Norton, 1998), 168.

6 Benjamin H. D. Buchloh, "Residual Resemblance," in *Formalism and Historicity: Models and Methods in Twentieth-Century Art* (Cambridge, Mass.: MIT Press, 2015), 471–508.

7 Scott Bukatman, *The Poetics of Slumberland: Animated Spirits and the Animating Spirit* (Berkeley: University of California Press), 7, 2.

8 Walter Benjamin, "On the Mimetic Faculty," in *Walter Benjamin: Selected Writings: Volume 2, 1927–1934*, ed. Gary Smith, Howard Eiland, and Michael W. Jennings (Cambridge, Mass.: Belknap Press of Harvard University Press, 1999), 720–722; Miriam Bratu Hansen, *Cinema and Experience: Siegfried Kracauer, Walter Benjamin, and Theodor W. Adorno* (Berkeley: University of California Press, 2011), 147, 148.

9 Hansen, *Cinema and Experience*, 147.

10 Hansen, 150.

11 One path we could productively follow to think about the question of children's culture that I am raising here is to read the works explored in *Out of Sync and Out of Work* in relationship to the "story" that Mark McGurl tells in "Gigantic Realism: The Rise of the Novel and the Comedy of Scale," *Critical Inquiry* 43, no. 2 (Winter 2017): 403–440. There he writes, "This is a story about giants, about giants in literature, but also, and more important, about the disappearance of giants from literary history, or rather, their migration from the mainline of that history to its margins, such that the phenomenon traditionally described as the rise of the novel occurs

largely unburdened by the supersized beings who live on in children's literature and cinema and advertisements for frozen vegetables" (403). The path McGurl's essay lays out might lead us to Jack Halberstam's *The Queer Art of Failure* (Durham, N.C.: Duke University Press, 2011). Embracing an admirably "low-theoretical" approach, Halberstam is focused on modes of the kind I am, especially animation, which "allow for the fact that [children] are always already anarchic and rebellious, out of order and out of time" (27). With regards to Miéville and not just children's but also childish culture in particular, see Joe Sutliff Sanders, "'Blatantly Coming Back': The Arbitrary Line between Here and There, Child and Adult, Fantasy and Real, London and UnLondon," in *China Miéville: Critical Essays*, ed. Caroline Edwards and Tony Venezia (Canterbury, Conn.: Gylphi Limited, 2015), 119–138.

12   Moishe Postone, *Time, Labor, and Social Domination: A Reinterpretation of Marx's Critical Theory* (New York: Cambridge University Press, 1993), 294, 300.

13   Fredric Jameson, *Postmodernism, or, The Cultural Logic of Late Capitalism* (Durham, N.C.: Duke University Press, 1991), 25; Andreas Huyssen, *Present Pasts: Urban Palimpsests and the Politics of Memory* (Stanford Calif.: Stanford University Press, 2003), 10.

14   Jameson, *Postmodernism*, xx–xxi.

15   Michael B. Schiffer, "The Explanation of Long-Term Technological Change," in *Anthropological Perspectives on Technology*, ed. Michael B. Schiffer (Albuquerque: University of New Mexico Press, 2001), 216–217; David Harvey, *Seventeen Contradictions and the End of Capitalism* (New York: Oxford University Press, 2014), 93; Robert Brenner, *The Economics of Global Turbulence: The Advanced Capitalist Economies from Long Boom to Long Downturn, 1945–2005* (New York: Verso, 2006), chapter 2. See also the highly useful article on which Brenner draws, Marvin Frankel, "Obsolescence and Technological Change in a Maturing Economy," *American Economic Review* 45, no. 3 (June 1955): 296–319. For a more extended account of the relationship between obsolescence and innovation, see Joel Burges, "Obsolescence/Innovation," in *Time: A Vocabulary of the Present*, ed. Joel Burges and Amy J. Elias (New York: New York University Press, 2016).

16   On the contradiction between these two spheres, especially the contradiction between production and realization, see Harvey, *Seventeen Contradictions*, 79–85. For Marxists, these spheres constitute a contradictory unity because, as Harvey explains, capitalism "can either maximize the conditions for the *production* of surplus value, and so threaten the capacity to *realize* surplus value in the market, or keep effective demand strong in the market by empowering workers and threaten the ability to create surplus value in production" (81). Also see Joshua Clover, "World-Systems Riot" (unpublished manuscript, 2012), accessed February 12, 2015, http://krieger.jhu.edu/arrighi/wp-content/uploads/sites/29/2014/03/World _System_Riot_2_CHS.pdf (site discontinued), 10–11.

17   Giles Slade, *Made to Break: Technology and Obsolescence in America* (Cambridge, Mass.: Harvard University Press, 2006), 9.

18   Paul M. Gregory, "A Theory of Purposeful Obsolescence," *Southern Economic Journal* 14, no. 1 (1947): 24–45.

19   Slade, *Made to Break*, 45.

20   Karal Ann Marling, *As Seen on TV: The Visual Culture of Everyday Life in the 1950s* (Cambridge, Mass.: Harvard University Press, 1994), 139–141.

21   Peter Dicken, *Global Shift: Reshaping the Global Economic Map of the Twenty-First Century*, 4th ed. (London: Sage, 2003), 104–105.

22 Aaron Benanav and John Clegg, "Misery and Debt: On the Logic and History of Surplus Populations and Surplus Capital," in *Contemporary Marxist Theory: A Reader*, ed. Andrew Pendakis, Jeff Diamanti, Nicholas Brown, Josh Robinson, and Imre Szeman (New York: Bloomsbury, 2014), 592. On this topic, also see Stanley Aronowitz and William DiFazio, *The Jobless Future*, 2nd ed. (Minneapolis: University of Minnesota Press, 2010).

23 Karl Marx, *Grundrisse: Foundations of the Critique of Political Economy* (Rough Draft), trans. Martin Nicolaus (New York: Penguin Books), 706.

24 Joshua Clover, *Riot. Strike. Riot: The New Era of Uprisings* (New York: Verso, 2016), 25.

25 The phrase "tendentially jobless" appears in Benanav and Chegg, "Misery and Debt," 602.

26 Brenner, *Economics of Global Turbulence*, 99–163. On neoliberalism, see David Harvey, *A Brief History of Neoliberalism* (New York: Oxford University Press, 2005). For more on 1973 as a year of "signal crisis" from the perspective of a much longer *durée*, see Giovanni Arrighi, *The Long Twentieth Century: Money, Power, and the Origins of Our Time* (London: Verso, 2009).

27 Jasper Bernes, *The Work of Art in the Age of Deindustrialization* (Stanford, Calif.: Stanford University Press, 2017), 19.

28 Benanav and Clegg, "Misery and Debt," 586, 596; Aronowitz and DiFazio, *Jobless Future*, 6.

29 Berry Bluestone and Bennett Harrison, *The Deindustrialization of America: Plant Closings, Community Abandonment, and the Dismantling of Basic Industry* (New York: Basic Books, 1982). This paragraph summarizes material from chapters 2 and 3, with quotations from pages 6 and 27.

30 Bluestone and Harrison, *Deindustrialization*, 6.

31 Aronowitz and DiFazio, *Jobless Future*, 47–48.

32 I borrow the phrase "quantum measures" here from Aronowitz and DiFazio, *Jobless Future*, chapter 10. These percentages are based on a chart comparing real output per hour of all persons in the manufacturing sector to employment in the manufacturing sector generated by FRED, using data from the U.S. Bureau of Labor Statistics, Manufacturing Sector: Real Output Per Hour of All Persons [OPHMFG], September 22, 2016, retrieved from FRED, https://fred.stlouisfed.org/series/OPHMFG; U.S. Bureau of Labor Statistics, Manufacturing Sector: Employment [PRS30006013], September 22, 2016, retrieved from FRED, https://fred.stlouisfed.org/series/PRS30006013. My calculation of percentage change is based on information on how to do so from the Federal Reserve Bank of Dallas (https://www.dallasfed.org/research/basics/indexing.aspx). The 85 percent figure, derived from the FRED site as well, appears in Farhad Manjoo, "How to Make America's Robots Great Again," *New York Times*, January 25, 2017, https://www.nytimes.com/2017/01/25/technology/personaltech/how-to-make-americas-robots-great-again.html?_r=0.

33 Figure 34.1 in Benanav and Clegg, "Misery and Debt," 594.

34 David F. Noble, *The Forces of Production: A Social History of Automation* (New York: Oxford University Press, 1984), 58; Karl Marx, *Capital: A Critique of Political Economy*, vol. 1, trans. Ben Fowkes (New York: Penguin, 1976), 568.

35 For a wager on a related historicism, see Ian Baucom's *Specters of the Atlantic: Finance Capital, Slavery, and the Philosophy of History* (Durham, N.C.: Duke University Press, 2005), especially chapter 1.

36 Jason E. Smith, "Nowhere to Go: Automation, Then and Now (Part Two)," *Brooklyn Rail*, April 1, 2017, http://brooklynrail.org/2017/04/field-notes/Nowhere-to-Go-Automation-Then-and-Now-Part-Two; Frey and Osborne, "The Future of Employment," 72.

37 Frey and Osborne, "Agiletown," 9.

38 Smith, "Automation, Then and Now (Part Two)."

39 Robert Gordon, *The Rise and Fall of American Growth: The U.S. Standard of Living since the Civil War* (Princeton, N.J.: Princeton University Press, 2015), 596; Robert Gebeloff and Karl Russell, "How the Growth of E-Commerce Is Shifting Retail Jobs," *New York Times*, July 6, 2017, https://www.nytimes.com/interactive/2017/07/06/business/ecommerce-retail-jobs.html. Also see Smith, "Automation, Then and Now (Part Two)"; and Richard Susskind and Daniel Susskind, *The Future of the Professions: How Technology Will Transform the Work of Human Experts* (New York: Oxford University Press, 2015).

40 This paragraph summarizes chapter 17 of Gordon's *Rise and Fall*, with quotations coming from pages 585 and 581.

41 Jaron Lanier, *Who Owns the Future?* (New York: Simon and Schuster, 2013), 2; entries for Anderson and Selznick at Wikipedia, both entries accessed June 2017, https://en.wikipedia.org/wiki/Wes_Anderson#cite_ref-telegraph2014_9-0 and https://en.wikipedia.org/wiki/Brian_Selznick; Peter Marks, "Citing Chains, Eeyore's Books Calls It Quits," *New York Times*, August 1, 1993, http://www.nytimes.com/1993/08/01/nyregion/citing-chains-eeyore-s-books-calls-it-quits.html. For another domain in which obsolescence has become legible culturally, see Daniel M. Abramson, *Obsolescence: An Architectural History* (Chicago: University of Chicago Press, 2016).

42 James Boggs, *The American Revolution: Pages from a Negro Worker's Notebook* (New York: Monthly Review Press, 2009), 35; John Maynard Keynes, "Economic Possibilities for our Grandchildren (1930)," in *Revisiting Keynes: Economic Possibilities for Our Grandchildren*, ed. Lorenzo Pecchi and Gustavo Piga (Cambridge, Mass.: MIT Press, 2008), 17–26; Walter Benjamin, "Surrealism: The Last Snapshot of the European Intelligentsia," in *Selected Writings, Volume 2, 1927–1934*, eds. Michael W. Jennings, Howard Eiland, and Gary Smith, trans. Rodney Livingstone et al. (Cambridge, Mass.: Belknap Press of Harvard University Press, 1999); "General Ludd's Triumph," in *Writings of the Luddites*, ed. Kevin Binfield (Baltimore, Md.: Johns Hopkins University Press, 2004), 99.

Chapter 2   Reading by Residual Means

1 Maura Nolan, "Medieval Habit, Modern Sensation: Reading Manuscripts in the Digital Age," *Chaucer Review* 47, no. 4 (2013): 465–476.

2 Raymond Williams, *Marxism and Literature* (New York: Oxford University Press, 1977), 122. For an important elaboration of Williams, see any of the essays gathered together in the far-ranging collection edited by Charles Acland, *Residual Media* (Minneapolis: University of Minnesota Press, 2007).

3 Quoted in Christian Thorne, "The Revolutionary Energy of the Outmoded," *October* 104 (2003): 108.

4 Leah Price, *How to Do Things with Books in Victorian Britain* (Princeton, N.J.: Princeton University Press, 2012), 22, 9.

5 Brian Selznick, *The Invention of Hugo Cabret: A Novel in Words and Pictures* (New York: Scholastic Press, 2007). Hereafter cited parenthetically.

6   On the "computerization of culture," see Lev Manovich, *The Language of New Media* (Cambridge, Mass.: MIT Press, 2001).

7   "Suture" is a technical term in film theory that describes how, as Kaja Silverman writes, "the viewer's exclusion from the site of cinematic production is covered over by the inscription into the diegesis of a character from whom the film's sounds and images seem to flow, a character equipped with authoritative vision, hearing, and speech." The paradigmatic act of suturing, which orients the spectators diegetically such that they feel they are part of a world from which they are absent, a world that was made elsewhere, is the shot / reverse shot. The shot / reverse shot is special because it "purports to show what was missing from the first shot," with one shot depicting someone looking, then the next shot providing the object of the look. While Hugo is akin to the film character that authorizes spectators to inscribe themselves into a cinematic diegesis, that inscription is arguably not a completed act of suturing—thus my "almost"—because there is no shot of the figure at whom he looks: the reader-spectator of *Invention*. To draw on Price again, this remediated close-up of Hugo looking at us is thus a moment when the textuality of *Invention* becomes bookish. Kaja Silverman, *The Acoustic Mirror: The Female Voice in Psychoanalysis and Cinema* (Bloomington: Indiana University Press, 1988), 12, 13.

8   A part of the very idiom of media studies at this point, remediation is a concept advanced most influentially by Jay David Bolter and Richard Grusin in *Remediation: Understanding New Media* (Cambridge, Mass.: MIT Press, 1999). Pavle Levi productively develops the notion of retrograde remediation on the basis of Bolter and Grusin, extending it to a consideration of the 1920s European avant-garde of what he calls "written films" (films of which we might take *The Invention of Hugo Cabret* to be a relative), in *Cinema by Other Means* (New York: Oxford University Press, 2012), 42–76.

9   Miriam Hansen, *Babel and Babylon: Spectatorship in American Silent Film* (Cambridge, Mass.: Harvard University Press, 1991), 211.

10   David A. Cook, *A History of Narrative Film*, 4th ed. (New York: W.W. Norton, 2004), 387–389.

11   According to Noël Burch, "The whole visual history of the cinema before World War I—and not only in France—thus turns upon the opposition between the 'Mélièsian' affirmation of the surface and the affirmation of depth already implicit in [*Arrival of a Train at La Ciotat*]." See *Life to those Shadows*, trans. Ben Brewster (Berkeley: University of California Press, 1990), 173.

12   Burch, *Life to those Shadows*, 165, 166, 168.

13   Burch, *Life to those Shadows*, 162–185; David Bordwell, Janet Staiger, and Kristin Thompson, *The Classical Hollywood Cinema: Film Style and Mode of Production to 1960* (New York: Columbia University Press, 1985), 227–230, 263–270; Patrick Keating, email message to author, June 14, 2016.

14   Bordwell, Staiger, and Thompson, 227; Keating, email.

15   Burch states that the apparent movement of the camera toward objects in Méliès's *Trip* is more likely the reverse: of the objects toward the camera (165).

16   Keating, email.

17   On the complexity of the set-up, see John Bengston, *Silent Visions: Discovering Early Hollywood and New York through the Films of Harold Lloyd* (Santa Monica, Calif.: Santa Monica Press, 2011), 104–118.

18   Jonathan Crary, *Suspensions of Perception: Attention, Spectacle, and Modern Culture* (Cambridge, Mass.: MIT Press, 1999), 13.

19 Tom Gunning, "Shooting into Outer Space: Reframing Modern Vision," in *Fantastic Voyages of the Cinematic Imagination: Georges Méliès's Trip to the Moon*, ed. Matthew Solomon (Albany: SUNY Press, 2011), 105, 106.

20 See André Bazin, "The Ontology of the Photographic Image," in *What Is Cinema?*, vol. 1, trans. Hugh Gray (Berkeley: University of California Press, 2005), 9–16.

21 See, for instance, Olivia Solon, "Self-Driving Trucks: What's the Future for America's 3.5 Million Truckers," *The Guardian*, June 17, 2016, https://www.theguardian.com/technology/2016/jun/17/self-driving-trucks-impact-on-drivers-jobs-us; Marc Levinson, *The Box: How the Shipping Container Made the World Smaller and the World Economy Bigger* (Princeton, N.J.: Princeton University Press, 2008).

22 Stephen Kern, *The Culture of Time and Space, 1880–1918* (Cambridge, Mass.: Harvard University Press, 2003), 65–88, 113–114; Wolfgang Schivelbusch, *The Railway Journey: The Industrialization of Space and Time in the Nineteenth Century* (Berkeley: University of California Press, 2014), 33–44.

23 In using the figure of hieroglyphs here, I am pointing back to a tradition of thought about mass culture as a form of hieroglyphic writing that I do not have the space to engage fully, but which has inflected my thinking about *Invention* and *Hugo*. As Miriam Hansen has made clear in *Babel and Babylon* (see chapter 8 in particular), this tradition can be traced back in film aesthetics by way of D. W. Griffith through Vachel Lindsay to major figures of the American Renaissance such as Poe, Emerson, and Whitman. But the key text for me here is Hansen's always dazzling essay, focused on the theorizing of this scriptural form in the culture industry, "Mass Culture as Hieroglyphic Writing: Adorno, Derrida, Kracauer," *New German Critique* 56 (Spring–Summer 1992): 43–73.

24 Price, *How to Do Things*, 9; Carl Benedikt Frey and Michael A. Osborne, "The Future of Employment: How Susceptible Are Jobs to Computerizaton?" Oxford Martin School, Program on the Impacts of Future Technology and Department of Engineering Science, University of Oxford, Oxford, United Kingdom, 2013, 71.

25 See Tom Gunning, "An Aesthetic of Astonishment: Early Film and the (In)Credulous Spectator," in *Viewing Positions: Ways of Seeing Film*, ed. Linda Williams (New Brunswick, N.J.: Rutgers University Press, 1995), 114–133.

26 Walter Benjamin, "The Work of Art in the Age of Its Technological Reproducibility: Second Version," in *Walter Benjamin: Selected Writings: 1935–1938*, vol. 3, ed. Howard Eiland and Michael W. Jennings (Cambridge, Mass.: Belknap Press of Harvard University Press, 2002), 101–133. For an important account of how this essay's idea of cinema as a "room-for-play" fits more broadly into Benjamin's thinking and depends on a counterpoint between *Spiel*, or "play," and *Schein*, or "semblance," see Miriam Bratu Hansen, *Cinema and Experience: Siegfried Kracauer, Walter Benjamin, and Theodor W. Adorno* (Berkeley: University of California Press, 2011), 183–204.

27 Walter Benjamin, "On the Mimetic Faculty," in *Walter Benjamin: Selected Writings: 1927–1934*, vol. 2, ed. Gary Smith, Howard Eiland, and Michael W. Jennings (Cambridge, Mass.: Belknap Press of Harvard University Press, 1999), 720.

28 Benjamin, "On the Mimetic Faculty," 721.

29 Moishe Postone, *Time, Labor, and Social Domination: A Reinterpretation of Marx's Critical Theory* (New York: Cambridge University Press, 1993), 298.

30 Joshua Romphf, "From Magician to Technician: Labor and the Art of Film Projection" (master's thesis, University of Rochester, 2013), 39–40; David Bordwell,

Pandora's Digital Box: Films, Files, and the Future of Movies (Madison, Wis.: Irving Way Institute Press, 2012), 6–8; Carole Pearson, "Infamous Players: Film Projectionists Battle the Big Boys," *Our Times* 21, no. 4 (August–September 2002): 33.

31 Bordwell, *Pandora's Digital Box*, 8, 92–96.

32 Bordwell, 94.

33 See Matthew Garrett, "Subterranean Gratification: Reading after the Picaro," *Critical Inquiry* 42, no. 1 (Autumn 2015): 97–123.

34 Carole Pearson, "Infamous Players," 33.

35 More than any other section of this chapter, in this one I move between the novel and film. There are two things to note about this decision. First, I attempt to distinguish between the two whenever possible if there is an important difference, but at times I have written over some of those differences where they seem less pressing to the argument. Second, the inclusion of *Hugo* points to how many of the works I examine double their audience in various ways. While *Invention* is primarily for children, *Hugo* seems more like a movie for adults than kids in many respects.

36 I borrow the phrase "twilight of irregular employment" from Aaron Benanav, "Research Statement," accessed June 1, 2016, https://aaronbenanav.files .wordpress.com/2015/11/benanav-research-statement.pdf. On wageless life, see the following essays: Michael Denning, "Wageless Life," *New Left Review* 66 (November–December 2010): 79–97; Margaret Ronda, "'Not Much Left': Wageless Life in Millennial Poetry," *Post45*, October 9, 2011, http://post45.research.yale .edu/2011/10/not-much-left-wageless-life-in-millenial-poetry/; Kathleen M. Millar, "The Precarious Present: Wageless Labor and Disrupted Life in Rio de Janeiro, Brazil," *Cultural Anthropology* 29, no. 1 (2014): 32–53, http://dx.doi.org/10.14506/ ca29.1.04.

37 This is the simplest form of metadiegetic narration that one can imagine, in which a character provides a narrative explanation in the form of dialogue to other characters. See Gerard Genette, *Narrative Discourse: An Essay in Method*, trans. Jane E. Lewin (Ithaca, N.Y.: Cornell University Press, 1983), 232.

38 Richard Abel, *The Ciné Goes to Town: French Cinema, 1896–1914*, updated and expanded ed. (Berkeley: University of California Press, 1994), 1–2, 14, 19, 20–24, 36, 58; also see 156–160. Selznick probably drew more extensively on Gaby Wood's lovely nonfiction work, *Edison's Eve: A Magical History of the Quest for Mechanical Life* (New York: Anchor, 2002), 175–212.

39 Hal Foster, *Compulsive Beauty* (Cambridge, Mass.: MIT Press, 1993), 159.

40 Wood, *Edison's Eve*, 207.

41 Nancy Rexford, "The Perils of Choice: Women's Footwear in Nineteenth-Century America," in *Shoes: A History from Sandals to Sneakers*, ed. Giorgio Riello and Peter McNeil (New York: Berg, 2006), 151–158.

42 Denning, "Wageless Life," 95, 79. For more on child labor, see Mike Davis, *Planet of Slums* (New York: Verso, 2007), 186–188.

43 Denning, "Wageless Life," 85, 90.

44 Denning, "Wageless Life," 90; Davis, *Planet of Slums*, 186–187.

45 Denning, "Wageless Life," 83–84.

46 Aaron Benanav and John Clegg, "Misery and Debt: On the Logic and History of Surplus Populations and Surplus Capital," in *Contemporary Marxist Theory: A Reader*, ed. Andrew Pendakis, Jeff Diamanti, Nicholas Brown, Josh Robinson, and Imre Szeman (New York: Bloomsbury, 2014), 596; Aaron Benanav, "Precarity

Rising," *Viewpoint Magazine*, June 15, 2015, https://viewpointmag.com/2015/06/15/precarity-rising.

47 Benanav and Clegg, "Misery and Debt," 592.

48 Williams, *Marxism and Literature*, 122–124.

49 Joel Burges, "Adorno's Mimeograph: The Uses of Obsolescence in *Minima Moralia*," *New German Critique* 40, no. 1 (2013): 77–80.

50 Peter Brooks, *The Melodramatic Imagination: Balzac, Henry James, Melodrama, and the Mode of Excess* (New Haven, Conn.: Yale University Press, 1976), 45.

51 Northrop Frye, *Anatomy of Criticism: Four Essays* (Princeton, N.J.: Princeton University Press, 1957), 44–45.

52 Joshua Clover, "Enjoy the Silents," review of *The Artist* and *Hugo*, *Film Quarterly* 65, no. 4 (June 2012): 7.

53 Clover, "Enjoy the Silents," 7.

54 Clover, 7.

55 Nathalie op de Beeck, *Suspended Animation: Children's Picture Books and the Fairy Tale of Modernity* (Minneapolis: University of Minnesota Press, 2010).

56 Fredric Jameson, *The Political Unconscious: Narrative as a Socially Symbolic Act* (Ithaca, N.Y.: Cornell University Press, 1981), 79.

57 Garrett, "Subterranean," 116.

58 Garrett, 97.

Chapter 3   Narrative by Obstinate Means

1 Karen Collins, "One-Bit Wonders: Video Game Sound before the Crash," in *Before the Crash: Early Video Game History*, ed. Mark J. P. Wolf (Detroit: Wayne State University Press, 2012), 119.

2 For more on the relationship between new and old tech in the making of *Wreck-It Ralph*, see Chris Carter, "Adapting 8-Bit Motion Style to 3D Computer Animation in *Wreck-It Ralph*," *Mediascape* (Fall 2013), http://www.tft.ucla.edu/mediascape/Fall2014_Adapting8BitMotion.html; and Barbara Robertson, "Triple Play," *Computer Graphics World* 35 (October–November 2012): 20–26.

3 In *Capitalism, Socialism, and Democracy* (New York: Harper Perennial, 1976), Schumpeter states in his chapter on "the process of creative destruction" that the "fundamental impulse that sets and keeps the capitalist engine in motion comes from the new consumers' goods, the new methods of production or transportation, the new markets, the new forms of industrial organization that capitalist enterprise creates." This is a process, moreover, that "unfolds through decades or centuries" and is only able to be judged from such a scale (83).

4 Mary Ann Doane, "Has Time Become Space?," in *Thinking Media Aesthetics: Media Studies, Film Studies and the Arts*, ed. Liv Hausken (New York: Peter Lang, 2014), 102.

5 Theodor W. Adorno, *Minima Moralia: Reflections on a Damaged Life*, trans. E. F. N. Jephcott (New York: Verso, 1974), 118.

6 "The Moving Contradiction: The Systematic Dialectic of Capital as a Dialectic of Class Struggle," *Endnotes* 2 (April 2010), https://endnotes.org.uk/issues/2/en/endnotes-the-moving-contradiction.

7 See chapter 3 for a more extensive discussion of this shift in film history from the photographic and indexical to the animated and the plastic as a result of the digital transition in film and the computerization of culture more broadly.

8 James Newman, *Best Before: Videogames, Supersession and Obsolescence* (New York: Routledge, 2012), 2. On competition in the process of creative destruction, see Schumpeter, *Capitalism*, 84–85.

9 Alan Liu, *The Laws of Cool: Knowledge Work and the Culture of Information* (Chicago: University of Chicago Press, 2004), chapters 11 and 12.

10 Peter Dicken, *Global Shift: Reshaping the Global Economic Map of the Twenty-First Century*, 4th ed. (London: Sage, 2003), 104–105.

11 Carly A. Kocurek discusses the simultaneity of an early period of video games, especially in the context of the arcade, and the significant economic changes of the 1970s in "Coin-Drop Capitalism: Economic Lessons from the Video Game Arcade," in *Before the Crash: Early Video Game History*, ed. Mark J. P. Wolf (Detroit: Wayne State University Press, 2012), 199–201, 204–205.

12 Mark J. P. Wolf, "Introduction," in *Before the Crash*, 4. To put these numbers in further context, see the entry for "Video Game Sales," especially the useful 2012-adjusted graph entitled "U.S. Video Game Market Revenues," last accessed September 1, 2016, http://vgsales.wikia.com/wiki/Video_game_industry?file=US _Inflation-Adjusted_Revenues.png.

13 Wolf, "Introduction," 4.

14 Gopal Balakrishnan, "Speculations on the Stationary State," *New Left Review* 59 (September–October 2009): 15.

15 Wolf, "Introduction," 5.

16 Horace Dediu and Dirk Schmidt, "Game Over," *Asymco*, September 9, 2013, http:// www.asymco.com/2013/09/09/game-over/.

17 Stephen E. Siwek, "Video Games in the 21st Century: The 2014 Report," *Entertainment Software Association*, last accessed September 1, 2016, http://www.theesa.com/ wp-content/uploads/2014/11/VideoGames21stCentury_2014.pdf, 1, 4; Newman, *Best Before*, 2–3.

18 Balakrishnan, "Speculations," 15–16.

19 Newman, *Best Before*, 42, 43.

20 Siwek, "Video Games," 1.

21 On these labor conditions, see Ian Williams, "'You Can Sleep Here All Night': Video Games and Labor," *Jacobin*, November 18, 2013, https://www.jacobinmag .com/2013/11/video-game-industry/; Nick Dyer-Witheford and Greig de Peuter, *Games of Empire: Global Capitalism and Video Games* (Minneapolis: University of Minnesota Press, 2009); Aubrey Anable, "Labor/Leisure," in *Time: A Vocabulary of the Present*, ed. Joel Burges and Amy J. Elias (New York: New York University Press, 2016), 192–208; Jane Wakefield, "Foxconn replaces '60,000 workers with robots,'" *BBC News*, May 25, 2016, http://www.bbc.com/news/technology-36376966.

22 Kocurek, "Coin-Drop Capitalism," 99, 200, 205.

23 I am using the concept of a "playbor force" more broadly to refer to both waged and unwaged labor in the video game industry here than the two scholars who coined the term do. As Dyer-Whiteford and de Peuter write in *Games of Empire*, while employing the concept to refer to unwaged work, that industry has depended on "the deepening involvement of various forms of free, voluntary, immaterial playbor as a costless means of renewing industry profits" (32). See also Dyer-Witheford and de Peuter, *Games of Empire*, 23–27.

24 Aaron Benanav and John Clegg, "Misery and Debt: On the Logic and History of Surplus Populations and Surplus Capital," in *Contemporary Marxist Theory: A Reader*, ed. Andrew Pendakis, Jeff Diamanti, Nicholas Brown, Josh Robinson,

and Imre Szeman (New York: Bloomsbury, 2014), 596. The phrasing about labor being "too much and too little" occurs in the *Endnotes* essay entitled "The Moving Contradiction."

25   Carter, "Adapting 8-bit."

26   Robertson, "Triple Play," 23–26.

27   Fredric Jameson, The Political Unconscious: *Narrative as a Socially Symbolic Act* (Ithaca, N.Y.: Cornell University Press, 1981), 100. It is worth noting here that I have wondered if all prior modes of production do "structurally coexist" in *Wreck-It* in the differing worlds of the video games depicted.

28   Fredric Jameson, "The End of Temporality," *Critical Inquiry* 29, no. 4 (2003): 716; Andreas Huyssen, *Present Pasts: Urban Palimpsests and the Politics of Memory* (Stanford, Calif.: Stanford University Press, 2003), 23; Mary Ann Doane, *The Emergence of Cinematic Time: Modernity, Contingency, the Archive* (Cambridge, Mass.: Harvard University Press, 2003), 11.

29   Devin Fore, "The Time of Capital: Three Industrial Novels," in *Realism after Modernism: The Rehumanization of Art and Literature* (Cambridge, Mass.: MIT Press, 2012), 81, 82, 83, 95.

30   "Strike and Sabotage at the *Washington Post*," *Fifth Estate*, November 1975, http://www.fifthestate.org/archive/267-november-1975/strike-sabotage-wash-post; "The Post and the Presses," editorial, *Washington Post*, October 3, 1975, A10; Robert G. Kaiser, "Dispute over New Work Rules, Violence Keeps 2 Sides Apart," *Washington Post*, October 12, 1975, 16.

31   "Strike and Sabotage."

32   As quoted in Cal Winslow, "Overview: The Rebellion from Below, 1965–1981," in *Rebel Rank and File: Labor Militancy and the Revolt from below in the Long 1970s*, ed. Aaron Brenner, Robert Brenner, and Cal Winslow (New York: Verso, 2010), 23.

33   Kaiser, "Dispute over New Work Rules," 16.

34   "Strike and Sabotage."

35   See both Arne L. Kalleberg, Michael Wallace, Karyn A. Loscocco, Kevin T. Leicht, and Hans-Helmut Ehm, "The Eclipse of Craft: The Changing Face of Labor in the Newspaper Industry," in *Workers, Managers, and Technological Change: Emerging Patterns of Labor Relations*, ed. Daniel Cornfield (New York: Plenum Press, 1987); and Michael Wallace and Arne L. Kalleberg, "Industrial Transformation and the Decline of Craft: The Decomposition of Skill in the Printing Industry, 1931–1978," *American Sociological Review* 47, no. 3 (June 1982): 307–324.

36   Kalleberg et al., "The Eclipse of Craft," 57.

37   Kalleberg et al., 61.

38   E. J. Hobsbawm, "The Machine Breakers," *Past & Present* 1 (February 1952): 57.

39   Hobsbawm, "Machine Breakers," 57.

40   Hobsbawm, 59.

41   Hobsbawm, 59, 60.

42   Joshua Clover, *Riot. Strike. Riot: The New Era of Uprisings* (New York: Verso Books, 2016), 20.

43   Hobsbawm, "Machine Breakers," 61, 62.

44   Hobsbawm, 63, my emphasis.

45   Devin Fore, introduction to *History and Obstinacy*, by Alexander Kluge and Oskar Negt, ed. Devin Fore, trans. Richard Langston et al. (New York: Zone, 2014), 36. I lean heavily on Fore's masterfully far-reaching and beautifully written introduction

in my understanding of obstinacy. For arguments related to Kluge and Negt on obstinacy, see Sara Ahmed, *Willful Subjects* (Durham, N.C.: Duke University Press, 2014) and Bliss Cua Lim, *Translating Time: Cinema, the Fantastic, and Temporal Critique* (Durham, N.C.: Duke University Press, 2009).

46 Fernand Braudel, "History and the Social Sciences: The *Longue Durée*," in *On History*, trans. Sarah Matthews (Chicago: University of Chicago Press, 1980), 34.

47 Fore, introduction, 37.

48 Robert Brenner, *The Economics of Global Turbulence: The Advanced Capitalist Economies from Long Boom to Long Downturn, 1945–2005* (New York: Verso, 2006), 56.

49 See Kalleberg et al., "Eclipse of Craft"; Wallace and Kalleberg, "Industrial Transformation"; and Brenner, *Economics of Global Turbulence.*

50 Kalleberg et al., "Eclipse of Craft," 48; Wallace and Kalleberg, "Industrial Transformation," 311.

51 On "unconscious history," see Braudel, "History and the Social Sciences," 39.

52 Moishe Postone, *Time, Labor, and Social Domination: A Reinterpretation of Marx's Critical Theory* (New York: Cambridge University Press, 1993), 292.

53 Clover, *Riot. Strike. Riot*, 69.

54 David F. Noble, *Progress without People: New Technology, Unemployment, and the Message of Resistance* (Toronto: Between the Lines, 1995).

55 E. P. Thompson, *The Making of the English Working Class* (New York: Pantheon, 1963); Kirkpatrick Sale, *Rebels against the Future: The Luddites and Their War on the Industrial Revolution—Lessons for the Computer Age* (Reading, Mass.: Addison-Wesley, 1995); Peter Linebaugh, *Ned Ludd and Queen Mab: Machine-Breaking, Romanticism, and the Several Commons of 1811–12* (Oakland, Calif.: PM Press, 2012).

56 "Luddite," "Luddites," and "Luddism," Google N-Gram Viewer, accessed November 12, 2017, https://books.google.com/ngrams.

57 Guy Debord, *The Society of the Spectacle*, trans. Donald Nicholson-Smith (New York: Zone, 1994), 85–86.

58 Debord, *Society of the Spectacle*, 31.

59 David Harvey, *Seventeen Contradictions and the End of Capitalism* (New York: Oxford University Press, 2014), 108.

60 Fredric Jameson, *Valences of the Dialectic* (London: New York, 2009), 580, 582.

61 Brenner, *Economics of Global Turbulence*, chapter 2. See as well the highly useful article on which he draws, Marvin Frankel, "Obsolescence and Technological Change in a Maturing Economy," *American Economic Review* 45, no. 3 (June 1955): 296–319.

62 On the "fall out of history," which is Jameson's phrase, see *Valences of the Dialectic*, 576–577. The importance of the spatial thinking that Jameson encourages is that it pulls us away from the faded industrial "cores" to the more recently industrialized "peripheries," fronts on which this book encounters one of its own limits to the extent that the works it considers remain largely within the boundaries of the United States and the United Kingdom. Even if a text like *The Invention Hugo Cabret* mediates the global phenomenon of wageless life, the spatially far-flung and globally unequal features of that life are issues to which I have only been able to gesture in this book.

63 Northrop Frye, *Anatomy of Criticism: Four Essays* (Princeton, N.J.: Princeton University Press, 1957), chapter 1, especially 163–165.

64 On "character space" and the related idea of "character system," see Alex Woloch's important study *The One vs. the Many: Minor Characters and the Space of the Protagonist in the Novel* (Princeton, N.J.: Princeton University Press, 2003).

65 Paul Ricoeur, "Narrative Time," in *On Narrative*, ed. W. J. T. Mitchell (Chicago: University of Chicago Press, 1981), 170.

66 I found Laura Marks's essay "Video Haptics and Erotics" useful in writing this sentence. See *Touch: Sensuous Theory and Multisensory Media* (Minneapolis: University of Minnesota Press, 2002), 1–20.

67 Scott Bukatman, *The Poetics of Slumberland: Animated Spirits and the Animating Spirit* (Berkeley: University of California Press, 2012), 135; Wendy Hui Kyong Chun, *Programmed Visions: Software and Memory* (Cambridge, Mass.: MIT Press, 2011), 87. For a salient concept of the "daemonic agent," see Angus Fletcher, *Allegory: The Theory of a Symbolic Mode* (Princeton, N.J.: Princeton University Press, 2012); and for a compelling account of angelic and demonic views of class struggle, see G. M. Tamás, "Telling the Truth about Class," *Socialist Register* 42 (2006): 228–268.

68 Ricoeur, "Narrative Time," 170.

69 Frye, *Anatomy of Criticism*, 163.

70 On zaniness, especially as it relates to labor in contemporary capitalism, see Sianne Ngai, "The Zany Science," *Our Aesthetic Categories: Zany, Cute, Interesting* (Cambridge, Mass.: Harvard University Press, 2012). To pursue the queer reading of this work, for which I unfortunately don't have room here, see as a useful framework Jack Halberstam, *The Queer Art of Failure* (Durham, N.C.: Duke University Press, 2011), chapters 1 and 6 especially. The gendered and generational dynamics here refract what Jasper Bernes calls "the feminization of speedup" in *The Work of Art in the Age of Deindustrialization* (Stanford, Calif.: Stanford University Press, 2017), chapter 4; and what Heather J. Hicks calls "the culture of soft work" in *The Culture of Soft Work: Labor, Gender, and Race in Postmodern American Narrative* (New York: Palgrave Macmillan, 2009).

71 Frye, *Anatomy of Criticism*, 165.

72 Lauren Berlant and Sianne Ngai, "Comedy Has Issues," *Critical Inquiry* 43, no. 2 (2017): 236.

73 Frye, *Anatomy of Criticism*, 165.

74 Both quotations from Thorne in this paragraph are from "The Revolutionary Energy of the Outmoded," *October* 104 (2003): 114.

75 Thorne, "Revolutionary," 107.

Chapter 4 Cinema by Dated Means

1 Patrick Keating, email message to author, 2010.

2 The term "boiling" is not consistent across the industry, but it appears in reporting about *Fantastic* and in online discussions among animators and other sources. The respective descriptions of boiling as an "unwanted effect" come from Barry J. C. Purves, *Stop-Motion Animation: Frame by Frame Film-Making with Puppets and Models*, 2nd ed. (New York: Bloomsbury, 2014), 162; and as "random fluctuations" from the entry for "boiling" at http://www.encyclo.co.uk, quoted by Michal Poniedzielski at https://forums.creativecow.net/thread/2/990013, accessed May 28, 2015 (site discontinued). For another relevant online thread, see http://ask.metafilter.com/112149/Is-this-cartoon-boiling, accessed May 28, 2015. Also see

"The *Fantastic Mr. Fox* Animates Hong Kong Fantastically," *Neon Punch*, February 5, 2010, www.neonpunch.com/tag/fantastic-mr-fox/ (site not currently accessible); and Chris Lee, "Fur Flies on 'Mr. Fox,'" *Los Angeles Times*, October 11, 2009, http://articles.latimes.com/2009/oct/11/entertainment/ca-mrfox11.

3 Obviously, the ideals of classical filmmaking will govern animation as a cinematic mode differently than the norms they generate in live-action films, especially since animation often draws attention to that which is less visible in live action. This is not only a function of the influential distinction advanced between classical cinema and the cinema of attraction but also a result of animation as such. For a helpful source on these questions, see Paul Wells, *Understanding Animation* (New York: Routledge, 1998).

4 Roger Ebert, review of *Fantastic Mr. Fox*, RogerEbert.com, November 24, 2009, http://www.rogerebert.com/reviews/fantastic-mr-fox-2009.

5 A. O. Scott. "Don't Count Your Chickens," review of *Fantastic Mr. Fox*, *New York Times*, November 12, 2009, http://www.nytimes.com/2009/11/13/movies/13fantastic.html.

6 On these stylistic tendencies in postclassical cinema, see David Bordwell's "Intensified Continuity: Four Dimensions," in *The Way Hollywood Tells It: Story and Style in Modern Movies* (Berkeley: University of California Press, 2006), 121–138.

7 Scott, "Don't Count Your Chickens."

8 For a brief account of the shot from *Hugo*, see Jim Thacker, "FMX 2012: The Hugo Shot That Nearly Killed Us," Cgchannel.com, May 12, 2012, http://www.cgchannel.com/2012/05/fmx-2012-the-hugo-shot-that-nearly-killed-us.

9 See, for instance, Richard Susskind and Daniel Susskind, *The Future of the Professions: How Technology Will Transform the Work of Human Experts* (Oxford: Oxford University Press, 2015), 71–78.

10 Scott, "Don't Count Your Chickens."

11 Susskind and Susskind, *Future of the Professions*, 73, 77–78.

12 Wai Chee Dimock, *Through Other Continents: American Literature across Deep Time* (Princeton, N.J.: Princeton University Press, 2006), 124.

13 David Bordwell, *Pandora's Digital Box: Films, Files, and the Future of Movies* (Madison, Wis.: Irving Way Institute Press, 2012), 24–25.

14 John Belton, "Digital Cinema: A False Revolution," *October* 100 (Spring 2002): 100. Turning to animation is a major critical and journalistic trope for describing how the tardy transition to digital means has reconstituted the ontology of the cinematic image. Examples of this trope can also be found in the following: Bordwell, *Pandora's Digital Box*, 31; J. Hoberman, *Film after Film, or, What Became of Twenty-First Century Cinema* (New York: Verso, 2013), 5; Lev Manovich, *The Language of New Media* (Cambridge, Mass.: MIT Press, 2001), 302.

15 Bordwell, *Pandora's Digital Box*, 8. While the glosses on *Avatar, X-Men,* and *Hugo* are mine, this paragraph otherwise synthesizes and thus significantly simplifies a wide body of work on new media and digital cinema, many of them already cited in note 13 above. See as well David Rodowick's compelling *The Virtual Life of Film* (Cambridge, Mass.: Harvard University Press, 2007). The gesture to the "plasmatic" here is to Sergei Eisenstein's work in *Eisenstein on Disney*, ed. Jay Leyda, trans. Alan Upchurch (Calcutta: Seagull, 1986).

16 The first quotation here is from Bordwell, *Pandora's Digital Box*, 217; the second from Belton, "Digital Cinema," 104. In chronological order, Belton's essays include the just cited *October* article; "Painting by the Numbers: The Digital Intermediate,"

Film Quarterly 61, no. 3 (2008): 58–65; "Introduction: Digital Cinema" and "Digital 3D Cinema: Digital Cinema's Missing Novelty Phase," *Film History* 24, no. 2 (2012): 131–134, 187–195.

17 Belton, "Digital Cinema," 100–101.

18 Belton, 104, 105.

19 Belton, "Painting by the Numbers," 58, 61.

20 David Harvey, *Seventeen Contradictions and the End of Capitalism* (New York: Oxford University Press, 2014), 94, 95. On the problem of economic growth in relationship to digital innovation in particular, see Robert Gordon, *The Rise and Fall of American Growth: The U.S. Standard of Living since the Civil War* (Princeton, N.J.: Princeton University Press, 2016), 566–604.

21 Belton, "Digital Cinema," 100–101.

22 I derive the term "digital omnivores" from Carmela Aquino and Sarah Radwanick, "Digital Omnivores: How Tablets, Smartphones and Connected Devices are Changing U.S. Digital Media Consumption Habits," whitepaper issued by comScore, October 10, 2011, http://www.comscore.com/Insights/Presentations-and-Whitepapers/2011/Digital-Omnivores.

23 For more on the costs of the digital transition in general, see Bordwell's *Pandora's Digital Box*, from which I also derive the detail about the built-in obsolescence of a digital projector being as grimly short as three years in contrast to analog projectors (72). On the complex interrelationships of turnover time, fixed capital, and moral depreciation—all of which relate to obsolescence as a decrease in the utility of some machine as a result of the dialectics of technological change tied to value revolutions in capitalism—see David Harvey, *A Companion to Marx's Capital, Volume 2* (New York: Verso, 2013), 67–142.

24 Max Horkheimer and Theodor W. Adorno, *Dialectic of Enlightenment: Philosophical Fragments*, trans. Edmund Jephcott (Stanford, Calif.: Stanford University Press, 2002), 111.

25 Bordwell, *Pandora's Digital Box*, 9; Belton, "Introduction," 131.

26 Benj Edwards, "The Digital Watch: A Brief History," *PC Magazine*, April 15, 2012, http://www.pcmag.com/slideshow/story/296609/the-digital-watch-a-brief-history/.

27 Nora's claim is of a piece with his critical generation, which sees historical perception as being in crisis and temporality as being at an end. See Pierre Nora, "Between Memory and History: Les Lieux de Mémoire," *Representations* 26 (Spring 1989): 7–24.

28 Bordwell, "Intensified Continuity," 121–124.

29 Aubrey Anable, "Labor/Leisure," in *Time: A Vocabulary of the Present*, ed. Joel Burges and Amy J. Elias (New York: New York University Press, 2016), 197.

30 On the waning of historical affect, see Jameson, *Postmodernism*, 1–54, especially 16–25. The phrase that Jameson uses again and again is actually "the waning of affect," but it is clear that historical affect is of central importance.

31 Robert Brenner, *The Economics of Global Turbulence: The Advanced Capitalist Economies from Long Boom to Long Downturn, 1945–2005* (New York: Verso Books, 2006), 37–40, 99, 100.

32 Robert Brenner provides a description of these intertwined economic shifts and political upheavals in "Structure vs Conjuncture: The 2006 Elections and the Rightward Shift," *New Left Review* 43 (2007): 33–59.

33 Jameson, *Postmodernism*, 17; Cornel West, "The New Cultural Politics of Difference," *October* 53 (Summer 1990): 93–109; Eric Lott, *Love and Theft: Blackface Minstrelsy and the American Working Class* (Oxford: Oxford University Press, 1993). See Jack Halberstam, *The Queer Art of Failure* (Durham, N.C.: Duke University Press, 2011), 182–186.

34 Devin Fore, introduction to *History and Obstinacy*, by Alexander Kluge and Oskar Negt, ed. Devin Fore, trans. Richard Langston et al. (New York: Zone, 2014), 36.

35 Matthew Fulkerson, *The First Sense: A Philosophical Study of Touch* (Cambridge, Mass.: MIT Press, 2014), 103. For a related discussion, see Elaine Scarry, *The Body in Pain: The Making and Unmaking of the World* (New York: Oxford University Press, 1985), 165–167.

36 For Laura U. Marks's influential accounts of "haptic visuality" in contemporary visual culture, see *The Skin of Film: Intercultural Cinema, Embodiment, and the Senses* (Durham, N.C.: Duke University Press, 2000) and *Touch: Sensuous Theory and Multisensory Media* (Minneapolis: University of Minnesota Press, 2002). See also Fulkerson, *First Sense*, 86, 117, 144.

37 Fulkerson, *First Sense*, 60–62, 124–125.

38 Information on influences culled from: "*Fantastic Mr. Fox* Animators Interview: Ian McKinnon, Andy Biddle and Andy Ghent," interview by Lesa Keddle, *Den of Geek*, March 2, 2010, http://www.denofgeek.com/movies/15459/fantastic-mr-fox -animators-interview-ian-mckinnon-andy-biddle-and-andy-ghent; "Wes Anderson Interview for *Fantastic Mr. Fox*," interview by Craig McLean, *The Telegraph*, October 20, 2009, http://www.telegraph.co.uk/culture/film/6387593/Wes-Anderson -interview-for-Fantastic-Mr-Fox.html; "Wes Anderson Talks *Fantastic Mr. Fox*: The Director on Moving into Stop-Motion," interview by Joe Utichi, *Rotten Tomatoes*, October 21, 2009; "Wes Anderson Interview *Fantastic Mr. Fox*," interview by Steve Weintraub, *Collider*, November 27, 2009, http://collider.com/wes-anderson -interview-fantastic-mr-fox/; "The *Fantastic Mr. Fox* Animates Hong Kong Fantastically" (see note 2 above); Michael Specter, ed., *The Making of "Fantastic Mr. Fox": An American Empirical Picture by Wes Anderson*, introduction and interviews by Michael Specter, set photography by Ray Lewis (New York: Rizzoli International, 2009).

39 "*Fantastic Mr. Fox* Animators," interview by Lesa Keddle.

40 "*King Kong*: Shading Fur," Renderman, accessed May 30, 2016, https://renderman .pixar.com/view/kingkong-shadingfur.

41 Raymond Williams, *Marxism and Literature* (New York: Oxford University Press, 1977), 121–127. I discuss the residual at length in chapter 1. "By emergent," writes Williams, "I mean, first, that new meanings and values, new practices, new relationships and kinds of relationships are continually being created. But it is exceptionally difficult to distinguish between those which are really elements of some new phase of the dominant culture . . . and those which are substantially alternative or oppositional to it: emergent in the strict sense, rather than merely novel" (123). There are few grounds on which I can demonstrate what *Fantastic* does with the boiling fur to be "emergent in the strict sense," especially in a broadly techno-aesthetic sense beyond this film in particular, except to say, with Williams, that such judgments are "always complex" because "*no mode of production and therefore no dominant social order ever in reality includes or exhausts all human practice, human energy, and human intention*" (125, emphasis in the original). The liveliness of the fur feels,

to me, like a moment in which human practice, energy, and intention reveal their inexhaustibility by way of the boiling's residual and emergent qualities.

42 "*Fantastic Mr. Fox* Animators," interview by Lesa Keddle.

43 "Wes Anderson Interview," interview by Craig McLean; "*Fantastic Mr. Fox* Animators," interview by Lesa Keddle; "Wes Anderson Talks," interview by Joe Utichi.

44 Specter, *Making of "Fantastic,"* 14–15.

45 The process genre is a mode of film that organizes itself around showing us how things are made, seeking to absorb us in representations of processes that involve kinetic action as related to technical knowledge and the form-giving power of labor as a skilled act of social reproduction. I derive this definition from Salomé Aguilera Skvirsky, "Cinema, Labor, and the Process Genre" (conference paper, Annual Meeting of the American Comparative Literature Society, Cambridge, Mass., March 2016).

46 "Wes Anderson Interview," interview by Craig McLean.

47 "*Fantastic Mr. Fox* Animators," interview by Lesa Keddle.

48 Lee, "Fur Flies."

49 Barbara Robertson, "One Step at a Time," *Computer Graphics World* 33, no. 1 (January 2010), http://www.cgw.com/Publications/CGW/2010/Volume-33-Issue-1-Jan-2010-/One-Step-at-a-Time.aspx.

50 The information and quotations in this paragraph largely come from Lee, "Fur Flies."

51 Thacker, "FMX 2012"; and Mike Seymour, "*Hugo*: A Study in Modern Visual Effects," *Fxguide*, December 1, 2011, https://www.fxguide.com/featured/hugo-a-study-of-modern-inventive-visual-effects/.

52 Mark McGurl, "Real/Quality," in *Time: A Vocabulary of the Present*, ed. Joel Burges and Amy J. Elias (New York: New York University Press, 2016), 218.

53 See—and there are more examples than these in the book—Specter, *Making of "Fantastic,"* 45, 47, 75, 81, 82.

54 McGurl, "Real/Quality," 218.

55 Karl Marx, *Capital: A Critique of Political Economy*, vol. 1, trans. Ben Fowkes (London: Penguin in association with New Left Review, 1990), 340–416. For online exposés of the working conditions, including the hours of VFX laborers, see Maggie Kraisamutr, "It Ain't Easy Being Green-Screened: One VFX Artist Speaks Out at Risk of Being Erased and Replaced," *IndieWire*, March 1, 2013, http://www.indiewire.com/2013/03/it-aint-easy-being-green-screened-one-vfx-artist-speaks-out-at-risk-of-being-erased-and-replaced-40537/; and Amid Amidi, "Guest Commentary: The Life of an Indian Visual Effects Artist," *Cartoon Brew*, February 21, 2013, http://www.cartoonbrew.com/ideas-commentary/guest-commentary-the-life-of-an-indian-visual-effects-artist-78220.html. For more on VFX, see Michael Curtin and John Vanderhoef, "A Vanishing Piece of the Pi: The Globalization of Visual Effects Labor," *Television & New Media* 16, no. 3 (February 2014): 219–239; and Allen J. Scott, "Multimedia and Digital Visual Effects: An Emerging Local Labor Market," *Monthly Labor Review* (March 1998): 30–38.

56 Joshua Clover, *Riot. Strike. Riot: The New Era of Uprisings* (New York: Verso Books, 2016), 155.

57 Clover, *Riot. Strike. Riot*, 134.

58 "*Fantastic Mr. Fox* Animators," interview by Lesa Keddle.

59 Theodor W. Adorno, *Minima Moralia: Reflections on a Damaged Life*, trans. E. F. N. Jephcott (New York: Verso, 1974), 221.

60 Joshua Clover, "World-Systems Riot" (unpublished manuscript, 2012), http://krieger.jhu.edu/arrighi/wp-content/uploads/sites/29/2014/03/World_System _Riot_2_CHS.pdf (site discontinued), 11.
61 Clover, *Riot. Strike. Riot*, 26.
62 Clover, 16.
63 Clover, *Riot. Strike. Riot*, 106–112. Also see John Walton and David Seddon, *Free Markets and Food Riots: The Politics of Global Adjustment* (Cambridge, Mass.: Blackwell Publishers, 1994).
64 These estimates are calculated on the basis of a chart comparing average adjustable- and fixed-rate mortgages between 2000 and 2008 from First American Loan Performance. Unfortunately, while I retain the chart in my research (and the chart indicates where it got its data), I can no longer locate the source of the chart itself. However, more information on the complex issue of interest rates can be found in the following article from a Federal Reserve Bank of Chicago publication: Gene Amromin and Anna L. Paulson, "Default Rates on Prime and Subprime Mortgages: Differences and Similarities," *Profitwise News and Views*, September 2010, 1–10. See table 1 especially for information on originating interest rates for subprime lenders between 2004 and 2007. See as well Souphala Chomsisengphet and Anthony Pennington-Cross, "The Evolution of the Subprime Mortgage Market," *Federal Reserve of St. Louis Review* 88, no. 1 (January–February 2006): 31–56. See figure 16 especially for information on interest rates for subprime lenders between 1995 and 2004.
65 Lauren Berlant, *Cruel Optimism* (Durham, N.C.: Duke University Press, 2011); Annie McClanahan, "Bad Credit: The Character of Credit Scoring," *Representations* 126, no. 1 (2014): 31–57.
66 Seth Lerer, *Children's Literature: A Reader's History from Aesop to Harry Potter* (Chicago: University of Chicago Press, 2008), 29, 36; James Simpson, trans., *Reynard the Fox* (New York: Liveright, 2015); Specter, *Making of "Fantastic,"* 5.
67 Clover, *Riot. Strike. Riot*, 29.
68 Clover, "World-Systems Riot," 13.
69 While Walton and Seddon discuss the twentieth century in the cited work, the most famous account of the eighteenth-century food riots is to be found in E. P. Thompson, "The Moral Economy of the English Crowd," *Past & Present* 50 (February 1971): 76–136.
70 Walton and Seddon, *Free Markets*, 51.
71 Clover, *Riot. Strike. Riot*, 155, 161–162, 167.
72 Fredric Jameson, "Class and Allegory in Contemporary Mass Culture," *Signatures of the Visible* (New York: Routledge, 1992), 44; and Jameson, *Postmodernism*, xx–xxi.
73 On what we might call the current semantic obsolescence of the concept of the "bourgeoisie," see Franco Moretti, *The Bourgeois: Between History and Literature* (New York: Verso, 2013), 1–24. As Moretti notes, over the course of the centuries, this class has porously encompassed the self-employed businessperson, the propertied ruling class, and the white-collar employee and civil servant (3).
74 Quoted in Clover, *Riot. Strike. Riot*, 153.
75 Clover, *Riot. Strike. Riot*, 150.
76 This can only be a tremor of the commune, I think, because in the end, the market remains here, containing them in what Foxy calls, however ironically, "real estate." As Clover writes, "The coming communes are likely to emerge first not in walled cities or in communities of retreat, but in open cities where those excluded from the

formal economy and left adrift in circulation now stand watch over the failure of the market to provide their needs" (*Riot. Strike. Riot*, 191).

77 Clover, *Riot. Strike. Riot*, 180.

78 Jack Halberstam sees a more critical relationship to this "tall tale of masculine derring-do" in *Fantastic* in a suggestive reading of the film at the end of *The Queer Art of Failure* (183). For a more extended reading of gender in the film, see Adrienne Kertzer, "Fidelity, Felicity, and Playing around in Wes Anderson's *Fantastic Mr. Fox*," *Children's Literature Association Quarterly* 36, no. 1 (2011): 4–24.

Chapter 5   Politics by Obsolete Means

1 China Miéville, "Socialist Irrealism: An Interview with China Miéville," interview by Jayna Brown, *Social Text*, January 4, 2012, http://socialtextjournal.org/periscope _article/socialist_irrealism_an_interview_with_china_mieville/; China Miéville, *London's Overthrow* (London: Westbourne Press, 2012), 18.

2 Miéville, *London's Overthrow*, 41.

3 Miéville, 15–16, 18, 31–32, 42–44.

4 Miéville's sense of the *totality*, a word he uses fluently due to his own theoretical and political investments, comes across in "Socialist Irrealism."

5 See Elaine Scarry's account of how "absence [occasions] the introduction of [images] into mental life" on a daily basis, pointing to how imagining works in the quotidian conditions of everyday life, in *The Body in Pain: The Making and Unmaking of the World* (New York: Oxford University Press, 1985), 162–164.

6 The "standpoint of labor" is a phrase that entered my head in reading Moishe Postone's *Time, Labor, and Social Domination: A Reinterpretation of Marx's Critical Theory* (New York: Cambridge University Press, 1993).

7 Scarry, *The Body in Pain*, 164.

8 China Miéville, *Iron Council* (New York: Ballantine, 2004), 74. Hereafter cited parenthetically.

9 David Harvie and Keir Milburn, "The Moral Economy of the English Crowd in the Twenty-First Century," *South Atlantic Quarterly* 112, no. 3 (Summer 2013): 559, 563; Joshua Clover, *Riot. Strike. Riot: The New Era of Uprisings* (New York: Verso, 2016), 138–142.

10 Annie McClanahan, *Dead Pledges: Debt, Crisis, and Twenty-First-Century Culture* (Stanford, Calif.: Stanford University Press, 2016), 186–187.

11 The phrase "twilit core" appears in Clover, *Riot. Strike. Riot*, 3.

12 Clover, *Riot. Strike. Riot*, 146.

13 Paul Gilroy, "1981 and 2011: From Social Democratic to Neoliberal Rioting," *South Atlantic Quarterly* 112, no. 3 (Summer 2013): 551–558.

14 On the neoliberal shift from the 1970s forward in British economic policy and political orientation, along with its relationship to the United States, see David Harvey, *A Brief History of Neoliberalism* (New York: Oxford University Press, 2005), 39–63. Also see Susan Watkins, "A Weightless Hegemony: New Labour's Role in the Neoliberal Order," *New Left Review* 25 (January–February 2004): 5–33.

15 "Vote 2001: Results and Constituencies: Regent's Park and Kensington North," *BBC News*, accessed March 7, 2018, http://news.bbc.co.uk/hi/english/static/ vote2001/results_constituencies/constituencies/474.stm. On Left Unity, see their website, http://leftunity.org/appeal, where their manifesto can be found, as well as their open letter to the *Guardian*, "Left Unity Ready to Offer Alternative,"

August 12, 2013, http://www.theguardian.com/politics/2013/aug/12/left-unity
-alternative.

16 Harvey, *Brief History of Neoliberalism*, 58; China Miéville, "Trembling on the Verge:
An Interview with China Miéville (Part Two)," interview by Joe Macaré, *Truthout*,
August 28, 2012, http://www.truth-out.org/news/item/11167-trembling-on-the
-verge-an-interview-with-china-miéville-part-2.

17 Watkins, "Weightless Hegemony," 26.

18 Watkins, 12.

19 Harvey, *Brief History of Neoliberalism*, 59; Watkins, "Weightless Hegemony," 32. For
an account of the strike that models this form of struggle on the basis of a specific
history of it in which the state plays a major mediating role, see Edward Shorter
and Charles Tilly's classic study *Strikes in France, 1830–1968* (New York: Cambridge
University Press, 1974).

20 Clover, *Riot. Strike. Riot.*

21 Beverly Silver, *Forces of Labor: Workers' Movements and Globalization since 1870*
(New York: Cambridge University Press, 2003), 39, 42–43, 66–69; Figure 34.1 in
Aaron Benanav and John Clegg, "Misery and Debt: On the Logic and History
of Surplus Populations and Surplus Capital," in *Contemporary Marxist Theory: A
Reader*, ed. Andrew Pendakis, Jeff Diamanti, Nicholas Brown, Josh Robinson, and
Imre Szeman (New York: Bloomsbury, 2014), 594; Frey and Osborne, "The Future
of Employment: How Susceptible Are Jobs to Computerizaton?" Oxford Martin
School, Program on the Impacts of Future Technology and Department of Engineering Science, University of Oxford, Oxford, United Kingdom, 2013, 9. Deloitte
tends to want to put a rosy view on these numbers in various ways that seem suspect
to me, as in Ian Stewart and Debapratim De, "Technology and People: The Great
Job-Creating Machine," *Deloitte*, August 2015, http://www2.deloitte.com/content/
dam/Deloitte/uk/Documents/finance/deloitte-uk-technology-and-people.pdf;
and Angus Knowles-Cutler, "From Brawn to Brains: The Impact of Technology
on Jobs in the UK," *Deloitte*, September 2012, https://www2.deloitte.com/uk/en/
pages/growth/articles/from-brawn-to-brains-the-impact-of-technology-on-jobs-in
-the.u.html.

22 Jason E. Smith, "Nowhere to Go: Automation, Then and Now (Part Two)," *Brooklyn Rail*, April 1, 2017, http://brooklynrail.org/2017/04/field-notes/Nowhere-to
-Go-Automation-Then-and-Now-Part-Two.

23 Clover, *Riot. Strike. Riot*, 144.

24 Watkins, "Weightless Hegemony," 6.

25 Watkins, 32.

26 Watkins, 32–33.

27 Watkins, 31–32.

28 Hannah Arendt, *Between Past and Future: Eight Exercises in Political Thought* (New
York: Penguin, 1977), 10.

29 Watkins, "Weightless Hegemony," 32.

30 China Miéville, *Perdido Street Station* (New York: Ballantine, 2000), 44.

31 Christian Thorne, "The Grassy-Green Sea," *Early Modern Culture* 5 (October
2005), http://emc.eserver.org/1-5/thorne.html.

32 Marian Bratu Hansen, *Cinema and Experience: Siegfried Kracauer, Walter Benjamin, and Theodor W. Adorno* (Berkeley: University of California Press, 2011), 150.

33 "Blunderbuss, n." and "dirigible, n.," *OED Online*, September 2016, http://www.oed
.com/view/Entry/20643 and http://www.oed.com/view/Entry/53344; Wikipedia

contributors, "Blunderbuss" and "Airship," *Wikipedia*, accessed September 2016, https://en.wikipedia.org/wiki/Blunderbuss and https://en.wikipedia.org/wiki/ Airship; Robert Friedel's more scholarly accounts of aviation and weaponry in chapters 14, 19, and 26 of *A Culture of Improvement: Technology and the Western Millennium* (Cambridge, Mass.: MIT Press, 2007); Ernest Edwards, *The Heliotype Process* (Boston: James R. Osgood, 1876); Wolfgang Schivelbusch, "The Mechanization of Motive Power," in *The Railway Journey: The Industrialization of Space and Time in the Nineteenth Century* (Berkeley: University of California Press, 2014), 1–15; Benedict Anderson, "Cultural Roots" and "The Origins of National Consciousness," in *Imagined Communities: Reflections on the Origin and Spread of Nationalism* (New York: Verso, 1983), 9–46.

34 Jameson, *Valences of the Dialectic*, 529, 532.

35 Dora Apel, *Beautiful Terrible Ruins: Detroit and the Anxiety of Decline* (New Brunswick, NJ: Rutgers University Press, 2015).

36 Barbara Foley, *Radical Representations: Politics and Form in U.S. Proletarian Fiction, 1929–1941* (Durham, N.C.: Duke University Press, 1993), 327. Foley's focus is 1930s proletarian fiction in the United States, but this definition applies nicely to *Iron*.

37 For a useful account of the "aristocracy of labor," see Eric Hobsbawm's 1970 essay, "Lenin and the 'Aristocracy of Labor,'" *Monthly Review* 64, no. 7 (December 2012), http://monthlyreview.org/2012/12/01/lenin-and-the-aristocracy-of-labor.

38 Jodi Dean refers to communism as a "signifying stress" throughout *The Communist Horizon* (New York: Verso, 2012).

39 David Harvey, *Seventeen Contradictions and the End of Capitalism* (New York: Oxford University Press, 2014), 111; Guy Debord, *The Society of the Spectacle*, trans. Donald Nicholson-Smith (New York: Zone, 1994), 86; Jasper Bernes, "Logistics, Counterlogistics, and the Communist Prospect," *Endnotes* 3 (September 2013), https://endnotes.org.uk/articles/21; McClanahan, coda to *Dead Pledges*.

40 Clover, *Riot. Strike. Riot*, 77.

41 Joshua Clover and Aaron Benanav, "Can Dialectics Break BRICS?" *South Atlantic Quarterly* 113, no. 4 (2014): 745, doi: 10.1215/00382876-2803624. The writings of many of the thinkers cited here, especially that of Clover, contain a complex relationship to norms of action. As far as I understand the argument, Clover does not intend to be normative but materialist, attuned to the possibilities of historical conditions as they exist, to the facts on the ground as that which determine the shape of struggle. It is nonetheless striking that the language of his and others' arguments about strategizing and imagining struggle often sparks in readers the sense that a normative claim about how they should act is being advanced. There is thus work to be done on this question, in an article that I envision, yet to be written, called "Structural Outrage." There the complicated nexus of norm and history might be worked through.

42 See Plato's "Meno," in *Five Dialogues*, 2nd ed. (Indianapolis: Hackett, 2002). Also see Gregory Vlastos, "*Anamnesis* in the *Meno*," in *Studies in Greek Philosophy: Socrates, Plato and Their Tradition*, vol. 2 (Princeton, N.J.: Princeton University Press, 1995), 147–165.

43 Karl Marx, "Part III: Consequences of June 13, 1849," in *The Class Struggles in France, 1848 to 1850*, Marxists.org, https://www.marxists.org/archive/marx/works/ 1850/class-struggles-france/ch03.htm.

44 Rosa Luxemburg, "The Mass Strike," in *The Essential Rosa Luxemburg*, ed. Helen Scott (Chicago: Haymarket, 2008), 168.

Index

Page numbers in *italics* refer to figures.

About the Author

JOEL BURGES is an assistant professor of English at the University of Rochester. He teaches in the Department of English, the undergraduate program in film and media studies, the undergraduate program in digital media studies, and the graduate program in visual and cultural studies. With Amy J. Elias, he is coeditor of *Time: A Vocabulary of the Present*.

Printed and bound by CPI Group (UK) Ltd, Croydon, CR0 4YY

16/04/2025

14658333-0002